Towards A Church Architecture

726.5 H22t   73-15337
Hammond
Towards a church architecture

kansas city, missouri

Books will be issued only
  on presentation of library card.
Please report lost cards and
  change of residence promptly.
Card holders are responsible for
  all books, records, films, pictures
or other library materials
  checked out on their cards.

TOWARDS A CHURCH ARCHITECTURE

Towards a Church Architecture

EDITED BY Peter Hammond

THE ARCHITECTURAL PRESS
LONDON

© *Architectural Press* 1962
Printed and bound in Great Britain by
STAPLES PRINTERS LIMITED
at their Rochester, Kent, establishment

Contents

 Acknowledgements 8
 Foreword 9
 Note on Contributors 13
1 A Radical Approach to Church Architecture 15
 Peter Hammond
2 Modern Architectural Theory and the Liturgy 38
 Nigel Melhuish
3 Meaning and Understanding 65
 Robert Maguire
4 Material Fabric and Symbolic Pattern 78
 Keith Murray
5 A Liturgical Brief 91
 H. Benedict Green
6 Church Architecture and the Liturgy 107
 Charles Davis
7 The Theological Basis of Church Architecture 128
 James A. Whyte
8 Liturgy and Society 191
 Patrick McLaughlin
9 The Church and the Community 206
 Patrick Nuttgens
10 Architectural Seriousness 220
 Lance Wright
 Appendix 245

Illustrations

129 Rudolf Schwarz, Corpus Christi, Aachen.
132 Rudolf Schwarz, Chapel of St Albert, Leversbach.
134 Rudolf Schwarz, Church of the Holy Family, Oberhausen
137 Rudolf Schwarz, St Christopher, Cologne-Niehl
140 Rudolf Schwarz, St Anthony, Essen
143 Rudolf Schwarz, St Andrew, Essen
144 Rudolf Schwarz, St Michael, Frankfurt am Main.
145 Emil Steffann and Klaus Rosiny, 'Maria in den Benden', Düsseldorf-Wersten.
148 Emil Steffann, St Lawrence, Munich
149 André Le Donné, Church of the Sacred Heart, Mulhouse
152 André Le Donné, St Clare, Porte de Pantin, Paris.
154 Robert Maguire and Keith Murray, St Paul, Bow Common, London
159 Robert Maguire and Keith Murray, St Matthew, Perry Beeches, Birmingham.
161 Rainer Senn, Chapel at St André, near Nice.
162 Rainer Senn, project for a pentagonal timber chapel.
164 Rainer Senn, Our Lady of Lourdes, Pontarlier.
167 Rainer Senn, Seminary chapel, Pelousey, near Besançon.
169 Rainer Senn, project for a prefabricated church.
171 Rainer Senn, Church at Villejuif, Paris.
172 Kaija and Heikki Siren, Chapel at Otaniemi, Finland.
176 Mies van der Rohe, Chapel, Illinois Institute of Technology, Chicago.

Acknowledgements

Acknowledgments are due to Verlag Aschendorff, Dr Theodor Klauser, and the German Liturgical Commission for permission to translate from the original German, and to reproduce their directives for church building (translated from *Richtlinien fur die Gestaltung des Gotteshauses aus dem Geiste der römischen Liturgie*, compiled by Theodor Klauser at the order of, and in collaboration with, the German Liturgical Commission Verlag Aschendorff, Munster, Westphalia, 1955. Also to the Reverend William Wenninger, Chairman of the Diocesan Liturgical Commission of Superior, Wisconsin, for permission to reproduce the *Diocesan Church Building Directives* issued by that Commission.

Also to the following for permission to reproduce illustrations: Dipl.-Ing. Frau Maria Schwarz and F. H. Kerle Verlag, pp. 129–44; Emil Steffann and Klaus Rosiny, pp. 145–7, photographs Konrad Mahns; Emil Steffann, p. 148, photographs 30 Inge Bock-Fetzer, 31 Gustl Vogel; André le Donné, pp. 149–53, photographs 32, 34, 35, 36, 37 Yves Guillemaut, 33, 41, 42 Chevojon, Robert Maguire and Keith Murray, pp. 154–60, photographs 44, 45, 47 H de Burgh Galwey, Arphot (*by courtesy of The Architectural Review*), 46, 49, 50, 52 Norman Gold; Rainer Senn, pp. 161–71, photographs 61, 64, 66, 67, 69, 70, 71, 72, 73 Walter Grunder; Kaija and Heikki Siren, pp 172–5, photographs 74 Havas, 75, 76, 77 Pietinen; Ludwig Mies van der Rohe, p. 176, photograph 81 Hedrich-Blessing.

Foreword

This book is a by-product of a discussion which has been going on within the New Churches Research Group since its foundation in 1957. Most of the essays which it contains originated in papers read at conferences organized by the group during the last three years, though several of them have been completely rewritten in the light of subsequent debate and criticism. The NCRG has from the outset been an inter-denominational body, drawing its membership from most of the major Christian communities; it also includes a number of architects who would not describe themselves as Christians at all, but who recognize that many of the problems which the group has tried to face are problems affecting modern architecture in general: not merely a single building type, which, whatever its importance in the past, may seem today to be of somewhat marginal concern. The contributors to this symposium include five Anglicans, four Roman Catholics and a Presbyterian, and, granted that the present debate about church design cuts right across denominational frontiers, differences of opinion are inevitable. I have made no attempt to reconcile conflicting views or to gloss over such differences where they exist. The purpose of the book is to stimulate further discussion and to raise fundamental questions, not to provide an agreed statement.

But while the reader will have no difficulty in detecting occasional differences of emphasis or opinion, what is surely more remarkable is the fact that ten writers, who if they do not represent the full diversity of denominational allegiance to be found within the somewhat ill-defined frontiers of the NCRG, are at any rate drawn from several very diverse traditions, should find so large a measure of common ground. It seems to me significant that wherever the problems of church design are being discussed today at a really fundamental level, and in a theological context, one finds a substantial measure of agreement, not only in regard to basic principles, but even where particular applications are concerned.

Towards a Church Architecture

So far as the book has a thesis, it can be summed up in the title of the first essay: the first essential for church builders today is a radical approach, an approach which, paradoxical as this may seem, involves forgetting all about architecture – at any rate in the early stages of the design process. The second essential is architectural seriousness and everything that is said here about the need for analysis and the consideration of human activities assumes the need for a deeply serious architecture.

In a talk which formed part of a series arranged by the NCRG in collaboration with the University of London in the autumn of 1959, Peter Smithson proposed the following 'spiritual exercises' for churchmen and architects; they bear very closely on the theme of this book:

For churchmen
  i. Keep on hammering away at the 'functional' requirements being met.
  ii. Try to make committees and architects scrutinize their proposals, so that even if they cannot invest every part of the building with meaning, in the deepest sense, they can at least eliminate the obviously meaningless.

and for architects
  i. Remember that what is most important is the 'general solution': that the formal organization should serve first that which is 'central to the problem', as Mies van der Rohe would say.
  ii. That the great baroque churches are not at all theatrical in the expressionist (or Gordon Craig) sense, but rather communicate their meaning primarily by space, and by absolute consistency of plastic language. And these tools are still available – in fact are the *only* tools of architecture.
  iii. That there is no reason why the technology and materials of churches should be in any way different from normal building, in fact they *have* to be the same (the ideation of the commonplace and so on).

In other words, we should be heading towards rather plain brick boxes with no tricks.

That is a very convenient summary of the theme of these essays and the illustrations have been chosen primarily to show what this can mean in practice. All the buildings illustrated are parish churches

Foreword

or churches designed to serve needs not substantially different from those of a parochial community; they do not include monastic buildings, pilgrimage or mortuary chapels, or other churches with functions radically different from those of the typical *domus ecclesiae*. Apart from the two Anglican parish churches illustrated on pages 154–60 and the chapels at Otaniemi and Chicago illustrated on pages 172–76, all the buildings shown are designed for the celebration of the liturgy according to the Roman rite. I suspect that a good many English Free Churchmen would feel far more at home in a church like the one at Perry Beeches (pages 159–60) or in Rainer Senn's chapel for a Catholic seminary at Pelousey (pages 167–8) than they would in the First Presbyterian Church at Stamford, Connecticut (see page 24), as I remarked in an earlier essay on church architecture, 'one of the ironies of the present situation is that *the classic principles of Anglican worship* are being given far more convincing architectural expression in modern Roman Catholic churches on the Continent than in Anglican buildings in London, Coventry or the New Towns' Similar ironies abound today in every situation where the leaven of the new reformation is at work: the need for a radical approach is not confined to the realm of church architecture.

Hull, March 1962   Peter Hammond

Note on Contributors

CHARLES DAVIS was born in 1923 and studied at St Edmund's College, Ware. After ordination in 1946 he went to Rome for further theological study at the Gregorian University. Since 1952 he has been professor of dogmatic theology at St Edmund's College, Ware. He is editor of *The Clergy Review* and a regular contributor to this and other periodicals. He is author of *Liturgy and Doctrine: the Doctrinal Basis of the Liturgical Movement*.

HUMPHREY BENEDICT GREEN was born in 1924. He read greats and theology at Merton College, Oxford, studied for ordination at Cuddesdon College, and then worked for five years in a suburban parish before joining the staff of King's College, London. Since 1960 he has been a member of the Community of the Resurrection, Mirfield. He is a contributor to several theological reviews.

PETER HAMMOND was born in 1921 and studied at the Bromley College of Art, Merton College, Oxford, the University of Salonica and Cuddesdon College. After ordination in 1951 and a period on the staff of St Thomas, Regent Street, he became rector of a small country parish near Cirencester, where the NCRG was founded in 1957. Since January 1962 he has been lecturer in the history of art and complementary studies at the Regional College of Art, Hull. His publications include *The Waters of Marah* and *Liturgy and Architecture*.

PATRICK MCLAUGHLIN was born in 1909. He read P.P.E. at Worcester College, Oxford, and was ordained in 1935. After seven years parochial work in Birmingham and Essex, and a period as secretary of the Church Union committee for social action, he became warden of St Anne's House, Soho, and vicar of St Thomas, Regent Street: two of the liveliest centres of the movement for reform within the Church of England during the 'fifties. He was one of the founders of the *Parish and People* movement and is author of *The Necessity of Worship*.

ROBERT MAGUIRE was born in 1931 and studied at the Architectural Association School, London. With Keith Murray, he has worked for some ten years on problems of church design, both theoretically and practically. The partnership's first building was St Paul's church, Bow Common.

NIGEL MELHUISH was born in 1927 and trained as an architect at Cambridge and the R.W.A. School in Bristol, where he wrote an unpublished thesis on *Church Architecture and the Liturgical Movement* which anticipates much of the discussion of the last five years After eight years' varied experience as an assistant he is now in private practice.

KEITH MURRAY was born in 1929 and studied at the Central School of Arts and Crafts, London. He has been managing director of a firm of church furnishers and has practised as a designer under the name of Keith Fendall. He is now in partnership with Robert Maguire.

PATRICK NUTTGENS was born in 1930 and is the son of a stained glass artist. He studied at the Edinburgh College of Art and Edinburgh University, where he was a lecturer in architecture from 1957 until 1961. He is now director of the Institute of Advanced Architectural Studies in the University of York. He is author of a book on the Scottish church architect Reginald Fairlie.

JAMES WHYTE was born in 1920 and studied at Edinburgh University and New College, Edinburgh. He ministered in two Scottish parishes before taking up his present post as professor of practical theology and Christian ethics in the University of St Andrews in 1958. He is also chairman of the Scottish Pastoral Association.

LANCE WRIGHT was born in 1915 and studied at University College, London, and the A.A. School of Architecture. From 1947 to 1953 he was a lecturer at the Royal West of England Academy School of Architecture, Bristol. Since 1951 he has been a member of the Lay Apostolate Group, an informal group set up by the Roman Catholic hierarchy of England and Wales to develop the part of the laity in the Church. Since 1953 he has been technical editor of *The Architects' Journal* and *The Architectural Review*.

1. A Radical Approach to Church Architecture

PETER HAMMOND

In talking about modern church architecture one is talking about something the very existence of which is open to question. If anything that can properly be described as modern church architecture exists at all today it does so only in embryonic form. There are plenty of new churches: they have been going up in their hundreds during the last few years all over the world, from Finland to Australia. How many of these churches can really be called *modern* buildings is another matter altogether. The great majority are essentially backward-looking; they merely take the formal concepts of the past and deck them out in a new and brightly coloured wrapper; they are like glossy paperback editions of minor nineteenth-century classics, and they are frequently issued with extravagant blurbs.

There are a few churches which do not fall into this category. They are almost invariably unpretentious structures which bear little resemblance to the popular image of a modern church. Frequently they are constructed of traditional materials. They offer little scope to the artist. The fact remains that they hint obscurely at possibilities as yet unrealized; and, significantly, they all reflect preoccupations which are social and theological rather than formal or stylistic.

Where church architecture is concerned we are, it seems to me, still very much in the period of 'towards an architecture'. So far as an embryonic church architecture does exist today, it is largely as the result of a movement which is not directly concerned with architecture at all, but which seeks to create within the Church a deeper understanding of its own nature and function in the modern world. This movement of reform and renewal first sprang up in Belgium during the years immediately preceding the First World War. It quickly spread to Germany, where the Benedictine abbey of Maria Laach was from the outset its focal point, and then to Austria. Since the Second World War it has developed out of all recognition, and the papal encyclical *Mediator Dei*, issued in 1947, the restoration of the Easter Vigil and the international liturgical congress held at Assisi in 1956 all bear witness to the way in which the general principles of the movement – if not all of their particular applications – have come to be widely accepted within the Roman Catholic Church. In other Christian communities too, the movement is now a force to be reckoned with: indeed, one of its most striking characteristics is its capacity for transcending denominational frontiers and for establishing a surprising measure of common ground between Christians of very diverse traditions.

The character of this liturgical movement, as it is commonly known, has unfortunately been widely misunderstood. In English-speaking countries in particular, where the influence of the movement has so far been slight, its significance has long been obscured by certain widely-held misconceptions. It has, to take only three examples of such misconceptions, been regarded as a misguided attempt to restore the outward observances of the primitive Church; as a programme of specific practical reforms; even, strange as this may seem to anyone who has known the movement from within, as the latest fashion in church furnishings: an esoteric cult of spiritual nudity and bare stone altars, slap in the middle of the congregation.[1] Such misconceptions have arisen mainly as the result of a failure to distinguish between

[1] The idea that the liturgical movement is 'nothing more than a fleeting phase of ecclesiastical fashion' has recently been given a new lease of life by Peter F. Anson's fascinating, but in some ways profoundly misleading book *Fashions in Church Furnishings 1840–1940*, Faith Press 1960. Mr Anson is not interested in theology and he entirely fails to recognize the biblical, doctrinal and pastoral roots from which the movement has sprung. Nobody reading his book would suppose that the liturgical movement *had* any doctrinal basis. Only once does he hint that fundamental issues are involved, when, on p. 357, he writes that 'the only solution (to the chaos of the 'thirties) was *a return to the basic principles of Christian worship*' (my italics). But we hear no more about basic principles; instead, we learn a few pages later 'So started yet another fashion in church furnishings, based on *a return to the age of the Catacombs*' (my italics). That, as Mr Anson is well aware, is not precisely what Continental theologians mean when they talk about a *retour aux sources*. For a very different interpretation of the significance of the liturgical movement see Louis Bouyer, *Life and Liturgy*, Sheed & Ward 1956, and Charles Davis, *Liturgy and Doctrine*, Sheed & Ward 1960.

A Radical Approach to Church Architecture

basic principles and detailed (and sometimes ill-considered) practical applications.

In fact, the whole basis of the liturgical movement has from the earliest days been doctrinal and pastoral. So far from being concerned only with outward observances and ceremonial frills, this movement of reform and renewal has led in the course of the last fifty years to a radical reassessment of the whole content of the Christian faith. The movement is concerned with the fundamentals of doctrine: with issues no less basic than those which were at stake in the controversies of sixteenth century· the resurrection and the paschal mystery as the central theme of the Christian message; the theology of the Church, the Bible and the sacraments; the activity of the Holy Spirit; the character and function of the Christian layman; and the nature of the Christian assembly as the mystery of the Church realized in one particular place and time. It has led to so many practical reforms, has reached out to so many points on the periphery of the Church's activity, precisely because it goes theologically deep. It affects our whole understanding of the Christian mystery; it touches the life of the body of Christ at its deepest and most hidden levels. Based as it is on a far more critical appreciation both of early Christian tradition, and also of its development during the Middle Ages, than was attainable four hundred, or even one hundred years ago, the liturgical movement is the latest, and by far the most promising attempt that has yet been made to cure a sickness which has vexed the whole body of the western Church – Catholic *and* Protestant – for many centuries. Its full significance can be grasped only when it is set in its proper theological context: when it is seen against the background of the revolutionary developments which took place in the western half of Christendom during the Middle Ages, and which, despite the efforts of earlier reformers, have continued to exercise a powerful influence right down to the present day.

In Germany, by the mid-'twenties, the debate about church building was already being drawn into a wider debate concerning the Church itself, its nature, its structure, the worship that is its distinctive activity, and its function in the modern world. The nascent liturgical movement was beginning to provide the radical theological thinking that was so desperately needed, not only by church architects but by all who were seeking to embody authentic Christian tradition in forms of equal authenticity. Architecture was beginning

Towards a Church Architecture

to be related to theology and it was becoming clear, that in order to understand the purpose of the *domus ecclesiae*, one must first seek to understand the purpose of the *ecclesia* itself: that the first necessity for church builders was to forget all about architecture and to study the anatomy of Christ's body, the structure of the temple built of living stones.

Architectural revivalism was dead, but it was impossible to create a new church architecture merely by accepting the technological revolution. It was necessary to go deeper. The new technology was capable of providing the Church with a living language. So much was clear from Perret's church at Le Raincy and Karl Moser's Antoniuskirche at Basle, where the means and forms of our time had been used with transparent honesty and immense rigour. What technology could *not* provide was the substance of the discourse· the meanings and values that architecture must express. That could come only from a new understanding of Christian tradition. As the German architect Rudolf Schwarz wrote in 1937: 'It does not suffice to work honestly with the means and forms of our time. It is only out of sacred reality that sacred building can grow. What begets sacred works is not the life of the world but the life of faith – the faith, however, of our time. . . . The substance of all church building is the living Church. The "structure" is her "visibleness", so much so that the building itself, taken together with all its contents as a living unity, is the revealed form, the revealed structure of the Church.'[2]

Before architects could hope to exploit the possibilities for church building of the new world of forms opening up all around them, before the unchanging substance of Christian tradition could again be expressed in the language of the living, there had to be a recovery within the Church of the meaning of the Church. The need was urgent. All too frequently churchmen seemed to have lost their hold on truths which were central to their faith, while they continued to

---

[2] *Vom Bau der Kirche*, Heidelberg 1938; English translation by Cynthia Harris. *The Church Incarnate, the Sacred Function of Christian Architecture*, Henry Regnery Company, Chicago, 1958, pp. 10 and 212. Now that this book is at last available in English it should be required reading for everyone concerned with church building. Mies van der Rohe has called it 'one of the truly great books . . . a book which illuminates the whole problem of architecture itself'. See also Schwarz's last published work: *Kirchenbau, Welt vor der Schwelle*, F. H. Kerle Verlag, Heidelberg, 1960.

cling tenaciously to much that was at best peripheral. The first step towards a church architecture was 'a renewal of the religious consciousness of Christian people'.³

By the late 'twenties the signs of renewal were multiplying rapidly. The German liturgical movement centred on Maria Laach, together with the biblical renewal stemming from Klosterneuburg in Austria and the Belgian movement for reform, with its strongly pastoral emphasis, promised to bring about a radical transformation in the Church's understanding of itself and its mission. The riches of authentic Christian tradition were being laid bare. The accretions which had obscured the true meaning of the *ecclesia* were being stripped away. There was a general return to essentials, to the great central truths of the Christian message.

The effect of this theological and liturgical renewal on church design can be seen from two remarkable churches which Rudolf Schwarz, himself deeply involved in the growing debate between the theologians and the architects, built during the years 1928-33: the Fronleichnamskirche at Aachen and the chapel of St Albert at Leversbach, near Düren.⁴ Here at last church architecture has recovered its true function. Once again the church has become a house for the people of God: an instrument for forming a human community, which is itself an instrument for the restoration of all things in Christ. These churches are essentially liturgical and pastoral tools. The peripheral distractions have gone and the true purpose of the building is disclosed. The incipient revolution in church architecture begun by architects like Perret and Moser has been carried a stage further. If the Antoniuskirche had brought about a *technical* revolution in church building, Schwarz's church at Aachen 'started another one, deeper and more radical. It makes architects develop, as a new problem, the essential church out of its *theological, liturgical* and *practical* conception.'⁵

The significance of these churches lies in the fact that they are the product of a really radical approach to architecture: an approach

³ Charles Davis, op. cit., p. 18.
⁴ See illustrations, pp. 129-133. The photograph of the interior of the chapel at Leversbach was taken before the war. It has subsequently undergone a rather unfortunate transformation.
⁵ H. A. Reinhold, 'The Architecture of Rudolf Schwarz,' *Architectural Forum*, January 1939, p. 24.

which starts not from formal concepts but from the analysis of human activities. In the case of a church, it is hardly necessary to add, such an approach involves asking some very fundamental questions about the nature of these activities and that of the community which takes part in them. One may begin by asking 'what is a church for?', but if one is going to be radical one cannot stop there; it is necessary to ask 'what is *the* Church for?', what sort of a community is it?', 'what are its distinctive structures?', 'what is the inner meaning of the various activities to which it appears to attach such importance?', 'what is the relationship between what goes on inside the church building and the Church's mission to society at large?', and so on. Unless architecture and theology are in deep communication with each other – as they were in Germany between the wars – it is unlikely that these questions will be answered. A radical approach to architecture must involve the client, no less than the architect, in some hard thinking and analysis. The churches at Aachen and Leversbach could never have been built had not the nascent liturgical renewal already compelled the Church in Germany to re-examine its traditions and to rediscover the sources of its life.

Modern church architecture began with a rediscovery of essentials. 'For the celebration of the Lord's supper,' wrote Schwarz, 'a moderately large, well-proportioned room is needed, in its centre a table and on the table a bowl of bread and a cup of wine. . . . That is all. Table, space and walls make up the simplest church. . . . There have been greater forms of church building than this one, but this is not the right time for them. We cannot continue on from where the last cathedrals left off. Instead we must enter into the simple things at the source of the Christian life. We must begin anew and our new beginning must be genuine.'[6] If we are to build on the foundations that were laid in Germany during the 'twenties and the early 'thirties, then we too must be prepared to forget about architecture and to enter into the simple things at the source of the Christian life. There is no other way to build real churches, churches which will reveal the structure of the *ecclesia* itself.

In an essay which appeared towards the end of 1959 Sir John Summerson asserted that there is now, what there was not as recently as the late 'thirties, a real school of modern design in Britain. He

[6] Op. cit., p. 35 f.

hastened to add that what he had in mind was not 'Englishness' or national character or anything of that sort, but rather the existence of a very general agreement among serious architects in this country as to what is the right *approach* to modern building. 'This agreement', he went on, 'goes deeper than a sharing of stylistic conventions, which come and go fashionwise; it is an agreement to be radical, to be continuously critical of results and to go back again and again to the programme and to wrestle with its implications till it yields an answer which has the stamp of reality. This radicalism is the great thing in English architecture today. Once lose it and "English modern" becomes just so much provincial back-wash from the Channel and the Atlantic.'[7]

Shortly after reading this essay I happened to be present at a meeting between a parish priest, faced with the task of building a new church, and the architect whom he had chosen. I would stress the fact that, by English standards at least, this was an exceptional project in that the client had made a real effort to take his responsibilities seriously. He and his people had done a great deal of preliminary study; there had been visits to other new churches in the diocese; a lecturer from the local university had talked about the liturgical movement and shown slides of recent churches on the Continent; a written programme had been drawn up, circulated and twice revised. The architect had been chosen with unusual care. Although he had never built a church, and was unknown to the archdeacon and the diocesan advisory committee, he had designed several secular buildings in the neighbourhood which had greatly impressed the parochial church council. Now, after a year of intensive discussion, the parish had decided that the time had come to present their requirements to the architect. This was the purpose of the meeting.

The parish priest began by explaining that what he proposed to do was to run through the brief, as he called it, section by section, starting with the church itself and going on to consider the ancillary buildings, which included a large hall, a committee room and a parsonage house. He would assume that the architect was quite happy unless he interrupted the reading to ask questions. The architect agreed and the briefing began: the church must consist of a single, unobstructed space, without aisles. The altar must be its focal point, and there must be seating for three hundred persons and a choir of

[7] Foreword to Dannatt, *Modern Architecture in Britain*, Batsford 1959.

Towards a Church Architecture

thirty at the west end of the nave, behind the congregation. A choir gallery was permissible. The sanctuary must be clearly defined but it need not be contained in an apse; the pulpit should stand on the north side of the nave and there must be a coherent visual relationship between altar, pulpit, lectern and priest's desk; the font should not be placed near the entrance to the church but should stand in full view of the congregation....

Had I been the architect, and not a mere observer, the briefing would not have proceeded very far without interruption. I should have wanted to ask· *in what sense* is the altar to be the focal point of the building? what exactly is the choir going to *do*? what is the functional basis of these 'coherent visual relationships'? and so on. None of these questions was asked. The architect listened attentively and made occasional notes, but he appeared to be quite satisfied. Within less than ten minutes we had turned from the church to the parish hall without a single question asked. But at this point the architect suddenly came to life: 'you say you need a large hall, now before we go any further, what are people going to *do* in this building?' Immediately the whole atmosphere changed, and in no time at all client and architect were discussing the nature of badminton. Instead of talking about architectural concepts – aisles, galleries, apses, etc. – they were dealing with the problem at the deeper level of human needs and activities

I mention this experience because it seems to me to go a long way towards explaining why, out of all the hundreds of new churches built within the last ten years, there are so few which can truthfully be described as modern buildings. Modern architecture is not simply a matter of stylistic conventions, new materials and structural systems. It is also the product of a radical approach to building which breaks through the crust of formal concepts to the underlying social realities. No matter what the building in question may be, whether it is a house, a school or a factory, the first step in the design process will be to ask basic questions about the human activities, relationships and values which the building exists to serve and to articulate. In other words, one has to start by trying to empty one's mind of formal concepts, by forgetting all about architecture, in order to study the specific activity or 'ritual' from which the building derives its purpose.

Thus, the design of a house will start from the consideration of a particular pattern of family life; that of a school, from the analysis of a curriculum; that of a factory, from the patient unravelling of a manufacturing process, and so on. Applied to a church, this kind of approach will involve forgetting all about apses, spires and stained glass. It will mean thinking not merely about the visual relationship between font and altar but also about the theological relationship between baptism and eucharist; not about pulpits and lecterns but about the ministry of the word. It will mean, above all, asking basic questions about the nature of the Christian community itself, its distinctive and characteristic activities and its relation to society at large. Until such questions have been faced it is worse than useless to discuss the pros and cons of hyperbolic paraboloids or central altars. A brief which is not based on really radical functional analysis will inevitably be little more than a statement of the client's prejudices and unexamined assumptions: though even a document of this nature can have its value, provided that it is treated as a starting point for discussion and that the architect is brought into the debate at a sufficiently early stage – and is prepared to ask questions.

So far as the best secular architecture of the last few years is concerned, the sort of approach which I have outlined can now be taken for granted. Whether or not the modern movement has created a valid and independent *style*, and this is perhaps debatable, it certainly seems to have produced an *approach* to building that is now so widespread as to be something of a commonplace among serious architects.

Church architecture is another matter. Here the old pictorial approach to architecture still persists almost unchallenged, disguised though it may be by a veneer of 'contemporary' detail, and, more recently, by the adoption of fashionable and supposedly 'liturgical' plan forms.[8] A radical approach to architecture is all very well where the parish hall is concerned: the design of the church itself is likely to be governed by considerations which have very little connection

[8] I feel bound to question Fr H. A. Reinhold's confident assertion that 'whether a church is truly modern or only overlaid with modern trappings that catch the eyes is infallibly tested by the floor plan'. (*The Dynamics of Liturgy*, the Macmillan Company, New York, 1961, p. 88.) I can think of quite a number of recent churches which look very interesting from the point of view of the plan, but which are non-starters as buildings. Post-war churches in Germany could provide some striking examples.

Towards a Church Architecture

with human activities. An architect designing a school, a university hall of residence or a shopping centre will, almost as a matter of course, adopt the sort of approach which I have described. But *the same architect*, given the chance to build a church, often seems quite prepared to throw all familiar disciplines and procedures to the winds. Not only in Britain but throughout the English-speaking world an ecclesiastical commission is still likely to result in this curious form of architectural schizophrenia; to be regarded as a sort of architectural holiday: an opportunity to escape from the restraints of normal design procedure into the less exacting world of fantasy and individual self-expression.

Churches are built to 'express' this and to 'symbolize' that. We have churches which look like hands folded in prayer; churches which symbolize aspiration or the anchor of the industrial pilgrim's life; churches which express the kingship of Christ; churches shaped like fishes, flames, and passion-flowers. There are still very few churches which show signs of anything comparable to the radical functional analysis that informs the best secular architecture of our time. Except in those countries of western Europe where the impact of the liturgical movement has forced church architects, and still more their clients, to re-examine first principles, ecclesiastical architecture is still dominated by pictorial and romantic preoccupations, it still tends to be regarded as a species of abstract sculpture unrelated to human needs. Of the thousands of 'modern' churches built since the Second World War, the overwhelming majority are primarily studies in composition: not functional structures designed to serve and articulate the communal activities which provide the one valid reason for building churches at all.

'More than most buildings do,' wrote a Canadian architect in 1959, 'the modern church offers a chance for an exercise in pure form. The basic space must be a large single volume. Then there is the symbol of cross or star which may be integrated in or opposed to the main mass, and there is a possible belfry.'[9] In a booklet describing the genesis of the First Presbyterian Church at Stamford, Connecticut, we are told how the early drawings showed 'the Sanctuary evolving at first as a great Druidical mass of heavy stone and prismed glass. Then as the long building ... took shape, the Sanctuary began to

[9] William Goulding in *Canadian Art*, vol. XVI, no. 4, 1959, p. 254.

A Radical Approach to Church Architecture

resemble an early symbol of Christ. And so evolved a new shape for a church of our time. . . . Cathedrals in the past were built around the shape of a cross traced on the ground. The Sanctuary is inspired by an ancient symbol of Christ. . . . To early Christians the Greek word for fish, *ichthys*, had a secret meaning. . . . Often the sign of the fish was drawn on the sand and on the walls of hiding places. . . . The fish became a symbol of the Christian faith. When seen from a distance the Sanctuary resembles this sign of hope which early Christians left on the walls of the catacombs as a symbol of spiritual victory.' Without questioning the assertion, made elsewhere in the fascinating booklet from which this quotation is taken, that 'the architectural concept and design of this church were unique and somewhat daring', one may well ask what all this whimsical symbolism has to do with the planning of churches, or indeed with serious architecture of any kind.

The familiar controversies about 'style' have effectively obscured the nature of the gulf that now separates ecclesiastical architecture from modern architecture in general. Neither the so-called traditionalists who, as has been remarked, are in reality much less the heirs of tradition than of revivalism, nor the advocates of what is commonly, though vaguely, referred to as the contemporary idiom, or the modern style, are fundamentally concerned with the human activities from which the *domus ecclesiae* derives its true purpose. They share an approach to church architecture which is essentially romantic. Their only real differences concern the superficial appearance of a building, the basic characteristics of which are taken for granted. There are plenty of recent churches which draw upon the whole rag-bag of contemporary clichés – random windows, *Betonglas*, skeletal bell towers, monumental crosses and the rest – but which are no more than caricatures of modern buildings. The most cursory examination will show that they reflect preoccupations of an entirely different order from those manifested in the design of our post-war schools, to take an outstanding example of a radical approach to architecture. Most of our new churches are in fact quite as ill-adapted to their true purpose as the revivalist buildings of an earlier generation. Uninformed by any serious attempt to think out afresh the nature of the activities which they ought properly to serve, they are, to adapt a saying of Bishop Gore's, 'ingeniously devised instruments for defeating the objects which they are supposed to promote'.[10] Their incidental differences at the stylistic level are of marginal importance.

The new Anglican cathedral at Coventry, for example, illustrates no less clearly than its revivalist predecessors at New York, Liverpool and Guildford the isolation of ecclesiastical architecture from any kind of theological or social context, the subordination of function to visual effect. No effort seems to have been made to analyse the purpose of a cathedral church in a setting which differs *toto cælo* from that within which the great mediaeval cathedrals were created; or, if it has, then the analysis has not been radical enough.[11] To try to build a cathedral today is like trying to run before one can walk. It will be time enough to think about cathedrals when we have succeeded in creating a few genuine 'liturgical sheds' of the most modest kind. If, however, the attempt had to be made, then the only responsible way to have gone about it would have been to try to formulate an adequate programme to have asked, for example, what is a bishop? what are his essential functions in a society which is no longer coterminous with the *ecclesia* itself? what is the precise character of his liturgical and pastoral ministry? and so on. One might do worse than to start from the ordination service: here surely is something that belongs to the *esse* of the bishop's liturgy, unlike so many of the peripheral activities which merely illustrate the extent to which the character of the Christian shepherd and father in God has been obscured by that of the mediaeval statesman and administrative official. One would certainly have to go on to ask some very basic questions about the diocese and its relationship to the parish, as well as about the commonly accepted pattern of cathedral worship, which often seems

---

[10] See G. L. Prestige, *The Life of Charles Gore*, Heinemann 1935, p. 265.
[11] It is of course only fair to the architect of the cathedral to point out that the commission was awarded as the result of a competition He could have no hand in formulating the programme, which was simply a statement of the client's supposed requirements. It can be taken as axiomatic today that what the client needs and what he thinks he needs are never the same. While a competition may sometimes be valuable as a means of discovering a young and unknown architect, it rules out from the start the kind of architect-client relationship which is essential for the formulation of an adequate programme. The architect *cannot* ask questions. The client will inevitably be presented with a design which has undergone a premature crystallization. The architect will be producing perspectives at a time when he ought to be drawing diagrams.

to be based on assumptions which would be entirely rejected by modern liturgical scholars. The architectural implications of this kind of radical analysis might well be surprising.

The new cathedral at Coventry does indeed provide a very striking example of the way in which the old pictorial approach to church architecture persists today beneath a wide variety of stylistic conventions. The sanctuary, for instance, instead of being considered as an organized space within which certain members of the one priestly community carry out their specific liturgical functions, is conceived first and foremost as part of a sort of two-dimensional backdrop which forms a visual focus for the gaze of a remote and passive congregation. The altar may legitimately be described as the focal point of the building, but only in the sense that it is the central element in what is essentially a two-dimensional composition (the fact of its being free-standing makes little difference) This is a debasement of the Lord's table into a mere ornament. Here the function of the altar is primarily visual: *it is something to be seen from a distance.* Its relationship to the worshipping community is far less important than its relationship to the great tapestry on the east wall. It is significant that the holy table is well over twenty feet long. Such an altar, considered not as an element in a composition but as something to be *used*, simply does not make sense; it is entirely unrelated to human scale. An altar over twenty feet long seems to call for a celebrant thirteen or fourteen feet high. and for all its alleged comprehensiveness it may reasonably be doubted whether the Church of England is equal to meeting such a demand. This, however, has clearly been a minor consideration. The dimensions of the holy table have nothing to do with use or usefulness [12]

[12] Compare Sir Edward Maufe on a Franciscan chapel in Holland: 'The secondary altars, on each side, greatly improve the value of the design, seeming to stabilise the thrust of the arch and bring the composition to rest'; and on Dominikus Bohm's church at Frielingsdorf: 'This is a beautiful interpretation of a modern church interior. The eye is led up to the altar, the rood and the east window. . . . The simple means used to obtain this dramatic composition are worthy of much thought'. *Modern Church Architecture*, Incorporated Church Building Society 1948, pp. 43 and 31. It was not until the later Middle Ages, and then only in western Europe, that the dimensions of the altar ceased to be related to human scale. In eastern Christendom, where the old tradition that the holy table should be free-standing has survived to this day, even in small churches, together

Towards a Church Architecture

The competition for the new Roman Catholic cathedral at Liverpool afforded some notable examples of the subordination of functional considerations to the craving for visual effect. Among the commended designs was one described by the assessors as 'an impressive design which would have succeeded as a structure *for general cultural purposes*', the nature of which they did not attempt to elucidate, but which can hardly have included the celebration of the eucharist, since it appeared to be impossible to *use* the high altar at all.

This primacy of the visual is ultimately the product of a defective understanding of the nature of the Christian assembly and the activities in which it engages. To treat the eucharistic liturgy as a solemn spectacle performed on a distant stage by a handful of professional actors for the edification of an amorphous crowd of spectators is to misconceive its essential character it is not that kind of activity. A church is essentially a place for *doing*, for corporate *action* in which all are participants and each has his appropriate function to perform, it is not a sort of jewelled cave in which the solitary individual may find some kind of worship experience, and where his emotions may be kindled by the contemplation of a remote spectacle The only remedy for fundamental misconceptions of this nature lies in the study of the worshipping community itself.

The first step towards a church architecture for our time is to recognize that a Christian church is essentially a house for a community and that it has no independent meaning apart from that community The revolutionary significance of the early churches of Rudolf Schwarz lies above all in the way in which they reassert this fundamental truth, that the church building is '*a house for* divine worship, not the autonomous architectural expression of religious feeling'.[13] Once this is accepted, then it is readily apparent that the first necessity for the church builder must be to understand what the *ecclesia* itself is and does.

As long ago as 1920 Professor Clement Rogers, in an extremely perceptive essay on *Pastoral Theology and Art*, which seems to have been entirely ignored by those responsible for building new churches

with the practice of concelebration, a more or less cubic form is still normal. As may be seen from the illustrations, the present liturgical renewal has led to a widespread return to ancient tradition.

[13] H. A. Reinhold, op. cit., p. 24.

A Radical Approach to Church Architecture

in this country, underlined the disastrous consequences of dissociating architecture from meaning and treating objects significant in themselves as mere pieces of ornamentation. We need, he wrote, in a passage curiously prophetic of later events in Germany, 'to recover the conception of a church as a place of worship. We must make a careful study of the intimate connection of liturgiology and church building. We must secure a full realization on the part of architects of the use to which a church is to be put, and an equally full realization on the part of the clergy of the inner spiritual value of a beautiful church, and the bar to spiritual growth that is presented by a bad one – a hindrance all the more serious because, fixed by wood and stone, it is continuous and unalterable.' It is depressing to reflect that, so far as the English-speaking world is concerned, this passage is just as relevant today as it was forty years ago.[14] Our most urgent need is still to recover the conception of a church as a house for a community, the form of which must grow out of the characteristic actions in which that community manifests (or should manifest) its essential nature. It is still necessary to insist that the building exists for the people who are themselves the temple of the living God; that it is not a shrine or a monument to some abstract concept of religion but a liturgical and pastoral instrument for the furtherance of the Church's apostolic task.

I have already considered the need 'to secure a full realization on the part of architects of the use to which a church is to be put': to make architects realize that a church, no less than a school, a hospital or a factory, is a building with certain precise and, to some extent at least, analysable functions; that it is not an autonomous architectural *tour de force*, providing a unique opportunity for throwing off the restraints and disciplines of normal design procedure.

[14] This essay seems to have been written towards the end of the First World War It was subsequently printed in a volume of lectures published by the Oxford University Press in 1920 with the title *Pastoral Theology and the Modern World*. I am grateful to Roger Williams for bringing this book to my notice Professor Rogers's criticisms of the church architecture of his day, and his proposals for remedying the situation by 'a continued and general bringing together of the architectural and ecclesiastical world', anticipate to a remarkable degree the thesis of my own book *Liturgy and Architecture*, published forty years later. The resistance to new ideas is so great in ecclesiastical circles that one cannot but wonder whether it will not be necessary for somebody to restate the same thesis in the year 2000.

Towards a Church Architecture

It may well be asked whether it is reasonable to look for such a realization on the part of architects at a time when the Church itself seems to have so little understanding of its true function in the modern world. Surely the Church has a responsibility for briefing its architects, and the pathetic irrelevance of most of our modern churches stems in the last resort from the Church's failure to shoulder its responsibilities. How much guidance can an architect normally expect from an ecclesiastical client, particularly where fundamental principles are concerned? As Diana Rowntree has remarked, 'all that is best in our architecture today has its roots in the functional tradition. Few twentieth-century architects, whatever their theories, like to start on a design without a precise programme of their client's requirements. In the case of church design this programme is simply not forthcoming.... Many clergymen would be astounded to be asked by their architect, in all seriousness, what a church is for.' Is it altogether surprising if, 'in the absence of a clear brief, many of the more serious architects prefer not to tackle church design at all?'[15]. Can there in fact be any genuine renewal of church architecture without a prior renewal within the Church of the meaning of the Church?

The history of ecclesiastical architecture during the last half-century would seem to suggest a negative answer to all these questions. It can hardly be too strongly emphasized that the importance of the so-called liturgical movement, where church design is concerned, does not lie in the advocacy of specific formal solutions – circular or fan-shaped plans, central altars and so on – but rather in the way in which it compels the client to face fundamental questions about the Church and its worship in all their depth and complexity:[16] to dis-

[15] *The Challenge of Church Architecture* in the *Guardian* for February 4th 1960.
[16] As Reyner Banham has observed, 'To regard the liturgical movement as a most promising new source of valid forms in church architecture is to miss its point completely.... Its interest for the architect lies in the kind of brief it will give him when he is asked to design a church – not vaguely emotive in the recent atmospheric manner, not fanatically precise over trivia, as with the Ecclesiologists of the last century, but concerned with functions and people. Such a brief... puts the conceptual stages of church design on the same intellectual and imaginative footing as applies in the most forward areas of secular architecture at present.' *The Architectural Review*, vol. CXXVIII, no. 766, December 1960, p. 400.

criminate between what belongs to authentic Christian tradition and what is merely the legacy of a conventional pattern of church life which has not been subjected to the judgment of the word of God.

But the second need to which Clement Rogers drew attention is no less urgent today. Church design has received so little serious thought or attention from the Church as a whole mainly because the majority of the clergy simply do not realize its potentialities; do not realize that a well-designed church can provide them with an invaluable pastoral tool, or that a bad one is a bar to the growth of the communities committed to their charge. There is a widespread assumption within the Church that the design of the *domus ecclesiae* is essentially an 'artistic' matter which, however important it may seem to an aesthetically sensitive minority, is of quite marginal concern to the Church as a whole. Architecture, it is thought, is at best a sort of decorative backdrop to human activities: something which, while it may provide a more or less convenient or appropriate setting for the performance of various 'rituals', is incapable of exercising any decisive influence on the character and development of the activities in question. Closely linked to this attitude to architecture in general and its relation to human activity is the further assumption that what distinguishes modern architecture from that of earlier centuries is simply a matter of style or idiom. Just as a nineteenth-century architect could, at the whim of his client, substitute a Palladian elevation for a Gothic, or vice versa, without making any radical alteration in the general character of the building, so all that is necessary today is a sort of architectural face-lift. It may be that, in an age of unparalleled technological progress, the dictates of fashion, and the need for economy, will suggest changes not only in the decoration of the backdrop but also in the materials of which it is woven. But it remains a backdrop. Within the wide limits laid down in the relevant canons and rubrics the design of a church is a technical matter that may safely be left to the appropriate experts; it is governed to a great extent by aesthetic criteria, which the average parish priest can hardly be expected to understand. The form of the building has only the most tenuous connection with the activities for which it provides a setting.

The chief argument put forward for building churches 'in the modern style' is that the appearance of the building can undoubtedly have an influence on the public image of the institution. The contrast between a neo-gothic church, built of traditional materials, and the steel and glass college of technology on the other side of the road can, it is recognized, help to foster the unfortunate notion that the Church itself is no more than a curious anachronism. No doubt it can, but the problem is a good deal more complex than is realized by ecclesiastical dignitaries who are regularly reported as saying that they feel sure that the simple, clean lines of Mr X's new church, its aluminium spire and its extremely contemporary reredos, constructed of wrought-iron, copper-wire and plastic, will appeal to the younger generation, and show that the dear old C. of E. is at last facing up to the challenge of the atomic age. . . .

Whether we realize it or not, the relationship between architecture and the activities which it serves (or frustrates) is far closer than is imagined by those who would confine the importance of well-designed churches to the realm of public relations. The design of a church can never safely be left to the various specialists whose skills are needed for the fashioning of the building It is an evasion of responsibility to call in an architect and a team of artists, as one might summon a signwriter to repaint the notice board outside the church or a typographer to give a new look to the parish magazine, and to take no further interest in their activities, apart from seeing that they do not exceed an arbitrarily determined cost ceiling. It needs to be realized that the architecture of the building is capable of exercising a profound influence on the worshipping community's understanding of itself and its mission.

As I wrote in an earlier essay on church building, 'the man who builds a church is, in the last resort, playing a decisive role in the creation of a community. . . . A church that reflects a distorted or impoverished understanding of the corporate actions from which it derives its *raison d'être* will prevent those whose house it is from attaining to a full awareness of their calling. . . . A clericalized liturgy means a clericalized apostolate If, on the other hand, the layman has learned to accept his responsibilities as a member of an organic, priestly community, and as an active participant in the eucharist, this awareness will undoubtedly be reflected in due course in his whole attitude towards the Church and its apostolic mission. The surest way of bringing home to the laity that they *are* the Church – and not the passive recipients of spiritual consolation at the hands of a professional ministry – is to make plain the full implications of the eucharistic liturgy.'[17] Whether these implications are made plain or not will depend to a far greater extent than is commonly realized on the building within which the Christian assembly takes place.

What W. R. Lethaby said of the town as a whole is no less true of the individual buildings which house the diverse activities of its citizens. 'Man builds towns so that the towns shall build his sons ... the outward is always reacting again on the inward, so that the concrete becomes a mould for the spiritual.'[18] Our understanding of the various 'rituals' in which we take part is inevitably moulded by the buildings in which they are habitually performed. For good or for ill, architecture is always more than a mere backdrop. That is why the design of the houses which the Church sets apart for the celebration of the liturgy cannot be treated as a technical or artistic matter, cannot be governed by aesthetic criteria alone. It is of vital concern to the Church as a whole.

An architecture informed by Christian meanings and values, a church building which embodies a genuine understanding of what the Church, in the biblical sense of that word, is and does when it gathers to celebrate the liturgy, can be a powerful influence in the formation of the people of God. If we build real churches, then those churches will build our sons. Conversely, a church which reflects other values than those of authentic Christian tradition will militate against the building up of the body of Christ – and churches are usually built to last a long time. As Robert Maguire puts it.

> If you are going to build a church
> you are going to create a thing which speaks.
> It will speak of meanings, and of values,
> and it will go on speaking.
> And if it speaks of the wrong values
> It will go on destroying.
> There is a responsibility here.

There is indeed a responsibility, and it is one which the Church has hardly begun to face. We have built in haste, conscious only of short-term pastoral needs, churches which with rare exceptions speak, and will go on speaking, of meanings and values profoundly alien to those which the Church exists not merely to proclaim but also to manifest; churches which, in ways more subtle and subversive than we realize,

[17] *Liturgy and Architecture*, Barrie & Rockliff 1960, pp. 168–9.
[18] *Form in Civilization*, Oxford University Press, 2nd edition 1957, p. 1.

deny the doctrine preached from their pulpits, and obscure the essential meaning of the communal acts which they should serve and articulate.[19] Whatever the errors of the nineteenth-century ecclesiologists, they realized far more clearly than our modern church extension committees the potentialities of architecture as an instrument for transforming the Church's understanding of what it is and does. Their theology may have been defective, at least they grasped the fact that architecture needs to be related to theology; that the design of a church is a matter of urgent concern to the pastor, and indeed to the Church as a whole. We have failed to profit from their example.

Within the last thirty years, in the prison camps of occupied Europe, we have seen that it is perfectly possible for the Church to flourish with undiminished vigour even though it has no buildings, no set-apart places, at its disposal; indeed, as has often been pointed out in recent years, the experiences of returned prisoners of war who rediscovered the meaning of the *ecclesia* as a eucharistic fellowship in the German prison camps have played a considerable part in the remarkable development of liturgical reform since the Second World War. In this country too, more than one university chaplain has commented on the astonishing effect upon a student community of celebrating the eucharist in lecture rooms and hostels, with the congregation standing round a simple table, instead of in some neo-gothic edifice the whole layout and spatial organization of which effectively obscure the character and implications of the sacramental action. One hears of similar experiences from those who have been attempting to build up 'house-churches' in suburban parishes and isolated rural communities.

It would be a mistake to argue from experiences such as these that ecclesiastical architecture is of marginal importance to the Church as a whole. On the contrary, what happened in the prison camps, and is still happening in universities, suburban house-churches, worker-

---

[19] One of the many projected books which I shall probably never write is a volume of *Contrasts*, consisting largely of photographs and scriptural quotations, in which evangelical qualities such as humility, sincerity, truthfulness, poverty of spirit, etc. would be illustrated from the secular architecture of the last thirty years or so; while architectural manifestations of the whole catalogue of deadly sins – pride, sloth, luxury and the rest – would be illustrated from the ecclesiastical buildings of the same period. It would, alas, be all too easy to produce such a book.

priests' lodgings and *colonies de vacances*, underlines the destructive potentialities of an architecture unrelated to theology for the Church's conception of its mission. The significance of such experiences is surely that they show Christians rediscovering fundamental truths which have long been obscured by the buildings in which they habitually worship. While doctrinal error has stemmed in the first instance from a defective understanding of the Church, it has been perpetuated by churches in which erroneous doctrine has assumed visible and tangible form. The spiritual has indeed been moulded by the concrete; the meanings and values embodied in stone have continued to shape the worship and the piety of Christians even when the false teaching from which those meanings and values derive has been recognized and corrected. Whenever church architecture is treated as something peripheral to the Church's mission, whenever it is regarded as the preserve of a handful of specialists and is not related to the work of the theologian, the liturgist and the pastor, then it will almost inevitably become a destructive influence in the life of the Christian community.

It is to be hoped that somebody will one day undertake a systematic study of the ways in which the worship and outlook of western Christians have been warped by the great churches of mediaeval Europe and the buildings for which they served as a pattern in the nineteenth century. Such a work could be extremely illuminating. There is, it seems to me, every reason to suppose that the legacy of vast, dim naves, unrelated to human scale, has been a factor of major importance in the persistence of the psychological proletarianism that prevents the Church from manifesting its true nature today. Splendid as these buildings are, they embody a particular and transient relationship between the Christian community and society at large which did not survive the passing of the Middle Ages: they are essentially 'rhetorical assertions of the temporal triumph of Christendom';[20] *not* houses for the family of God. The understanding of the Church and its worship expressed in these churches would have seemed as alien to Christians of earlier centuries as it is unsatisfactory to ourselves, who have begun to rediscover the biblical insights into the nature of the *ecclesia* and to try to translate those renewed insights into action, both in and out of church. In the process, we have

[20] Robert J. Dwyer, Bishop of Reno, Navada. See *Liturgical Arts*, vol XXVII, no. 1, November 1958.

begun to realize the extent to which our understanding of our mission has been moulded by buildings which, however magnificent as architecture, are nevertheless the product of a defective ecclesiology and a liturgical tradition in an advanced stage of decay.

Because our approach to church architecture has been almost exclusively aesthetic we have failed to appreciate the theological implications of a building which, for the majority of western Christians – and even for those who never enter a church except for christenings, weddings and funerals – remains the image *par excellence* of a Christian church. Even though mediaeval doctrines of the Church, the eucharist and the laity are no longer preached from the pulpits of our new churches, they are still implicit in the plan and spatial organization of the buildings themselves, despite the decorative clichés, the bright primary colours and the Festival of Britain light fittings. Sermons about the parish communion as a corporate action are all very well, more often than not they are rendered ineffectual by buildings which impose upon the central and normative act of the Church's life the character of something done 'up there' by a distant celebrant. Nave altars and similar expedients may help to counteract the influence of such buildings on worship; they cannot disguise the fact that most of the churches built in this country since the middle of the nineteenth century have been shaped by an ecclesiology which is hopelessly at variance with that of scripture and early Christian tradition: and which, if it were made explicit and expressed verbally, would be repudiated in no uncertain terms both by those responsible for the design of the buildings and those who use them Sunday by Sunday.

Architecture can never be dissociated from meaning. The architect who designs a spire a hundred and twenty feet high is, whether he grasps the fact or not, making an assertion about the Church's relationship to the community at large which needs to be substantiated. The Methodist chapel with a communion table in the form of a cube, richly vested with an embroidered frontal, speaks of a sacramental doctrine which, however deeply it may be embedded in the eucharistic hymns of the Wesleys themselves, would, I suspect, be rejected by most of their modern disciples. The conventional nineteenth-century layout of an Anglican parish church embodies a doctrine of the royal priesthood which finds little support either in the Book of Common Prayer or in the scriptural and patristic sources to which the Church of England professes to appeal.

A Radical Approach to Church Architecture

Everywhere today one finds Christians 'attempting to worship in buildings that imply beliefs they do not hold and patterns of worship they do not practise'.[21] Such are the consequences of isolating church architecture from the main stream of the Church's life and thought: of treating the design of the *domus ecclesiae* as an 'artistic' matter subject only to aesthetic criteria. If a church is not informed by a deep understanding of its true purpose, then it will inevitably speak of values other than those intended by its builders. The only remedy lies in what Clement Rogers called a continued and general bringing together of the architectural and ecclesiastical world; in the development of a genuine dialogue between the architect and the theologian; above all, in an approach to architecture which starts from the consideration of human activities, relationships and values, and not from formal concepts.

The prospect for church architecture in the 'sixties depends very largely on the extent to which we succeed in bringing to the design of the *domus ecclesiae* the same radicalism, the same readiness to go back again and again to the programme and to wrestle with its implications, which Sir John Summerson has noted as the hall-mark of serious modern architecture. If, instead of imitating the formal solutions of the pioneers of modern church building we seek to understand their fundamental approach; if we can tackle the problems of church design at least as radically, and with the same theological competence and discernment, as they were tackled in Germany during the 'twenties; then we may yet learn, slowly and patiently, to create churches which will build our sons, and which will lead those who use them to a renewed understanding of their calling as Christians.

[21] Marvin Halverson in *Religious Buildings for Today*, F. W. Dodge Corporation 1957, p. 5.

2. Modern Architectural Theory and the Liturgy

NIGEL MELHUISH

In this country a serious approach to the problems of church building has so far been almost entirely lacking, both in the architectural and in the ecclesiastical press. The renewal of church architecture abroad has been the subject of a few articles in the architectural journals, but in most of these there seems to have been a complete abandonment of the normal standards of architectural criticism. It is a commonplace of modern criticism that architecture is the most social of the arts, and that a building can be adequately assessed only in a social context. But in most of what is written about church architecture this doctrine is not applied. There is seldom any attempt to connect the problems of church building with the present situation of the Church, or with current developments in Christian theology and sociology. From a humanist point of view the reason for this is obvious: a new church is simply an anachronism, and modern religious art, however good, can never be more than a sort of highbrow entertainment. But for the Christian, sacred art is a matter of vital importance. His difficulty lies in the fact that religion today is usually seen as a department of life, having only a superficial connection with society at large. Yet if church architecture cannot be related to an understanding of the Church and its place in modern society, there cannot be any profitable discussion of Christian art.

A serious attempt to relate church building to the Christian position as a whole is to be found in the various periodicals devoted to sacred art which are published abroad, many of which have sprung from the liturgical movement, which is bringing about a transformation in the most diverse fields of Christian thought and activity. The movement is not confined to any one communion, and in many ways it is changing the traditional patterns of denominational Christianity. In this country the implications of the liturgical movement for art and architecture are only just beginning to be realized.

The position here was quite well described in an editorial of *The London Churchman*, in connection with that very depressing book *Sixty Post-War Churches*.[1] The writer says: 'It is odd to reflect that we are living in one of the great ages of church-building. Not so much, perhaps, on account of our piety, as because of the last war and the shift in population to new areas. Not for five hundred years have we seen so many new churches going up, and never, one imagines, in such extreme divergence of design. .. Here are churches of all shapes, from a cave to a star, built of everything from aluminium to asbestos, and all of them intended not for the amusement of art critics, but for the worship of ordinary people. Yet, this variety, stimulating as it is, raises a question. Have the architects any clear idea as to the *function* of the buildings they are designing? Have we who commission them?'

There are two points arising out of this. In the first place, it would probably be very surprising to most architects, and perhaps also to most clergymen, that so many churches have in fact been built since the war.[2] The great majority of new churches are so devoid of merit that they have been entirely ignored in the architectural press, and until the publication of *Sixty Post-War Churches* it was very difficult to find out anything about recent church architecture without making laborious investigations. Church architecture has been in a back-water, neglected both by the architectural profession and by the best minds in the Church. The second point, following on the first, is that an enormous programme of investment has been undertaken – and unhappily to a large extent completed – without any serious consideration of its purpose.

It is beginning to be recognized that the problem of church architecture in this country centres on the question of *function*: what is a church *for*? To start from the functional programme of a church building is to abandon the sentimental and aesthetic language in which these things are normally discussed, and to speak in terms which can at any rate begin to make sense to the modern architect as well as to the theologian. Historically, the buildings erected by the

[1] Incorporated Church Building Society 1957.
[2] It is hard to get accurate information, but the Church of England alone has built well over three hundred churches since the war, and in all kinds of church work (not including Coventry Cathedral) it must have spent something approaching fifteen million pounds.

Towards a Church Architecture

Christian Church have served different purposes at different times and places. What sort of buildings are called for at the present time? Enthusiasts for modern church architecture in this country generally avoid such questions and discuss the problem in terms of 'style'. It is argued that there is a perfectly good modern style of building, and that all would be well with church architecture if only the Church could be persuaded to adopt it. But this approach is theologically irrelevant and architecturally misleading. Style is a vague word, and architects are apt to find it embarrassing In the sense in which it applies to the great traditions of the past, it refers to a more or less well-established 'grammar' of building, associated with methods of construction which evolved very slowly over many centuries. Today, when the architect has to deal with an increasingly rapid development of new inventions and new structural techniques, there is nothing which can really be compared with the traditional styles. New methods of construction do not constitute a new style of architecture, though architectural propagandists sometimes appear to think so In this respect the situation in architecture is hardly less confused than in contemporary painting or sculpture, where it would be an obvious absurdity to talk about 'the contemporary style'. The question of what is meant by modern architecture is therefore not an easy one to answer; but unless some sort of answer can be found the growing demand for modern churches is likely to lead only to an endless attempt to be up to date: to follow the changing enthusiasms of the art-pundits, or even the latest novelties of the exhibition stand

At the present time there is a good deal of boredom with architectural theory. a feeling that much of the literature of the modern movement is discredited, that didactic talk is no longer of any use, and that buildings cannot be valued in terms of a purely literary propaganda. The emphasis on function in the liturgical movement comes at a time when the validity of the functional tradition in architecture is being widely questioned. Are we not moving beyond functionalism to a less utilitarian conception of architecture? To many people the South Bank Festival seemed to usher in a more 'human' approach to design, which was welcomed by Osbert Lancaster in an article called 'The End of the Modern Movement'. Since then there have been many buildings – some of them by the most famous modern architects – which seem far removed from the functional theories of the nineteen-thirties. At the same time there have been significant changes in the vocabulary of architectural criticism. Many of the old slogans are no longer heard, and there is much talk about the problem of symbolism: the word image occurs almost as often in architectural writing as it does in theology. It might seem that in using the language of function the liturgical movement is reverting to a way of thinking which architects have already abandoned.

The current dissatisfaction with functionalism usually derives from a too-limited idea of its significance in architectural practice. A crude utilitarianism has never characterized the work of the most influential modern architects. Architectural theory today is in a state of considerable confusion, and the reaction against a superficial rationalism has led to impatience with any attempt to provide a reasoned basis for design. But an architecture without critical standards is clearly in a weak position. In the nature of his work an architect is committed to theory: if he is not understood, he cannot retire into his studio and make things for the mantlepiece. An architect who adopts the role of outsider soon ceases to be an architect. he is bound to interpret his work, and in doing so he will normally depend to a large extent on ideas he has inherited. As a theory, the functional idea has often been formulated in a way which is open to obvious objections, but it is important to see what it was intended to do, and where it has proved inadequate.

The ideas which have influenced modern architecture might be classified under three main headings The first is the association of architecture with social and ethical idealism, going back to Pugin and Ruskin, and forming part of the whole revolt against individualism which began in the nineteenth century. The second is the application of scientific method to the problems of design, and all the scientific and 'scientistic' theories which have come to be associated with functionalism. Finally there are the art movements, including artnouveau, cubism, constructivism and the various movements of our own time. These things have not occurred in isolation from one another, since in the literature of the modern movement they are interconnected and sometimes confused. In the actual form which modern buildings have taken – the various styles or languages of modern architecture – it is the art movements which have been most important. But it is ethical and scientific ideology which has given the propaganda of the modern movement its characteristic tone.

When the ethical note first appears in architectural theory, it comes as a revolt against the whole conception of style as a matter of fashion or individual preference. In Pugin, the traditional forms are seen as rooted in certain patterns of belief and social order from which they cannot be separated. The question of architectural style is therefore not only one of taste, but of moral conviction. Both he and Ruskin took the architecture of the Renaissance as a symbol of *laissez-faire* capitalism: it had robbed the worker of freedom and initiative, and condemned him to a mechanical drudgery. Gothic architecture was held up as an ideal, since it revealed 'the life and liberty of every workman who struck the stone'.

Romantic mediaevalism now seems a strange thing, and it has done the Church a great deal of harm. But in their concern with the position of labour under industrialism, the Victorian mediaevalists stated a problem which has haunted architectural theory ever since. The problem lies at the centre of much Victorian thinking about social reform, and it was clearly stated by Marx in what he wrote about the alienation of labour. Explaining what he means by this, he says: 'First, the fact that labour is *external* to the worker, i.e. it does not belong to his essential being; that in his work, therefore, he does not affirm himself but denies himself, does not feel content but unhappy, does not develop freely his physical and mental energy, but mortifies his body and ruins his mind. The worker therefore only feels himself outside his work, and in his work feels outside himself. He is at home when he is not working, and when he is working he is not at home. His labour is therefore not voluntary, but coerced; it is forced labour. It is therefore not the satisfaction of a need; it is merely a *means* to satisfy needs external to it . . .'[3]

Ruskin and Morris denounced machinery, and refused to allow any artistic merit to things not made by hand. They saw that art must be rooted in the common life, but found no hope of such an ideal in a society based on industrial production. Ruskin eventually turned away from art criticism, and worked for social and economic reform; and as William Morris would never have anything to do with modern machinery, the products of his workshop were beyond the means of any but the well-to-do. For all its ideals of brotherhood, the Arts and Crafts Movement was never much more than a middle-class hobby.

[3] *Economic and Philosophic Manuscripts of* 1844, Foreign Languages Publishing House, Moscow; Lawrence and Wishart, London, n.d., p. 72.

Modern Architectural Theory and the Liturgy

In the nineteenth century, the worlds of work and culture were so completely separated that all the most advanced structures of the age, the great railway stations, bridges and exhibition halls, were built without the aid and generally without the approval of architects. But architects could not pretend to ignore machinery indefinitely: looking at the towers of Chicago, Frank Lloyd Wright proclaimed that 'if this power must be uprooted that civilization may live, civilization is already doomed'. Towards the end of the century the achievements of the engineers began to be recognized as the basis of a new architecture, and architects were exhorted to adopt modern machinery and modern methods of construction. And this was seen not only as an aesthetic, but as a moral question: the traditional styles were sternly condemned as instruments of reaction and privilege. In an age of machinery, the architect was to restore the connection between art and everyday labour: to redeem industrial work and give it a social and cultural significance. The manifesto of the *Deutscher Werkbund* speaks of 'ennobling industrial labour' and 'raising the morale of work'. From this sprang the concern of the modern movement with honesty in the use of structure and materials. Products which had hitherto been ignored or disguised were now given a value of their own. At the same time the function of a building acquired a new importance; for the design was not to come from a stylistic handbook, but from an imaginative understanding of modern life and of the human activities the building had to serve.

One of the most famous books of this period is Louis Sullivan's *Kindergarten Chats*, which came out in 1901. The architects of his time come under a scathing attack for their timidity in the face of industrialism; and in his conception of the architect's function he provides a remarkable summary of the idealism of the modern movement. The architect's task, he says, is 'to vitalize building materials, to animate them collectively with a thought, a state of feeling, to charge them with a subjective significance and value, to make them a visible part of the genuine social fabric, to infuse into them the true life of the people, to impart into them the best that is within the people as the eye of the poet, looking below the surface of life, sees the best that is within the people. . . .'[4] Sullivan was a keen student of biology, and he is best known for his saying that form follows

---

[4] Edition of 1934, Scarab Fraternity Press, p. 194.

function. Reyner Banham regards this as an example of 'nineteenth-century determinism' and dismisses it as 'an empty jingle'.[5] Torn out of its context and made into a propaganda slogan, this is no doubt what it has become. But *Kindergarten Chats* does not present a straightforward determinism: Sullivan sometimes sees architecture as a sort of poetry, and sometimes as a science. This mixture of romantic and scientific elements is often contradictory, because the scientific philosophy of his time – even in biology – was essentially mechanistic.[6] As a method, science was the application of Bacon's principle that 'men should put their notions by, and attend solely to the facts'; and such a programme is not easily combined with a romantic view of the imagination.

This conflict is not peculiar to Sullivan, and in one way or another it has been a feature of nearly all architectural theory since the beginning of the modern movement. Impressed by the scientific achievements of the age, architects first interpreted their work in terms of engineering (structural rationalism) and later on in the language of biology. hence 'form follows function' and all the talk about organic architecture. In their most logical statements these are deterministic theories in which the imagination is regarded as a poor substitute for scientific method. At the same time (and sometimes in the same breath) architects continued to speak of their work as art and to see the function of the building as subject-matter for the artist. In this case the design process is essentially imaginative: informed but not determined by an analysis of the practical requirements.

The tension between an intuitive and a scientific view of architectural design appears conspicuously in *The New Vision* by Laszlo Moholy-Nagy.[7] He was on the staff of the Bauhaus, and Walter

[5] *Theory and Design in the First Machine Age*, Architectural Press 1960, p. 320. This is one of the most valuable surveys of modern architectural theory which has so far appeared.
[6] 'One most significant fact of this period is the advance in biological sciences. These sciences are essentially sciences concerning organisms. During the epoch in question, and indeed also at the present moment, the prestige of the more perfect scientific form belongs to the physical sciences. Accordingly, biology apes the manners of physics. It is orthodox to hold, that there is nothing in biology but what is physical mechanism under somewhat complex circumstances.' A. N. Whitehead, *Science and The Modern World*, Cambridge 1946, p. 128.
[7] Brewer, Warren & Putnam, New York, 1936.

Gropius (rather oddly) called his book a standard grammar of modern design. In his attitude to social reform Moholy-Nagy starts from the same position as William Morris: 'the class struggle is in the last resort not about capital . . . but in reality it concerns the right of the individual to a satisfying occupation, work that meets the inner needs, a normal way of life and a real release of human powers.'[8] All this is in accordance with the Bauhaus programme of uniting industry and art, and *The New Vision* still provides one of the best accounts of the art movements which have influenced modern design. In his underlying philosophy, however, and in his main teachings about design, Moholy-Nagy owes more to H. G. Wells than to the utopians of the nineteenth century. All human behaviour is interpreted in terms of a mechanistic biology, and our plans for the future are to be guided by a clear understanding of biological function: 'every action and expression of man is the sum of components founded mainly on biological structure. . . . We are therefore much less interested today in the intensity and quality of expressions of "art" than in the elements that determine, with the force of ruling law, our function as human beings and the forms it takes.'[9] Reyner Banham writes that 'architecture – the ordering of space – is justified in Moholy's eyes in so far as it furthers the ascertainable biological needs of man';[10] and Moholy-Nagy lays it down as a basic principle of modern design that 'in all fields of creation, workers today are striving to find purely functional solutions of a technical-biological kind: that is, to build up each piece of work from the elements that are required for its function'.[11] The traditional forms must be abandoned, since they reflect a class-culture which is irrelevant in industrial society. An architecture firmly based on the objective laws of biology will again find a link with the common life, and the artist will be drawn out of his isolation.

The total impression left by *The New Vision* is a rather strange one: that while Moholy-Nagy speaks of uniting industry and art, what his

---

[8] Ibid., p. 15.   [9] Ibid., p. 8.
[10] Op. cit., p. 318. Dr Banham concludes that what emerges from *The New Vision* is 'a kind of non-Deterministic Functionalism, based no longer on the bare logic of structural Rationalism, but upon the study of man as a variable organism'. It is hard to know what to make of this, since in many passages a deterministic theory of design seems to have been just what Moholy-Nagy was after.
[11] Op. cit., p. 54.

theory really does is to exclude the artist altogether. The artist is welcomed into the factory at the main entrance, and then shown firmly out by the back door. However much you extend the meaning of the word biological – to cover man's psychological as well as his physical make-up – you still cannot describe the artist's work wholly in terms of scientific method. One might say that this is only a matter of words: that the imagination plays as vital a part in science as it does in art. The trouble is that what Moholy-Nagy writes about determination and objective laws implies a nineteenth-century view of science which allows no room for the imagination: there is certainly no place for aesthetic judgment. At the Bauhaus such ideas were never realized, nor were they ever wholly accepted as an aim. In its search for form in industrial design, the Bauhaus leaned heavily on the work of contemporary painters and sculptors; and in some places *The New Vision* seems a strained attempt to play down the achievements of the imagination in favour of utopian and mechanistic propaganda.

The Bauhaus was primarily a school of industrial design, though it was always intended to develop an architectural course there. In the modern movement the problem of architecture and of industrial design have always been closely connected, and in some ways this has led to a good deal of confusion. For example, the design of goods for mass production lends itself much more readily to a mechanistic interpretation than the design of most buildings: it is more easily thought of as *technical* problem. The problem itself is a full statement of all the requirements the product has to fulfil, and the answer to the problem is the design. The design process in this case is not an imaginative, but a purely logical one, and the solution to the problem is really determined by the way in which the problem is stated. All this is very remote from what actually went on at the Bauhaus, and it would be a misleading account of industrial design as it exists at present. But in this field art and technique are so intimately connected that it is easy to lose sight of the distinction altogether. In discussing the nature of scientific investigation Michael Foster pointed out that the ability to *produce* by scientific means depends on the ability to *specify*, but there are certain things which 'cannot be achieved by technical means, because we cannot specify in advance what would count as having achieved them'.[12] This is certainly true

[12] *Mystery and Philosophy*, S.C.M. Press 1957, p. 64. Cf. also the chapter on 'Art and Craft' in Collingwood's *Principles of Art*, Oxford, 1938.

of art, and however much the artist may be involved with technology, his work can never be given a purely technical interpretation. The confusion of art and technique which is implied in a good deal of writing about industrial design is really on a level with the discussions of mechanical painting and poetry, etc., which still take place on the lunatic fringe of popular science. In itself, however, the demand for a wider application of scientific methods in design is well founded, and it has always had a central place in modern architectural theory.

During the nineteenth century, and indeed until quite recent times, manufacturers of industrial goods decorated their products with all kinds of traditional motives to give them cultural prestige: things were deliberately designed to disguise the way they were made. William Morris's reaction was to reject machinery and work for a revival of handicrafts; but it was not long before his principles of 'fitness' and 'honesty' began to be applied to the design of goods for industrial production. This resulted in things which were obviously made by machinery and showed the best use of industrial processes. But artists sometimes spoke as if their products were even *designed* like machinery. i.e to a strict specification of functional requirements. This of course was not the case, since the form of the product was never completely determined by functional analysis. The pioneers of industrial design had an idealized conception: 'mechanical form', and in applying it they were sometimes quite as romantic as the Victorian manufacturers who put Doric columns on railway engines or Gothic tracery on the kitchen stove. Much of what looked like pure functional design (in the scientific sense) was therefore nothing of the kind: it was the product of a quite definite style. In architecture this is especially obvious, since the building industry during the inter-war period relied very largely on traditional materials and methods of construction. When Le Corbusier called the house a machine for living in, he was generally taken to be an advocate of an extreme scientific functionalism; yet his pre-eminence is due above all to his extraordinary command of modern architectural imagery.

The marriage of art and science in modern design has always been an uneasy one, and at the present time it is under a greater strain than ever. Advocates of a purely scientific method are apt to accuse the imaginative designer of falling into the subjectivism and individualism that the modern movement has always fought against. The conception of art as a co-operative enterprise has been a prominent feature of modern architectural theory, originating with Ruskin and Morris and culminating in the Bauhaus. During the nineteen-thirties teamwork was an accepted axiom of architectural propaganda. The Victorian idea of co-operation was based on a revival of the mediaeval outlook and tradition of craftsmanship, and its weaknesses were sufficiently exposed at the time by the followers of art for art's sake. The ideal was not maintained for long, and during the inter-war period teamwork was increasingly associated with a technological conception of architecture. The significance of this was not fully realized, because the architectural imagery of the time had a severely mechanistic character which effectively disguised its unscientific origins. Now that artists are less inclined to romanticize machinery, architectural symbolism has become richer and more chaotic, and no longer provides an illusion of rationality. To many people Whistler seems to have been right after all: co-operation in art is as dead as the Oxford collective poem and the group theatre of the nineteen-thirties. In the present state of aesthetic confusion it appears that an 'artistic' approach to architecture can only lead to a sequence of ephemeral experiments, without any social relevance. If the tradition of co-operation is to be maintained, it can only be in the context of science and technology, where every decision is subject to some kind of checking procedure. The scientific method makes no unverifiable assumptions, and takes its stand on the ascertainable facts. If the imaginative designer protests that his work is inspired by a study of function, no one is in a position to contradict him; but how can we be sure that he is not the victim of some private obsession? 'Symbolic form' may be all very well in an art gallery, but can we afford to have it in the street?

In architectural practice scientific methods have so far had a limited application, and the idea of a scientifically determined environment has always been somewhat remote from reality. In recent years, however, there has been something of a revolution in certain branches of industrial design, arising partly from the use of the mechanical computer, and partly from the scientific investigation of things which have hitherto been left to the artist These developments began during the last war, when the attempt was made 'to get away from trying to match men to machines by selection and training, and to design equipment in such a way that its operation was within the capacities of most normal people. This "fitting the job to the man" meant a collaboration of engineers with those trained in the fundamental human scientific disciplines of anatomy, physiology and experimental psychology. . . . The contribution of experimental psychology has come to be known as *human engineering* or *engineering psychology*. More recently the term *ergonomics* has come into use to cover both this and also the contributions of anatomy and physiology.'[13] Thus the study of 'biological function' – the central plank in Moholy-Nagy's platform – includes the findings of experimental psychology on such things as form and colour, noise and lighting conditions. All this coincides with the development of the mechanical computer and new ways of handling information. In the past, the most obvious objection to a purely scientific programme of design was the sheer weight of information to be handled by the designer. Even in the design of quite simple products, an almost countless number of alternatives would have to be considered before you could claim to have arrived at a perfectly functional solution: you could not do it even if you wanted to. By using a computer, however, this difficulty, at any rate in principle, may be considerably reduced.[14] A thorough programme of analysis can now be carried out for any problem which can be clearly specified.

So far the new techniques have been chiefly employed in the design of machinery and factory buildings, where the success or failure of the design is assessed in terms of output and efficiency; but they are clearly capable of being employed in many other fields where

[13] A. T. Welford, *Ergonomics of Automation*, H.M.S.O. 1960, pp. 4–5.
[14] In one of a series of articles on 'Automation and Design', Christopher Jones has written that 'the computer enables the designer to initiate and carry out the most arduous and protracted analysis of design problems, without resort to guesswork and without the tremendous labour of doing the computing and calculating involved in such an analysis. Not only can the computer be used for analysis of data, it can be used by the designer to try out and predict the consequences of using any of a large number of possible designs, so that the correct shape can be discovered with certainty. . . . A computer could be programmed to work painstakingly through the countless possibilities until the optimum design was discovered. There seems to be no theoretical reason why such a procedure – the replacement of informed but intuitive designing by logical analysis – cannot be extended to any design problem of any three dimensional complexity. . . .' *Design* magazine, August 1957.

similar considerations apply. They are already beginning to have an effect on teaching methods, and in the new school at Ulm, which was started on Bauhaus principles in 1953, the type of formal training developed under Gropius has given way to a curriculum which places a far greater emphasis on analytical study. Other schools are introducing similar changes, which will tend to produce a new type of design specialist with a predominantly scientific background. Some cutlery designed by scientific methods was illustrated recently in *Design* magazine. It looked well, but the critic writing in the paper had to report that in using it, some 'changes in habit' were necessary. Evidently in this field the new techniques have a long way to go. But it does seem possible that the disappearance of the industrial designer in his present form may be one of the changes which will follow the general introduction of automation. Until the techniques which are required by a strictly scientific procedure are fully developed, industrial design will continue to be an art, but Christopher Jones, writing in *Design*, anticipates a state of affairs in which 'the design and production of goods will have become as automatic and uninteresting as our present water supply'. If this forecast is correct, Ruskin's case against machinery will at last have become irrelevant. The programme of 'uniting industry and art' may turn out to have been a side-issue: part of the whole attempt to personalize industrial production which a writer like David Riesman regards as a temporary and disagreeable phase in our adjustment to machinery.[15]

At present the significance of all this for architecture is hard to assess. No one is satisfied with the technical training given in the schools of architecture, and proposals for revising the curricula are frequently discussed. What such discussions generally reveal is the complete absence of any agreement as to the relationship between architecture and the special sciences. Is an architect some sort of specialist or not? If not, what is he? Some of the claims now being made for scientific methods in design seem to regard architecture as a sort of alchemy. a backward and rather bogus practice which will disappear with the advance of science. Reyner Banham edited a series of articles in *The Architectural Review* dealing with recent developments in science, and he wrote as follows: 'No longer can architects assume that only the basest material functions of architecture come

[15] *The Lonely Crowd*, Yale University Press 1950, Chapter XIII, 'False Personalization'.

Modern Architectural Theory and the Liturgy

within the purview of science. If the magic of Late Gothic is now susceptible to scientific analysis... then a very large part of the psycho-physiological relationships between man and environment is likely to fall to the mathematician, not – as heretofore – the mystic.'[16] The impression one gets on reading this is that architects are concerned with something which could be done much better by scientists and technologists. So far as architects deal with technical problems, this hardly needs to be argued; but the passage seems to suggest that architecture *is* a technique: architects must clear their heads of art-nonsense and 'attend solely to the facts'. As our knowledge of man's relationship to his environment advances, the design of buildings will be increasingly governed by technology. A similar view is put forward in *Survival Through Design* by Richard Neutra, who describes architecture as 'an extension of human biology'.

If the whole significance of the functional tradition in architecture is *technological*, it seems that architects will either have to abandon it altogether, or give up any claims to art. The former course appears to have been widely adopted in a good deal of what passes for Plasticism or Expressionism: an American paper recently had a stern article about the dangers of what it called 'the new sensualism'. In the introduction to a new edition of *Pioneers of Modern Design*, Nikolaus Pevsner regretfully explains that he had to enlarge the references to Gaudi, because 'we are surrounded once again by fantasts and freaks'.[17] Church architecture, of course, provides an ideal outlet for all this, because church buildings are commonly supposed to have no function. The link between science and the imagination, which held precariously during the nineteen-twenties and 'thirties, is now in danger of snapping altogether: the architect almost seems to have a straight choice between the roles of technologist and 'divine idiot'. In this situation image and symbol have become key-words in architectural criticism. What is the nature of architectural symbolism, and can it be harmonized with the claims of scientific method? To many people imagery signifies all that is irrational, intuitive, undetermined: it can never be reconciled with the idea of architecture as a social service, or with the objectivism of science. Science and art are mutually exclusive: you just have to take your choice.

In some ways this brings us back to exactly the situation that

[16] *The Architectural Review*, March 1960, p. 188.
[17] Revised edition, Penguin Books 1960.

architects had to face at the turn of the nineteenth century. The pioneers of the modern movement set themselves firmly against the Victorian cult of genius and the whole split between work and culture. In doing so they adopted to a considerable extent the mechanistic scientific outlook of the time. Even when this had been largely abandoned by scientists, architects were still using deterministic analogies quite unsuited to their purpose.[18] Art and science lived together, but they never really spoke to one another. Today, science has moved a long way from the mechanistic assumptions of the nineteenth century, and the distinctions we habitually make in the discussion of art and science urgently need to be overhauled. The boundaries between reason and intuition, image and fact, etc., are no longer as clear as they used to be. Traditional empiricism insists that 'the facts speak for themselves'. that science tells us of an impersonal world which is 'there' whether we notice it or not. But our apprehension of facts is largely governed by language and convention: by our cultural background. One writer points out that 'the way we see a fact – i.e what we emphasize and what we disregard – is *our* work . . . if you want a simile, a fact is present, in much the same sense in which a character manifests itself in a face . . . just as we have to interpret a face, so we have to interpret reality. . . . Language, then, *contributes to the formation, and participates in the constitution* of a fact, which, of course, does not mean that it *produces* the fact.'[19] On the role of the imagination in science, Stephen Toulmin says that Einstein 'speaks of physical theories as "free products" of the human imagination. . .

[18] 'Surprise is often expressed that a Chinaman can be of two religions, a Confucian for some occasions and a Buddhist for other occasions. Whether this is true of China I do not know; nor do I know whether, if true, these attitudes are really inconsistent. But there can be no doubt that an analogous fact is true of the West, and that the two attitudes involved are inconsistent. A scientific realism, based on mechanism, is conjoined with an unwavering belief in the world of men and of the higher animals as being composed of self-determining organisms. This radical inconsistency . . . accounts for much that is half-hearted and wavering in our civilisation.' Whitehead, op. cit., p. 94.
[19] Friedrich Waismann, 'Verifiability' in *Logic and Language*, Basil Blackwell, Oxford 1955, pp. 140 ff. Later on, he says that 'a scientific theory is never a slavish imitation of certain features of reality, a dead, passive replica. It is essentially a *construction* which to a greater or lesser degree reflects our own activity.'

But we must not be tempted to go too far. This is not the work of the untutored imagination. It may be an art, but it is one whose exercise requires a stiff training.... One cannot teach a man to be imaginative, but there are certain kinds of imagination which only a man with a particular training can exercise.'[20] An account of science which speaks of participation and imagination is very different from the scientific orthodoxy which is normally taken for granted in architectural literature. The nineteenth-century view of science assumed a clear logical relationship between observation and theory: the mechanical analogy applied not only to the subject-matter of science, but even to its methods. Traditional empiricism is no longer an adequate account of science, and the scientist's participation in knowledge is recognized as a vital factor in all scientific discovery. The shift of emphasis from mechanism to the language and symbolism of science has brought a new understanding of the creative and social character of scientific knowledge. The detached observer, and the theoretical separation of subject and object, are no longer the unquestioned assumptions that they were in the eighteenth and nineteenth centuries

It would not be hard to find better analogies between art and science than were available to Sullivan, but they would not be very illuminating. Certainly it is no longer possible to make large statements about the laws which 'determine our function as human beings and the forms it takes' with any show of scientific relevance: like art, science involves more than careful observation and sharp logic. The real difficulty, however, is not the question of freedom or determinism, but the relationship between different kinds of symbolism. A new scientific 'picture' of experience is judged by whether it *works* or not as an organizing concept and as an instrument of prediction: it can be tested by anyone with the appropriate training. An architectural analogy on these lines would only be relevant if buildings were judged in terms of measurable efficiency. To speak of art as a way of 'knowledge' is apt to be frowned upon by philosophers of science, since art does not appear to 'inform' us about anything, and there is a sense in which it is impossible to say what a work of art *refers* to. Ernest Nagel writes that 'no unique system of symbols is required for the formulation of scientific knowledge; in short, formulations of knowledge in one symbolic medium are in principle

[20] *The Philosophy of Science*, Hutchinson's University Library 1953, p. 43.

translatable into formulations using other symbolic devices. . . . In this respect there seems to me a fundamental difference between the knowledge codified and communicated by scientific formulations, and what a number of writers are pleased to call the "truths" embodied in works of art.' He would not allow the words knowledge and symbol to be used of art, since 'the use of a common label for both sorts of things (whatever the sorts of thing that art objects convey may be) seems to me but a species of punning, and is bound to lead to intellectual confusions' [21] Artists are not likely to accept this limitation of their vocabulary, and no doubt the confusion will continue until the relationship between science and art is investigated by thinkers equally interested in both. At present, much of what is written about science sets a low value on art, and vice versa. A grave difficulty arises from the fact that it is hard to talk about art as cognitive without suggesting the theological conception of symbolism which underlies the great traditions of art in Europe and elsewhere.[22]

[21] 'Symbolism and Science' in *Logic without Metaphysics*, The Free Press, Glencoe, Illinois, 1956, pp. 104 ff. The book contains a criticism on the same lines of Susanne Langer's *Philosophy in a New Key*.

[22] For example·
(*a*) 'Maximus the Confessor . . . defines what he calls "symbolic vision" as the ability to apprehend within the objects of sense perception the invisible reality of the intelligible that lays beyond them . . . The mediaeval artist was committed to a truth that transcended human existence. Those who looked at his work judged it as an image of that truth, hence the mediaeval tendency to praise or condemn a work of art in terms of the ultimates of religious experience.' Otto von Simson, *The Gothic Cathedral*, Routledge and Kegan Paul 1956, p. xix
(*b*) 'Thus, for instance, positivistic rationalism uses symbols as conventional signs, as abbreviations of a concept or a series of concepts, as an explanatory scheme or logical design. . . The opposite to this "symbolism" of conventional signs and pragmatic images is the symbolism of religion and art, which is indeed the prototype of all true symbolism Here symbol denotes and represents (makes present) an invariable reality . . . It is not invented or made but is born and arises. It is not man who makes the symbol, but the symbol which utters itself through man.' Evgueny Lampert, *The Divine Realm*, Faber 1944, p. 109.
(*c*) 'If in painting and poetry the daily life of peasants seemed to reflect conditions ever present in the pastoral Heaven . . this is not a sentimental or romantic symbolism, but born of the conviction that "all the men and women of the world are His living forms", that reality is here and now

The natural philosopher of 'symbolic form' runs into the same sort of logical trouble as the natural theologian, and empiricists inevitably regard him as being in the same camp. In a recent article Harold Osborn concludes that among modern theories, the one which comes closest to explaining the value of art is the theory that art is a language of symbolic form; but 'the manner of this symbolism has not yet been adequately formulated, and it is therefore difficult to present or assess the theory'.[23]

In these circumstances it is difficult to attach any clear meaning to the word symbol in architectural theory, and easier to think of architecture as a branch of technology. In this case the function of the building will be seen as a set of observable phenomena, to be approached in the same way as the data of biology or the mechanical sciences. The architect's main task will be to assemble as much information as he can, either by direct observation and enquiry, or at second-hand. Unless the building is of a type with which he is already very familiar, most of this information will come from books· from studies of building-types, by-laws, research papers, commercial brochures and a mass of other literature. His client will be regarded as little more than a reliable source of information. Now in the course of this activity it easily appears that the architect is indeed concerned with facts, and not with human beings. He becomes a kind of manipulator, co-ordinating work-programmes, devising schedules and having interviews with specialists. Aesthetic considerations, if they are allowed at all, become the province of yet another specialist – a designer – whose contribution has to be born in mind. As the word architect has pre-technological overtones, the controlling figure might well be called something else: a manager or building co-ordinator. He will be an expert in some branch of technology, and he will also have special qualifications as an administrator As much of the work involved is a matter of logical calculation, there is no reason why it should not be done by a computer.

This is a not altogether inaccurate impression of a symposium

tangibly and visibly accessible.' Coomaraswamy, 'The Theory of Art in Asia' in *The Transformation of Nature in Art*, Harvard, 1934. Cheap edition Dover Publications, New York 1956, p. 45.
[23] 'Aesthetics as a Branch of Philosophy', *British Journal of Aesthetics*, November 1960.

Towards a Church Architecture

published in *The Architectural Review* for April 1960, on 'The Future of Universal Man'. As an attack on architects' professional complacency, much of what was said was no doubt justified. But one does not have to subscribe to an impossible ideal of universal competence to think that the separation of design and co-ordination is ultimately a confusion. The point is that without a design (and hence a designer) there would never be any co-ordination at all. One of the functions of the design is to define the problem to establish working relationships between the various specialists and provide a framework for logical thinking. It is quite unreal to divorce the work of research and analysis from whatever may be meant by design: if the collection of data is not interrupted by occasional bursts of invention, the filing cabinets will be overloaded and nothing will ever be done. During the research stage in a design project anyone is likely to have an unpleasant feeling that he doesn't know what he's doing; and it is only when a design has been sketched out (perhaps later to be abandoned) that he begins to find his way. Quite apart from aesthetics, this is true of any kind of research, scientific or otherwise. Even a 'factual' account of architecture implies more than logical calculation, and the computer offers no substitute for imagination.[24] The notion that we could predict the future if we knew the position of every particle in the universe has long been abandoned by science, but a similar idea persists in architecture: that if you knew all the relevant facts, you could determine the shape of your building The trouble is that 'relevance' is largely governed by the designer's statement of the problem: it depends on his point of view.

In scientific functionalism, the designer's point of view is that of the detached observer. In science this has been a useful and necessary

---

[24] One of the difficulties about the computer business is that the information-machine has become a new scientific model for interpreting human behaviour. Consequently if you talk about poetry with an electronics-man you are likely to find that what he means by poetry is the sort of thing that *could* be done by machinery. 'The fact is that we must distinguish between routine thinking (which involves the memory and judgment according to specific definable criteria) and creative thinking; and if we remember that the machine cannot exceed the limitations of its design and instructions, that is to say that it cannot create anything on its own, we shall not go far wrong ' Sir Ben Lockspeiser, *Man and his Machines*, Institute of Personnel Management 1960, p. 6

fiction, but in architecture it leads to theoretical dilemmas, and the sooner it is abandoned the better. One of the characteristics of the view represented by Moholy-Nagy is that it rejects the whole of our cultural inheritance. The old symbols, it claims, are no longer valid, no longer a vital or significant part of the common life A new culture – perhaps a new art – will come from a scientific study of the observable biological facts: such an approach provides the only basis for co-operative work which still remains to us. Like the observer in traditional empiricism, the designer works in a cultural vacuum: science is seen as an activity independent of history and indifferent to the social and religious climate of its time. This is a false account of science, though it is not without justification, in architecture it is little more than an affectation. In his attempt to see human activities as they are 'in fact', the biological functionalist seeks to divest them of any traditional interpretation or any customary meaning which attaches to them Now this is something which can be done in a laboratory, but not in real life. In normal society even the most utilitarian actions are charged with meaning and emotion. every movement tends to be a gesture. A person reveals himself not only in what he says, but also in what he does and how he does it: even in walking or sitting down, for example. But this, like language, is largely a matter of convention; it arises in company. Although biological functionalism is often accompanied by a concern with social reform, it treats people as if they were always alone.

A meal eaten alone, for example, is a utilitarian activity best carried out with a maximum of functional efficiency. But a meal eaten in common is something different: it tends to be a celebration or a ritual. It is this fact, we are told, that keeps the wheels of industry turning: no one *needs* a three-guinea lunch every day, but without such things it would be impossible to generate the good-will on which our prosperity depends. The expense-account racket may be a disgrace, but it is certainly a saner thing than the Victorian ethic of 'good hard grinding work'. The alienation of labour affects the manager no less than the factory-hand. It is difficult to use the word ritual without confusion today; but all human relationships depend on ritual, and no society exists without it. The evil of industrial work, as described by Ruskin and Marx, is that it has no connection with the symbolic activities which make life meaningful. It is the most commonplace functions – those which are most necessary to our physical existence – which tend to acquire the most universal significance. Such things are so familiar and so habitual that they easily become formalized. In the great agricultural societies of the past, all labour was a sphere of ritual, and by ritual every human activity became a significant part of social life Marx saw one of the consequences of alienation in the fact that 'man no longer feels himself to be freely active in any but his animal functions – eating, drinking, procreating, or at most in his dwelling and dressing-up, etc. . . Certainly eating and drinking are also genuinely human functions. But in the abstraction which separates them from the sphere of all other human activity and turns them into sole and ultimate ends, they are animal.'[25] It is this kind of abstraction which has brought the idea of a 'functional' architecture into disrepute: human activities cannot be adequately described in terms of 'ascertainable biological needs'.

All rituals are things done, and what they convey cannot be better expressed in any other way. The significance of a ritual can only be fully understood by a participant, and it can never be adequately translated for the benefit of an outside observer. The study of ritual as a 'phenomenon' in anthropology and the social sciences has put us in a dilemma. On the one hand the historical significance of ritual as source of art and a focus of cultural achievement is undeniable. In primitive society all art is 'liturgical' art, and this is largely true of the great traditions as well. But on the other hand the comparative study of ritual presents a history which is so unpalatable that it is hard to resist Frazer's estimate of primitive culture as 'a tragic chronicle of human error and folly, fruitless endeavour, wasted time and blighted hopes'.[26] If anything in the nature of ritual is detected in our own society it is either rationalized as 'necessary' or dismissed as compulsive and absurd. Apart from the rituals of totalitarian politics, which are more or less loathsome, the acknowledged rituals of everyday life are seen as a fit subject for ridicule. The social observer finds that we make rituals: 'out of going to school, out of work, out of having fun, out of political participation . . . as well as out of countless private compulsions'.[27] In this case the word make is not used in its

[25] Op. cit., p 73.
[26] *Aftermath* (supplement to *The Golden Bough*), Macmillan 1936, p. vi.
[27] Riesman, op. cit., p. 269.

normal sense of a *purposeful* activity, but in the sense of making a mistake. something involuntary, to be avoided, or if possible corrected. In common usage this is what the word ritual normally implies. But there are many activities in which we make something of necessity, and which are generally seen to be creative. A dinner-party makes something of hunger; and when thirsty men gather for a drink they are not only making money for the landlord. What is made on such occasions cannot be specified or catered for, but it adds up to whatever may be meant by friendship, brotherhood, solidarity, etc. Such activities may not be regarded as rituals, but that is what they are. Ritual, then, is not only the concern of anthropologists and psychiatrists, but the very stuff of society. Jane Harrison wrote that 'the ritualist is, to the modern mind, a man concerned perhaps unduly with fixed forms and ceremonies, with carrying out the rigidly prescribed ordinances of a church or sect The artist, on the other hand, we think of as free in thought and untrammelled by convention in practice. . . . Art and ritual, it is true, have diverged today; but . . . these two divergent developments have a common root, and neither can be understood without the other. It is at the outset one and the same impulse that sends a man to the church and to the theatre.'[28]

In current architectural theory a great deal is written about the architect's programme: the schedule of instructions setting out the requirements of the building in as much detail as possible. It is sometimes regarded as the 'source of design', though what this means is never very clear. Llewelyn Davies points out that it came into use during the nineteenth century, and he regards it as a 'disastrous innovation'; a consequence of the architect's failure to keep pace with the technical and social development. 'The architect of the Renaissance did not need a programme. If he was asked to design a church or a villa, the breadth of his education ensured that he would share with his client an understanding of what would be needed.'[29] The programme was a device which allowed the architect to avoid thinking about the purpose of the building: it set out the problem ready-made, and the designer's task was to solve it within the conventions of an established style. Architecture thus began to be thought of as a

---

[28] *Ancient Art and Ritual*, Home University Library, Oxford University Press 1951, pp. 9–10.
[29] *Architects Journal*, November 17th 1960.

Towards a Church Architecture

logical exercise in problems and solutions; and this habit still persists, though the traditional styles have long been abandoned and the task of framing the programme is now seen to be an essential part of the architect's work. To set out an adequate programme evidently needs a much greater knowledge of modern life than was considered necessary in the nineteenth century. But the Universal Man as conceived by the Renaissance is no longer a practical ideal even for men of outstanding genius; and it is here that the supposed conflict between design and co-ordination becomes most acute. Architectural offices at present may be ill-equipped to handle the complexities of modern building, but whatever answer may be found, the whole question is essentially one of organization. There is a sense in which the current discussion of information and technical expertise avoids the real problems of architecture altogether. Even if every known factor could be taken into account and all the available information assimilated, we could still be without any clear picture of the architect's task.

If the programme is given to the architect, his work can properly be described as finding solutions to problems; but this is not the case if he is responsible for framing the programme himself. We have seen that research and analysis cannot be divorced from design, so that to talk about working out a programme is hardly more than another way of describing the design process. The architect's work does consist very largely of formulating problems and solving them. if he cannot do this he cannot even begin: hence, most new churches are non-starters. But when he is given a commission it can only loosely be described as presenting a problem. An architect may have to consider '1000 sq. ft of wood-block flooring at so much a yard' or '1000 sq. ft of uniformly distributed load on four columns', and these are genuine problems which are the special business of the quantity-surveyor and engineer. But '1000 sq. ft of living space for Jack and Jill' is a different matter, and it is the special business of the architect. He has to do something which will involve all kinds of problems, but which in itself cannot be stated as a problem at all. The main reason for this is that the architect is always to some extent a *participant* in the activities he serves: they do not only appear as phenomena. During the course of his research he will come to know a great deal about them, but what he knows cannot be wholly reduced to the status of information, because it is largely a matter of *feeling*: in architecture there are no hard facts, whatever may be the case in science [30] Furthermore, a good building is always an enlargement of knowledge, and it is only in working on a design that the architect discovers what he knows. 'Theoretically the artist is a person who comes to know himself, to know his own emotion. This is also knowing his world, that is, the sights and sounds and so forth which together make up his total imaginative experience. The two knowledges are to him one knowledge, because these sights and sounds are to him steeped in the emotion with which he contemplates them . . .'[31] If architecture is seen as a form of participation, the co-operative idea acquires a new significance. The purpose of research work on a building project is partly to enable the architect to identify himself with his client's aims and intentions; and this requires insight as well as information. In this context the idea of architecture as a social service cannot be separated from architecture as an art.

What is involved here is an elusive but familiar aspect of many kinds of creative activity. One can imagine two people listening to a theme on the piano One of them is musical and the other is not; they both hear the same thing, but only one of them finds it meaningful. Yet if both of them have good hearing, the physical facts are the same. (In this analogy the architect is the musical one, and the other is the biological functionalist, missing the whole point.) If the musical one plays the trumpet, he may join in the music-making. The music then becomes richer, and in this sense it is changed; but the original theme remains while its musical possibilities are explored. In such activities as these the distinction between a subjective and an objective approach is difficult to apply. The musicians are united by a common theme and by a common understanding of music: both the theme and the musical tradition are outside them, and in this sense are perfectly objective; yet what they do with the theme cannot be described in

---

[30] Even in science the division between thought and emotion is illusory, as Collingwood shows in *The Principles of Art*: ' "The proposition", understood as a form of words expressing thought and not emotion, and as constituting the unit of scientific discourse, is a fictitious entity. This will be easily granted by any one who thinks for a moment about scientific discourse in its actual and living reality, instead of thinking only about the conventional marks on paper which represent or misrepresent it.' Oxford, 1938, p. 266.

[31] Collingwood, op. cit., p. 291.

Towards a Church Architecture

terms of problems and solutions. Similarly a building is the result of co-operation: the client provides the theme, and this is taken up and enriched by the architect.

When you come to the special nature of architectural imagery in the literature of the modern movement, you are confronted with talk about space: organic space, dynamic space, activated space and so on. At the end of *The New Vision*, Moholy-Nagy comes out with the following statement. 'A constant fluctuation, sideways and upward, radiant, all-sided, announces to man that he has taken possession, so far as his human capacities and present conceptions allow, of imponderable invisible and yet omnipresent space.'[32] After reading this, you begin to see why architectural theory is so unpopular. In itself, the word space means very little unless it is combined with a sense of 'place' and 'occasion'.[33] One of the best statements of this idea is in *Feeling and Form* by Susanne Langer.[34] What the architect creates is an 'ethnic domain'. a place which takes its character from the activities which go on in it, and at the same time gives form and expression to them. It is rooted in function, but in *human* function – and this is not what is spoken of by the biological functionalist. Architecture embodies the emotion and meaning which are always a part of human activity. A place in this sense can be created with great economy of means, and it need not have any permanence It may be an arrangement of chairs in a garden, or the inside of a caravan: anything which constitutes a human environment. On a different level, Stonehenge is an astonishing place, created by a ring of admittedly very large stones. In such elementary arrangements there is the basic impulse of all architecture. From this point of view architecture cannot be defined in terms of institutional qualifications or confused with what Reyner Banham condemns as traditional 'operational lore'.

Church architecture has for a long time been incomprehensible to the modern architect, because the subject has generally been discussed in terms of atmosphere and religious sentiment. On the other

[32] p. 181.
[33] 'Whoever attempts to solve the riddle of space in the abstract will construct the outline of emptiness and call it space. Whatever space and time may mean, place and occasion mean more.' Aldo van Eyck, quoted by Brian Housden in *The A.A. Journal* for December 1960.
[34] Routledge and Kegan Paul 1953.

hand, Christians have been inclined to regard all modern architecture as a product of materialism. The whole argument rests on the familiar division between thought and action, spirit and matter. The liturgical renewal has re-established the fact that Christian worship is essentially something done, and not only thought or said. During the early centuries of Christianity the eucharist was a corporate action in which every order in the Church had a special part to play. It was essentially a physical action: the meaning of it was not something independent of it – read *into* it – but something which grew out of the experience of doing it. In this conception there is no false opposition between the spirit and the body. the spirit is revealed in and through the body. And the word body connotes not only the individual human body, but also the Church. Physical action only becomes meaningful within a human relationship: the body only finds its true nature when it is incorporated into the body of society. The idea of community necessarily implies ritual, since no community can exist without some conscious expression of the common life. The primary symbols are always things done, and their symbolic value arises from the recognition of common necessity; they are founded on biological need, but they transcend it. Architecture is not so much the 'extension of human biology' as the extension of ritual; and the chief significance of functionalism is that it has given us a new sense of the simple and universal things which are the basis of all sacramental life.

When Christianity was established under Constantine, there began to be a gradual change in the understanding of the eucharist. Mass conversions led to the exclusion of the laity from most worship, which now became the special business of monks and secular clergy. In western Europe the eucharist became little more than an occasion for individual piety. lay people occupied their minds with private devotions which had nothing to do with what was going on at the altar. In this way the external forms of Christianity were divorced from individual belief and private prayer. Religion increasingly became a matter of private feeling and sentiment. Above all, there grew up a false and quite un-Christian separation of spirit and body, which obscured the social nature of the Church and distorted the whole meaning of the sacraments. In one way or another the Church has been suffering from these distortions ever since.

In its appeal to the early centuries of Christianity, the liturgical movement has given us a new understanding of the sources of the

Catholic-Protestant argument; it has established many points of contact between religious and secular thought, above all, its reaffirmation of the doctrine of the body of Christ has a close relationship to the modern quest for community. The new reformation sees architecture as an integral part of the life of the Church, and it has brought about a clearer understanding of the relation between art and religion. 'Indifference to art is the most serious sign of decay in any institution, nothing bespeaks its old age more eloquently than that art, under its patronage, becomes literal and self-imitating. Then the most impressive, living art leaves the religious context, and draws on unrestricted feeling somewhere else. It cannot do otherwise; but in doing so it loses its traditional sphere of influence . . . and runs the danger of never reaching beyond the studio walls where it was created'[35] Christian art grows out of the life and worship of the Church; and if the symbols we have inherited from past ages now seem to have lost their power, this is because they are no longer the living language of a community.

Rudolf Schwarz described the church building as at the same time 'an instrument of worship, a symbolic representation of the deepest relationships, and a sacred participation in creating the mystical body of the Lord'. As an instrument of worship, the building provides for the convenience of the worshippers, and this requires a close analysis of physical function As a symbol, it arises from an understanding of the liturgy; and this implies a degree of participation in something which is, essentially, done. But much work will have to be done before architecture can be seen as a 'sacred participation' in the life of the Church for too long it has been relegated to a position of minor importance, as if it had only an accidental connection with the Christian faith.

---

[35] Susanne Langer, *Feeling and Form*, Routledge and Kegan Paul 1953, p. 403.

3. Meaning and Understanding

ROBERT MAGUIRE

I

There is an argument which is increasingly heard. It runs:

> To build a new church in a style from a past age
> is backward-looking and sentimental.
> There is a modern architectural style.
> We must show forth the readiness of the Church
> to face the problems of the age in which we live
> By building churches in this style.

There is some truth in this generalized statement, as there usually is in generalized statements. But it reveals a misunderstanding of the nature of architecture. Architecture is not a matter of superimposed style, and by choosing a style to wear – like selecting the latest thing from the Vogue Pattern Book – you may appear for the moment to be up to date, but you do not thereby show yourself ready to face reality.

> Architecture articulates and presents meaning.

It does this by means which are peculiar to itself. It does not, like an advertisement, make an announcement which is comprehended in one visual experience.

We now have too many buildings, and among them too many churches, which make a bright announcement, and are afterwards found to speak of other values. Afterwards found: that is, in use, which is the experience of architecture in time, and in space.

> We walk around, into, and about in buildings.
> Not only once, but countless times: we *use* them.

The building remains substantially the same, yet the experience varies constantly, with one's own movement through its space, and with the changing time of day and season. To this experience the

Towards a Church Architecture

building brings what it has: the tangible – form and material of all its parts, and the intangible – its modulated space, the relationship of things within the space, the light which makes it sensible. And through this experience the building insinuates; all that it has, with no exception, is expressive of meanings, and hence of the values implicit in those meanings.

The meanings expressed (articulated and presented) are those of the purposes for which it is built, purposes which are a direct reflection of the nature of the institution which caused the building to exist. The values expressed are those held by the institution.[1]

A good school expresses the meaning of education in relation to society, and the values implicit in a particular pedagogic system.

A good hospital expresses the meaning of medical care in relation to society, and the values implicit in a particular medico-psychological system.

A good house expresses the meaning of family life in relation to society, and the values implicit in the way of life.

> If you are going to build a church
> you are going to create a thing which speaks.
> It will speak of meanings, and of values,
> and it will go on speaking.
> And if it speaks of the wrong values
> it will go on destroying.

There is a responsibility here.

---

[1] These statements hold good only when architecture is appropriate; when it is otherwise, it may be only the values held by the architect which are expressed Hence the importance of the architect's relationship with the institution.

I am aware that this kind of statement raises some difficult (and by no means new) issues For example is architecture necessarily 'good' architecture simply by being appropriate? Would an architecture really appropriate to some anti-social or immoral purpose (i.e truly expressive of the nature of that purpose) be 'good'? The answer obviously depends on whether 'good' is meant to refer to the depth of expression or to the thing expressed. One involves an aesthetic judgment, the other a moral judgment. Both are important, but they must be distinguished.

Another such issue is whether inappropriate architecture should be called architecture at all. This can quickly descend into an argument about the meanings of words.

II

There *is* a modern architectural style.
We now have an ironical situation: there is a Modern Architectural Style.

There used to be something loosely called the Modern Movement, 'movement' signifying something on the move, developing. The serious contributions to this movement showed the same profound concern, a concern with meanings and values in architecture.[2] More often than not these contributions were undiscriminating, biased, self-contradictory, or unrelated to reality. Nevertheless the basic concern was there, however misapplied.

There are still those who possess this concern. They are regarded with suspicion by Contemporary Architects. At a certain point speculative thought was deemed dispensable by lesser men, who required a neat intellectual structure as a security, an anchor for their little boats in a sea of shifting currents.

There are thousands of architects in this country who will refer to the principles 'of modern architecture'. Ask them what these principles are, and they will produce some meaningless generalizations.

'A building should express its function.
A building should honestly express its structure.
Materials should be used with honesty.
Techniques should be given expression.'
And perhaps a few more.

What do these words mean? What does expression mean in these contexts? How is one honest in a situation where morality does not enter in?

In almost every architectural school in this country, students are taught to design according to such 'principles': garbled versions of a few ideas from the early days of the Modern Movement, applied with an intellectual licence and without understanding. To meet the practical demands of the situation, a whole series of architectural devices has been developed (mostly borrowed out of context from photo-

[2] For a sensitive and discriminating account of this development see Reyner Banham, *Theory and Design in the First Machine Age*, Architectural Press 1960

graphs of serious buildings) which appear to answer to these 'principles', and are used in various combinations. The constant repetition of these devices gives an appearance of consistency to the products: hence the illusion of style.

The Modern Movement has undergone a premature crystallization.
We have a new *Beaux Arts*.
Its success is transforming our cities.[3]

III

I shall call this phenomenon modern architectural orthodoxy. This excludes certain people who continue to think, and to search for understanding. It also excludes others, who have reacted to the situation, and in doing so have reverted to a kind of personal cosmic expressionism.

Modern architectural orthodoxy attempts to derive *a working-method* for the architect *from critical standards*. It attempts, by pseudo-logical deduction, to obtain from what in its own terms architecture should be, a method of getting there.

The result of such an attempt is naturally a working method – if it can be called a method at all – which is founded on inhibitions. Statements of what architecture 'should be' or 'ought to have' postulate perfectionist standards, and to work constantly in an aim to perfection is to work in fear. fear of falling short of it. Canons of perfection do not in practice guide you towards what to *do*, but operate as negative admonitions·

'A building shall not express its structure dishonestly.'
(The 'principles' in their negative form reveal their meaninglessness more emphatically.)

---

[3]Cf. a letter written by P Morton Shand towards the end of his life and quoted by John Betjeman in an obituary article published in the *Architectural Review* for November 1960: 'I have frightful nightmares, and no wonder, for I am haunted by a gnawing sense of guilt in having, in however minor and obscure degree, helped to bring about, anyhow encouraged and praised, the embryo searchings that have now materialized into a monster which neither of us could have foreseen; Contemporary Architecture'.

Consequently the 'principles' of modern architectural orthodoxy are applied in practice like an extreme Protestant moral system. Criticism of buildings (still, in the main negative, which in the circumstances is easier) is heavily spiced with words like *dishonest* and *unethical*, and architects' retrospective justifications of their works are laden with words such as *honest* and *truthful*.

Moralistic justification has become a main part of the design process itself, and so designing a building has ceased to be a creative process informed by understanding, and has become intellectualized. Only a highly developed system of cerebral juggling can cope with the problems of convincing oneself and others that one has done the Right Thing at every juncture.

To propose criteria is useful. It was especially useful and necessary in the early days of the Modern Movement, when existing criteria were very questionable. But to set up criteria, particularly a set of meaningless criteria obtained through misunderstanding, and then to treat them as the basis of a working method, is doomed to failure.

> You cannot create architecture by trying to live up to what you think architecture should be.
>
> You can create architecture only through an understanding of what architecture does.
>
> Even then, you may only be a good architectural critic.
>
> You also need a creative capability beyond the understanding.

IV

Architecture can be created only through an understanding of what architecture does.

Architecture articulates and presents meaning, and values: it *expresses* these things.

It does not 'express' function, because function is not in itself capable of expression. The underlying meaning and values of 'functions' – purposes – are, however, capable of expression: capable, that is, of articulation and presentation.

Nor can a building express its structure, nor its materials, nor the techniques with which it was built.

These things are, however, of first importance in architectural expression, for they are (along with spatial modulation, the relationship of objects in space, etc.) the *means* by which a building makes its significant statements.

Towards a Church Architecture

The task before the architect can therefore be seen to be exacting, and particularly so when seen in the context of the age of advanced technology in which we live.

The architect must be capable of analysing 'user-requirements'. In order to organize these into a coherent pattern he has to use powers of discrimination: understanding begins to enter in.

In order to create architecture from this coherent pattern, he has to *achieve an understanding* of the meaning of it in relation to *people* (i.e. if you like, in the context of society, both in general and locally). Such an understanding will unavoidably involve coming to terms with the values implied in the use of the building.[4]

Further, in order to create architecture, the architect must understand the ways in which architecture articulates and presents meaning, and he has to have the creative capability to put these in train, in the context of the culture in which he lives.

And consequently he has to have a wide knowledge (to be conprehensive is now impossible) of the range of technological means available.

There are other demands of the architect. In order to *build* successfully, he must be a good constructor (which is different from having a knowledge of the range of technological means), a good organizer, and a good building economist.

Architecture is also good building.

v

It is possible to evolve a working method only from the existential[5] situation in which the architect finds himself.

Only by this means can the architect create. He cannot be creative while controlled by his own or anyone else's assessment of what ought to be

The only standards involved concern the person of the architect *as architect*, that is, he must have, to some degree, all or most of those abilities which make a person capable, simply, of being an architect.

---

[4] This, if taken seriously, may of course lead to personal difficulties which prevent the architect continuing.

[5] I use the word existential with some trepidation, knowing that it has connotations which may lead to misunderstanding. It is, however, the only word I can find which aptly describes the situation.

Meaning and Understanding

This may perhaps seem too obvious to require stating, but the question does arise as to whether (since we have so much poor architecture) the schools have not been training the wrong kind of people for a job which has been wrongly assessed.

Confronted with the task of designing a building, the architect has before him a very complex situation out of which he can create architecture.

> He has a client with needs to be met.
> He has a cost limit within which to work.
> He has a site, related to surrounding topography.
> There is a climate, the extremes of which impose their own limitations.
> There are the needs, in general and particular situations, of the human person.
> There is restrictive legislation.
> There is the whole range of technological means, the limits of which are now beyond his comprehension.
> And there is his responsibility to society, and to himself.

All these are 'given factors': given in the sense only that they exist, not in the sense that they are all known *or knowable*. Yet each one is formative of architecture.

In the face of this situation the architect has a responsibility to inform himself, that is, to increase his consciousness of the situation in those directions where this is most lacking, and in those in which this is of itself more urgent. Fully conscious appreciation of the entire situation is not possible, because much is not knowable.

There can be no perfection.

The situation itself has got out of hand, especially in view of the increasing rate of technological progress, and will continue to be so.

Those who still aspire to perfection can be seen placing their trust in a misunderstanding of 'scientific method'. The need for efficient classification of information, though in itself a true need and long overdue in being met, has become a hobby-horse for those who see classified information as the main instrument in the creation of architecture. The expectation seems to be that when the architect has the whole situation at his fingertips – all the sociological, statistical, technical, and graphic data 'authoritatively' stated and neatly indexed – he will then, and only then, be able to make the Right Decisions.

Towards a Church Architecture

Since fully conscious appreciation of the entire given situation is never possible, the architect relies heavily on unconscious appreciation: on intuition. In saying this I am not advocating a return to the romantic view of the artist as one who produces beautiful things out of a jealously guarded vagueness and confusion. The fact is that the architect must continue to live, to face reality; he cannot defer action simply because the situation which confronts him is not reasonable. Intuition is a necessary part of his equipment. he needs *intuitive grasp*, which is something neither vague nor confused.

Gaining a conscious appreciation means work. Energy must be deployed to the best advantage, and it is for each architect to decide where in the situation his powers of intuition are most lacking and so where he must do most analytical work. There are two fields, however, in which this work is essential. those which concern the purposes of the building, and the needs of the human person. The reason for this is not only that too little is known in these fields (although this is, perhaps surprisingly, generally so) but because underlying the purposes are the meanings and values which are to be expressed in architecture, and the purposes themselves are to be interpreted in the light of human needs. An understanding of meanings and values is necessary in order that appropriate architecture may be created, and hence the purposes (i.e people's needs in specific situations) served fully Purposes are not served fully merely by *convenience*.

The analytical statement of the purposes which a building is to serve has become known as the 'programme',[6] and it follows from what I have said above that a carefully considered programme is now a necessary first step in the creation of architecture, as much as in the designing of a building for convenience.

A programme is a written statement of a part of the whole given situation to the extent to which it has been objectified, or made conscious In the sense in which it is generally used, it refers to that part

---

[6] The concept of the programme was introduced into the public discussion of church design in this country by Keith Murray and myself as late as 1957. Before then it seems that the idea that churches have purposes worthy of serious enquiry was lacking in architectural circles. Since then, despite Peter Hammond's frequent expositions and warnings, programme has become a much-used but little understood word.

Meaning and Understanding

of the situation which concerns the purposes of the building; but the idea can obviously be extended to other parts of the situation. The site, for example. it may be in many cases useful to produce a full programme covering topography, geology, landscape character, etc. in order to bring about a better understanding of the possibilities of a site. And as design work proceeds, it is now essential to consider a cost programme: a technique for this has been developed in the last few years, but is still too seldom used.

But the situation being what it is, the programme for other aspects of the whole situation is bound to be limited.

In diagram form, the outlines of a working method so far look like this:

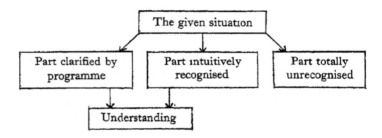

In so far as we are concerned with architecture, the object of this preliminary work is *understanding*. Buildings can be designed with little or no understanding; architecture can only be created through understanding.

In this sense, understanding involves seeing the meaning and values underlying the purposes of the building.

It involves seeing what is of greater and less importance in the *demands* which purposes make, in the light of those meanings and values.

It involves having a feeling for the ways in which architecture articulates and presents meaning; that is, the nature of architectural expression.

It involves discrimination between known technological *means*, so that appropriate means may be selected.

Towards a Church Architecture

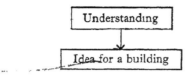

Out of such an understanding can come an idea. I use the word idea in an everyday sense: an 'idea for a building'. An idea, in this simple sense,[7] is born only of an understanding of the situation to which the idea is pertinent. In the context of architecture, the idea is *the essential building*, undeveloped yet rudimentarily complete. It is a three-dimensional image, and attempts to meet the demands, on many levels, of all aspects of the given situation *as understood*.[8]

> The distinctive quality of the idea is appropriateness
> A utility (circulation, space allocation, services, etc.) appropriate to purposes.
> An appropriate expression (articulation and presentation) of the meanings and values underlying purposes.
> Each achieved through the use of appropriate *means*·
> appropriate spatial relationships
> appropriate forms
> appropriate materials
> appropriate technology.

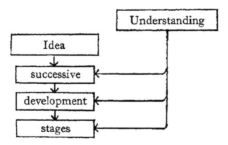

[7] Idea: 'an image of an external object formed by the mind': *Chamber's Twentieth Century Dictionary*.
[8] In *Programme and Idea*, a paper which I wrote in 1959 (*NCRG Papers* no. 2) and from which the present essay is a development, I spoke of the

Meaning and Understanding

In order to be translated into a building, an idea must be developed. In the development of the idea, reference must be made constantly to the understood facts of the situation. This may seem self-evident, but architects are notorious for allowing their first ideas to become *idées fixes*, and for developing them into buildings despite the fact that they do not 'fit' the situation. The constant reference back puts the idea under test at every stage of its development. According to the degree of its appropriateness at all levels, it may remain intact, it may evolve further, or it may have to be rejected.

The architect must remain open to this last possibility. It can be constructive, because the shortcomings revealed in the idea when under test are themselves means to increased understanding.

During the development stage, repetitions of the whole process, on a smaller scale, will have to be made in order to negotiate the detailed design of parts of the building or objects in it. But parts are interdependent and cannot easily be isolated, and so there tends to be simultaneous operation of the various stages of the process for various parts. The whole process of design is consequently very complex. In this state of affairs, understanding can again be seen to be central in the creative action: only through an understanding of the interrelation of parts can the idea be kept in balance and appropriate architecture result.

VI

That is the outline of a working method. It is a framework which needs filling in.

But it is no new thing. I believe that this is how architecture always is and always has been created, whether acknowledged or not. I believe that it is (in its fundamentals) simply a description of the process of architectural creation.

In a historical context, substitute a historically existential situation, with the relevant purposes, meanings, people, technology, etc; men (not necessarily architects, for vernacular architecture is included) with varying degrees of understanding: the creative process

---

'idea' as *containing solutions to the problems of the programme*. This is naive, and I am indebted to Nigel Melhuish for pointing to the fact that 'problems' and 'solutions' are perfectionist concepts in this context. Furthermore, I treated the programme in that paper as a statement embodying all there is to know of the given situation, which it plainly cannot be.

follows the same pattern. The development stages need not have been 'on the drawing board': they may have been worked out in the building of a number of buildings of the same type, as indeed is often still the case.

The creative process centres around understanding, which is an achievement which varies from person to person, and from time to time with the same person.

If a man's understanding of technological means is extremely limited, his 'ideas' are likely to be either technologically restricted (e.g. always conceived in terms of brick) or structurally unsound (e.g. using concrete arches as though they were stone arches).

If his understanding of the ways in which architecture expresses meanings is based only on a fondness for eighteenth-century classical architecture, then he has no real understanding of either. He may produce exquisite detail, but he will not express any meaning beyond his own nostalgia, and perhaps that of his client.

Many examples could be brought to show that where the process breaks down, it is due to a lack of understanding in one or several directions. The results, in the architecture, are easier to identify.

A building may express meanings, but in terms of a past culture; the meanings consequently have little validity for us (churches are very prone to this).

A building may be so much of our age that its technological means of realization have become ends in themselves; consequently it reveals only the structural prowess, conceitedness and disregard for human values, of its architect.

But although it is easy to point out examples of lack of understanding, it is important to remember that there is no ideal. There are only degrees of understanding, and no perfection.

When I call this description of the process of architectural creation a working method, I do not mean that one can *guarantee* architecture by following it. We cannot say: 'If we do this we shall get fine buildings.' But by making ourselves more aware of the way we work, we can achieve several things.

> We can cease to be governed by what we think architecture should be.
> We can be governed instead by what can be done.
> We can begin to see what can be done.

Meaning and Understanding

We can inform ourselves more fully where we see this to be most necessary.

We can come to terms with the fact that our own understanding is limited (even though we cannot know what these limits are)[9] and so not expect more of ourselves than what we can reasonably achieve.

We may even achieve fine buildings.

VII

A church architecture will express the meaning and values of the Church. Meanings underly purposes.

In a church the Church lives.
Lives corporately in doing these things:
It baptizes
It expounds and teaches
It celebrates the eucharist
It gives praise.

What is the meaning of baptism?
What is the meaning of the eucharist?
Of exposition, teaching, praise?
And how do these meanings relate to one another?

To look for this is theology.
That is not our job as architects
yet it is our responsibility as Christians.

As architects:
So to understand the meanings of these things
and so to understand the ways in which architecture
articulates and presents meanings
that architecture can be created.

---

[9] We cannot know this because we cannot account for the working of the Holy Spirit.

4. Material Fabric and Symbolic Pattern

KEITH MURRAY

> 'What is a church?' – Let truth and reason speak,
> They would reply, 'The faithful, pure and meek;
> From Christian folds, the one selected race,
> Of all professions, and in every place '
> 'What is a church?' – 'A flock,' our Vicar cries,
> 'Whom Bishops govern and whom priests advise;
> Wherein are various states and due degrees,
> The bench for honour and the Stall for ease;
> That ease be mine, which, after all his cares,
> The pious, peaceful prebendary shares.'
> 'What is a church?' – Our honest Sexton tells,
> ' 'Tis a tall building, with a tower and bells;
> Where priest and clerk with joint exertion strive
> To keep the ardour of their flock alive,
> That, by his periods eloquent and grave;
> This, by responses, and a well set stave·
> These for the living, but when life be fled,
> I toll myself the requiem for the dead . . .'
> *The Borough* by George Crabbe, 1810.

'We enter. The triple breadth of Nave and Aisles, the triple height of Pier arch, Triforium, and Clerestory, the triple length of Choir Trancepts and Nave, again set forth the Holy Trinity. And what besides is there which does not tell of our Blessed Saviour? And that does not point out "Him First" in the two-fold Western Door, "Him Last" in the distant Altar. "Him Midst", in the great Rood: "Him Without End" in the monogram carved on boss and corbel, in the Holy Lamb, in the Lion of the Tribe of Judah, in the Mystic Fish? Close by us is the font; for by Regeneration we enter the Church it is deep and capacious; for we are buried in Baptism with Christ: it is of stone; for he is the Rock: and its spiry cover teaches us, if we be indeed risen from its waters with Him, to seek those things that are above.'

J. M. Neale and B. Webb, Introduction to *Symbolism of Churches and Church Ornaments by Durandus*.[1]

---

[1] Leeds, 1843, pp. cxxx–cxxxi.

Crabbe was a country parson, and Neale and Webb the undergraduate founders and prime-movers of the Cambridge Camden Society. When Crabbe wrote, the romantic movement was well started; Gothic and the Picturesque were fashionable. In 1818, the fear of revolution had persuaded a Tory government of the utility of churches and an Act was passed, granting a million pounds for church building in populous districts. Two hundred and fourteen churches were built as a result of the Church Buildings Act of 1818. Of these, 174 were Gothic in style, as it was generally cheaper. Churches were large and dull, as the religion of the establishment was dull. Reason and utility had prevailed. In architecture, taste and elegance were the objects of design. Apart from a few extravagant but stylish monstrosities for the sophisticated, everything was well designed. After two hundred years in use, classical standards were well understood. Industrial design was particularly good. England must have been visually very comfortable in the 'golden age' of design.

Methodism, which was 'unreasonable' had been more than the establishment could stomach, and it had rejected it. Apart from some life in the missions, the Church of England seemed to be gently settling down to a good common sense view of religion. In 1833 John Keble's assize sermon at Oxford disturbed the peace, and in the same year Newman wrote the first Tract. By 1843, when Neale and Webb wrote their introduction to *Durandus,* the whole position was being transformed. The Tractarians were concerned especially for two things; to show that the Church of England was the ancient Catholic Church of the country; and to revive, in themselves and in the whole country, the longing for holiness. Holiness was not an intellectual attribute, the result of reason and conscious control, but a way of life, a quality of the complete person, body, mind and heart.

The early Tractarians were not very interested in Gothic architecture; and, though they were generally known as ritualists, they were not primarily concerned with ritual. They were, on the whole, scholars, careful men; but holiness and catholicity led them to worship; in particular to a deeper understanding of the eucharist. Neale and Webb felt that there was a connection between the spiritual lethargy and decadence which they fought, and the way that people worshipped. Their interest in architecture arose out of their belief in the significance of architecture for worship and their conviction that the change they hoped for in the Church, the full Christian life, would come about through the building up of the Church in worship. To achieve this, churches were needed which had a quality which modern churches seemed to lack, but which ancient churches possessed. They wrote: 'It is not that the rules of the science have not been studied, that the examples bequeathed to us have not been imitated, that the details are not understood. We have (though they are but few) modern buildings of the most perfect proportions, of the most faultless details and reared with lavish expense. It is that there is an undefined – perhaps almost undefinable – difference between a true "old church" and the most perfect of modern temples. In the former, at least till late in the Perpendicular era, we feel that, however strange the proportions, or extraordinary the details, the effect is church-like. In the latter we may not be able to blame; but from certain feelings of unsatisfactoriness, we cannot praise.'[2] They go on to discuss Pugin's idea of 'reality' in architecture. Pugin defined reality in two rules of design: first, that there should be no features about a building which are not necessary for convenience, construction or propriety; secondly, that all ornament should consist of enrichment of the essential construction of the building. While accepting these principles, Neale and Webb found them inadequate and suggested a further axiom. They wrote: 'We assert, then, that Sacramentality is that characteristic which so strictly distinguishes ancient ecclesiastical architecture from our own. By this word we mean to convey the idea that, by the outward and visible form, is signified something inward and spiritual: that the material fabric symbolizes, embodies, figures, represents, expresses, answers to some abstract meaning. Consequently, unless this ideal be itself true, or be rightly understood, he who seeks to build a Christian church may embody a false or incomplete and mistaken ideal but will not develop the true one.'[3]

By asserting that 'the outward and visible form signifies something inward and spiritual' they give the 'material fabric' a scandalous importance. Those who accepted this idea could no longer see churches in terms of good taste, and the whole meaning of a church became a great deal more significant; it gave architects a deeper sense of the value of their work and the creative function which buildings could fulfil in the life of the Church

[2] Introduction to *Durandus*, p. xviii.
[3] Ibid., p xxvi.

By the beginning of the nineteenth century the architect had become a man of sensibility ministering to the delicate tastes of civilized men, a sort of chef whose justification lay in pleasing his clients and himself. With this new understanding of the function of a church he became one responsible for embodying Christian truth through the church building: one of whom the Christian community could expect to make great demands. These powerful ideas liberated the Gothic Revival and gave it an entirely new character.

While the Gothic style had been chosen for churches because it was cheaper, or because it satisfied romantic tastes, churches were sometimes dull, but not disturbing. fitting very well into their surroundings. After, Neale, Webb and Pugin, Gothic churches were no longer integrated into their environment, they were set against it to transform it. Like Blake's poems they prophesy against the complacency of their environment. The new Gothic architecture asserted the spiritual potential of the material environment; it was an attempt to build Jerusalem.

> The fields from Islington to Marylebone
> To Primrose Hill and St John's Wood,
>   Were builded over with pillars of gold,
> And there Jerusalem's pillars stood.

The vision of Neale and Webb may seem as fantastic as that of William Blake, and their condemnation of the worship and architecture of the Church of England at that time disproportionate But they had seen the deprivation that their Church was suffering through the decline of worship, particularly eucharistic worship. They had realized the possibilities inherent in a true pattern of worship and its significance for the renewal of the life of the Church. They insisted that the Christian life involved the whole person – not only the rational, intellectual faculties; that in the eucharist in particular the deeper levels of the personality are integrated in the life of the Church.

Though the new significance which church architecture had acquired freed it from the inhibiting standards of taste, it created a vacuum. The classical system of design, applied to buildings of all sorts over a long period of time, had developed a well-understood vernacular which any local builder could use with considerable freedom. There are many Regency houses of great charm and originality built by local builders of no reputation. Even some pre-Ecclesiologist Gothic churches, such as St Michael s, Stockwell and St Luke's, Chelsea, though not in the classical vernacular, often have the charm and sense of proportion which is characteristic of eighteenth-century and early nineteenth-century building Architects and builders seemed to have an inborn sureness of touch, provided only that they accepted and worked within the classical system of design.

Though Neale and Webb could recognize the role of architecture and though they could show the architect the importance of the symbolic pattern for church building, they could not create a new system to replace the classical system of design which had provided the basis for all the architect's decisions, conscious and unconscious To do this they would have needed a profounder understanding of architecture than was possible then Most of the Ecclesiologists thought that by substituting an uncorrupted Gothic style of the best period for the eclectic, Gothic or classical style that was then being used for churches, they would achieve the revival of the true Christian architecture that they sought. This assumption suited most of the architects who supported the revival because it provided them with a set of cribs to replace the classical system of design and so enabled them to get on the Gothic Revival bandwagon. William Butterfield and G. E. Street are outstanding at the beginning of the revival because they tried to *understand* Gothic and were not content to copy.

William Butterfield was a friend of Neale and Webb and took very seriously their belief in the significance of architecture for worship, but he did not accept the easy answer of style. Sir John Summerson writes of him: 'His work is little appreciated in England today because of its extreme harshness of silhouette and texture. Trained as a builder he was the most pious and devoted of all Gothic men after Pugin. Unlike Pugin he lived a remote celibate life, wrote no books and could draw little better than a builder's clerk. But he set himself to build without affectation or antiquarianism a Gothic architecture for the Victorian age, using the ordinary thin pit-sawn timbers, the common bricks and tiles which were the builder's stock-in-trade. Out of these he made churches whose curious proportions and fierce ornamentation are often extremely moving.'[4]

[4] *Architecture in England since Wren*, Longmans, Green & Co. 1948, p. 13.

G. E Street was ten years younger than Butterfield and, though less austere, had much in common with him Street was closely connected with the inner circle of the Oxford Movement, particularly with the Revd W. J. Butler, who founded the Community of St Mary the Virgin at Wantage. Street also designed the convent at East Grinstead, founded by Neale, which was significantly one of his most outstanding buildings. Like Butterfield, Street was concerned with the whole process of building and with the symbolic aspect of the church. He designed churches for worship; his concern for symbolism was practical – unlike that of Neale and Webb, who at first, in the excitement of the discovery of the symbolic nature of worship, lumped together indifferently all sorts of symbolic interpretations and ideas without distinction. Whereas Neale and Webb saw the Holy Trinity set forth in the 'triple breadth of nave and aisles', Street objected to wide aisles as a hindrance to congregational worship.

Butterfield and Street are outstanding among Gothic Revival architects; their work is important for church building now, not only because their architectural thinking and practice influenced the modern movement through Street's pupils, William Morris, Philip Webb and Norman Shaw, but because their churches seem to show that there is a connection between a concern for worship and a convincing church architecture. No doubt they could not have achieved this coherence without considerable ability as architects; but the quality of their churches also stems from a belief in the reality of the worship which the buildings served, and a realization of the part which architecture could play in the life of the Church.

The revulsion against fancy dress styles of architecture towards the end of the nineteenth century was due to a growing recognition that good architecture can only be created if it is rooted in the life and culture which it serves. Many and varied pronouncements were made as to how such an appropriate relationship could be achieved, each concerned with one or more aspects of the rapidly changing ethos of the age, such as the changing social pattern or the advance of technology. Among those which have had a lasting significance are the concern for the basic elements of building – structure and materials, which are primarily a problem of the architect – and for function, in which both architect and client are involved.

The key word, function, is open to misunderstanding and has in fact been constantly misunderstood, not only by the architectural layman but also by architects. In the first place, both frequently deny function its full meaning, limiting it to the severely practical operation of a building; a failure to recognize that a building can have a comprehensible function which transcends circulation patterns, aspect or heating. And, in the second place, the curious notion is still current that a statement of function, however broadly based, can and should be transformed into a building by a process of purely logical development: a naive interpretation of Sullivan's dictum 'form follows function'. Such misunderstandings have had an unfortunate effect on recent church design, cutting it off from the best of modern architecture. As a consequence, those churches which owe anything at all to modern architectural developments are usually mere essays in 'the contemporary style', with basically Gothic plans, or rationalized solutions reflecting little feeling for the nature of the Church and its worship. There are exceptions, but they are rare among the mass of post-war church building.

Good architects are needed to design good churches, but good clients are almost as important. If our new schools are admired throughout the world it is largely because educators clarified their educational needs *and values* in such a way that a comparatively small group of sympathetic architects was able to give architectural expression to an *understanding* of the problems. As a result the schools provide good tools for teaching and an excellent architectural standard. It is important to see that the functions of a school are quite different to those of a church, and so the forms evolved for schools are not necessarily appropriate for churches. But the method of design based on the analysis and understanding of function is equally appropriate for both types of building. If there is one thing in particular that can be learned from school design, it is that care for apparently insignificant relationships and details in the design can give the whole a depth which is often lacking in more pretentious buildings.

The architectural values in a church building will arise naturally from those implicit in the worship and life of the Church. The search for a functional basis for the design of a church will therefore involve architect and client in an attempt to understand and relate various levels in the life of the Church, from the severely practical needs of the Christian community to the more subtle, theologically informed relationships of its liturgy. If we accept a functional basis for church design, the most urgent task for any church architect is to achieve as deep an understanding as possible of the nature of corporate worship and of its relationship to the other activities which the building serves. Without such an understanding the church itself and its relationship to the other buildings in the group will become an affirmation of values other than those intended by the Church.

The deeper levels of this understanding can only be developed from the architect's own experience of worship, related, through meetings and discussion, to the particular Christian community for which he is working. First, the symbolic pattern must be clarified. This pattern is important, even in the case of denominations which rely almost exclusively on verbal symbols to express doctrine, because there is a universal human tendency to think in symbolic associations, and even if such associations are not used *explicitly*, a doctrinal contradiction can be implied by an inexact symbolic relationship of parts or details

Symbolic patterns are means of communication and relationship. They arise wherever men, or, for that matter, birds or animals, live together in community. In the preface to *Bird Display and Behaviour*, Edward Armstrong writes: 'I have not hesitated to point out similarities between the behaviour of birds and other creatures varying from insects and fish to man. Indeed one of the outstanding impressions gained as a result of the study of behaviour patterns is the tendency for certain types of activity to recur in groups of organism widely separated from each other. These parallelisms are not to be explained as coincidence, but are due to the operation of fundamental psychological forces. The ritualization of activities, for example, characteristic of the human and subhuman animal alike, is only one amongst many indications of continuity of mental constitution at different levels.'[5]

Two things suggest themselves from the consideration of animal ritual patterns. one is the variety of symbolic means used and the subtlety of the patterns created; the other is the dynamic character of these patterns, so that the meaning of any element in the pattern is changed by changes in other aspects of the pattern. As Armstrong writes: 'The bird's world is comparable to a dynamic ever-changing relationship; in the words of Hippocrates, everything is in whole-part relationship, and part by part, the parts in each part operate

---

[5] Lindsay Drummond 1947, p. 12.

Towards a Church Architecture

according to their function.'⁶ The life of the bird is very simple and its ritual patterns are simple in comparison with those of men. The ideas and meanings it needs to convey seem to be largely, but not exclusively, concerned with the survival of the individual or of the group. Human symbolic patterns, even excluding language, express far wider ranges of meaning As Professor H S. Hooke writes in the introduction to *Water into Wine* by E. S. Drower, 'one of the most important developments of modern psychology has been the *Gestalt* psychology with its recognition of the importance of pattern in the growth of mental life. Nowhere is the importance and persistence of certain patterns so remarkable as in those modes of human behaviour which we call religion.'⁷

Symbolic patterns exist throughout any human society, but particular entities have characteristic patterns through which they live. the family, the law court, the parliament, the school, the church. Architecture plays a part in the symbolic pattern of each of these. Symbolic patterns are seldom thought up by a conscious process, but they are often revived, transferred, reformed and otherwise consciously influenced If their meanings are made conscious, the patterns are changed. The expressed meaning of part of a pattern becomes an extension of the pattern itself; a single action may have a variety of related meanings in the context of a particular pattern.

Today, in our life in the Church, we are often acutely aware of the verbal part of the symbolic pattern and subtle in ordering it, and yet show little real comprehension of the non-verbal. This is more surprising when we see that we have all sorts of symbolic patterns in our lives in which words, actions, clothes, hair styles, buildings, places, times and so on interact, modifying each other by their dynamic relationship. We find that in the ordinary life of society we have subtle powers of understanding and living through non-verbal, as well as verbal, symbolic patterns For instance, the black cap which the judge puts on when he pronounces the sentence of death illustrates some characteristics of symbolic patterns. At the Royal Commission on Capital Punishment (1949–53) Lord Chief Justice Goddard held that the black cap was put on as a token of sorrow. The judge covers his head in the manner of King David who covered his head

---

⁶ Ibid., p. 323.
⁷ John Murray 1956, p. vii.

on hearing the death of his son Absalom. The Lord Justice General of Scotland maintained in evidence before the Commission that the black cap was worn as official headgear by a representative of the Crown when performing a solemn duty with the full authority of his office. It is interesting in this context that while the Criminal Justice Bill was before Parliament in 1948, and the operation of the death penalty was suspended, the judges continued to pronounce the the death sentence formula, but they did not put on the black cap.

The black cap descends from the mediaeval biretta; it was the normal wear of judges in the sixteenth century; in the seventeenth, it was beginning to be archaic and its use was controlled by rules, by the eighteenth century, it had become inconveniently archaic and difficult to wear on top of a full wig. Though the rule that it should be worn on the prescribed occasions survived, it was in fact carried in the hand, as it is today. The particular meaning which the action of putting on the black cap has for us is due to its place in the context of the symbolic pattern of the courts.

The assumption of the black cap has caught the popular imagination. It is not very easy to say what it means to people outside the courts, but it seems to convey a sense of the gravity of the act of taking of life, whether the life of the murderer or the murdered, and so speaks of the value of life. This is an instance of the symbolic pattern of the law influencing understanding beyond the particular entity in which it works.

The interpretations by the two judges of the action as showing either the sorrow or the delegated authority of the judge are interesting as they emphasize the role-creating aspect of the action. The action enabled Lord Goddard to express not a personal emotion, which he may or may not have felt, but his sorrow as a judge fulfilling his function. When the Lord Justice General saw in the action a delegation of authority, he made explicit to himself and those who understood this meaning of the action, the impersonal nature of the condemnation to death.

Both judges used the act to enable themselves to function in a public role, where private judgments and feelings would be an intrusion. The assumption of the black cap illustrates both the esoteric and the exoteric character of the symbolic pattern. The act of putting on a black cap is in itself very insignificant and could only have such symbolic significance in the face of the actual event, which it foreshadows – the death of the murderer – and in the context of the whole pattern of the courts.

This discussion of a point in the symbolic pattern of the law may seem remote from the architecture of churches. Yet if Neale and Webb were right when they wrote that 'the material fabric symbolizes, embodies, figures, represents, expresses, answers to some abstract "meaning",' to understand symbolic patterns is important for church architecture. A feeling for and an understanding of the symbolic pattern is important for all those involved in the creation of any part of it. We cannot isolate architecture from the rest of the symbolic pattern of worship any more than we can isolate the robes of the judge from his actions or the architectural setting of the law.

Symbolic patterns, through which bodies live, should be distinguished from dramatic actions, pageants, plays and so on, which represent real or imaginary events. The church or court may be presented on the stage or screen, the same actions performed, the whole pattern simulated. The same black cap, put on by the same judge, in the same manner in a mock trial will recall the events of a real trial; it may move us, but it will still be unreal. Whereas for the drama the things which stimulate the imagination, the paste board and the wooden sword, are not only tolerable, but appropriate, they are for this reason unacceptable in the context of real life, whether of church, school, court or home. Pugin's concern for reality in church architecture is valid, not because make-believe architecture is dishonest but because the reality of the action demands that the elements in this symbolic pattern (architectural or otherwise) must be real. This reality is not a matter of materials (though it may influence their choice), or of craftsmanship, or of structural expression, but of a concern for the worship and its reality for life. Concern for and belief in the value of the pattern is essential to its life. So taste, as the primary value in the pattern, is its death. When architectural values are subordinated to the values implicit in the life of the Church they may be creative. When they dominate and are set above the values of worship they are frequently destructive.

Symbolic language may be simple or complex. An analysis of the use of such language in a particular instance may help to show something of its character. In the catholic tradition the eucharistic action is the uniting of the Church in worship, a sacred meal and a re-presenting of the sacrifice of Christ. The altar is by its form and position potentially a symbol of these realities. Its form can convey the meaning both of a table and of an altar; the former expressing the commemorative meal, the latter sacrifice. Its position in the eucharistic room can suggest either union or disunion in the action of the priestly people of God By the act of vesting the altar with a rich cloth the Church conveys reverence for the material object as a symbol of Christ its Head, High Priest and King. By stripping the altar on Good Friday its expresses the desolation of that day. Spreading a white linen cloth brings to mind the preparation for the Last Supper by the apostles.

In such an understanding the architect has a basis for design. He must therefore ask many questions, and the success of this part of his work will depend largely on his feeling for the problem: on an intuitive grasp of the kind of questions to ask. Why the architect? Because usually (there will be rare exceptions) the client, whether clergyman or committee, will have taken these things for granted; they are part of his own background and outlook. Moreover, the client will probably present his requirements in an apparently simple form which only obscurely incorporates the underlying meaning which things have for him: for example, 'the altar is to be the focus of the building and will have a frontal'. By asking questions the architect can find where meaningfulness lies and make it explicit in his design. Nothing but symbolic confusion can result from meaningless details and relationships; and the more artistically impressive they are, the worse the confusion. For example, if the altar is seen primarily as a *table* for the commemorative meal and has no significance as a symbol of Christ, a covering of richly embroidered cloth is meaningless and any kind of frontal will detract from the effectiveness of the symbol. The white linen cloth on the other hand may become even more symbolically expressive.

The Gothic Revival gained its power from the attempt to recapture the richness of worship, but its popular appeal was fed by the Romantic Movement· a literary rather than an architectural phenomenon. It created a popularly accepted image of a church, imposing a general pattern on the buildings of most denominations. That this popular image is still with us can be seen, for example, from the *Methodist Buildings Report* of 1958. Although the buildings illustrated in this document would generally be considered as 'contemporary' in style, they are practically all long and narrow, with the communion table set against a curtain at the end of a vista. This position gives the table a symbolic significance analogous to that of an altar – a significance which is further emphasized in some examples by the table having a cubic form, more suggestive of an altar than a table. Also the long, narrow, high building is far from ideal for preaching or for the development of the Christian community.

It is not only Methodists who are suffering from the consequences of romantic revivals. Anglicans and Roman Catholics, who theoretically believe in the participation of the laity in the liturgy, still worship in churches where the altar is often out of sight of many of the congregation. Even where the present liturgical movement has influenced church design, there is still a widespread failure to recognize that its insights can inform the functional basis for design *to a depth of understanding* sufficient to be really fruitful for both worship and architecture. To stress the importance of functional analysis of this kind is not to say that this is all that is needed to achieve good churches. But through a real comprehension of what a church is, and of the values implicit in the life and worship of the Christian community, we may hope to take a first step towards a church architecture which is genuinely rooted in the vitality of Christian tradition today.

Neale and Webb revived the mediaeval symbolic pattern of worship as a means for the sanctification of the Church of England. Looking back, their enthusiam and their inflexibility are difficult for us to understand unless we recognize their aim. For those who see the Gothic Revival as a mere change of fashion, or as a matter of taste, it will seem incomprehensible that clergy were willing to go to prison for what cannot but strike us as ceremonial *minutiae*. Often the particular issues which were at stake seem unimportant to us; but, as in so many controversies, the real ground of conflict lies deeper. The ritualists were defending not particular symbolic forms but the symbolic way itself.

5. A Liturgical Brief

H. BENEDICT GREEN

I offer no apology for the frankly theological matter of much of this essay A liturgical brief is virtually synonymous with a theological brief; the presuppositions on which the use and character of a church rest are theological ones, and if architects as such do not necessarily accept them, the fact that their clients do is at any rate the starting point of their own operations. I have naturally tried to eliminate both piety and technical theological language; but to avoid the use of the believers' family jargon altogether, or to signalize every lapse into it, would not have been possible without some cumbersome circumlocution, and I have preferred to stick to direct speech. It should be emphasized that what follows is a personal statement by an Anglican. I should like to believe that much in it would be assented to by members of other Christian communions which have felt the influence of the liturgical movement. But in any case personal bias is a less serious danger than the colourlessness of the agreed statement, which would be the alternative, and is far more easily discounted.

The fundamental question for church designers is the nature of Christian worship; and one cannot begin to understand Christian worship without first discovering what it took from Judaism and how it affected what it took – the ways of Jewish worship and the difference that the Christian dispensation necessarily made to them. Christian worship, like Christian faith, at once grew out of and transcended the Jewish chrysalis from which it emerged; but as the modes of Jewish worship were various, the Christian transformation of them had a multiple source. The worship of the Jews in the century in which Christianity emerged was centred on three foci: the Temple, the synagogue and the home; and all contributed to the new synthesis which emerged in the worship of the settled Christian Church.

The Temple had begun as no more than a local sanctuary with exceptional prestige (to say nothing of a streak of syncretism in its rites), but, at a date identified by most scholars with the religious reforms of King Josiah of Judah in 621 BC, it had been transformed into the sole central sanctuary of the Jewish kingdom, at which all sacrifice, and consequently all representative worship, had to be offered. These reforms, and the code of Deuteronomy in which they were incorporated, conditioned the thinking of the religious *élite* of the nation after their exile to Babylon not many years later; consequently, when the influence of these was able to be brought to bear again upon the religious life of the whole community, the pattern that emerged was that of a people with a single centre of worship, which Jews living at a distance made valiant attempts to attend, at least occasionally. The analogy of Mecca for contemporary Islam is only partial, for Islam has from the beginning been the religion of a dispersion, and Mecca the goal of its pilgrimage rather than the heart of its worship, which in any case is not sacrificial at all. But for Judaism the Temple came first; the Deuteronomic code set a local sanctuary at the heart of the religious life of a united nation, and it is really by reference to this that the Dispersion is so called. Since the destruction of the last Temple in AD 70, Judaism has had only a maimed worship, lacking its centre; and to this day only a truncated observance of the passover, for instance, is permitted to the scattered sons of Israel – for the full observance requires the sacrifice of a lamb, and there is one place only (and that in Muslim hands) where this can lawfully be effected.

The Christians of the first decades after the resurrection were apparently not averse to using the existing Temple, as Christ himself had done; but they rapidly developed a way of thinking about the Church with which any centrality of a localized sanctuary was ultimately incompatible. The events of AD 70 brought this incompatibility to a head. The fourth Gospel represents Jesus as saying, on the occasion of his symbolic purging of the Temple, 'Destroy this temple, and I will raise it up again in three days', and the evangelist immediately glosses 'but he spake of the temple of his body.'[1] The two concrete images here combined dominate the thought of the New Testament about the Church, which is both the body of Christ, the organism in which the Christian's life is lived, and the spiritual temple, the holy place in which his worship is performed – and he lives

[1] John ii, 19 and 21.

by worshipping The Holy Spirit is both the life of the body and the agency of God's indwelling of the temple. And as the body is, by expansion, that of Christ who is seated at the right hand of God, so the worship of the temple is the earthly embodiment of that of the heavenly places, as the sacrificial work of Christ has established it.

But if Christianity ultimately rejected the idea of a single sanctuary on which its forerunner was based, it did not therefore revert to the multiplicity of shrines which was normal in the pagan world into which it spread. Rather it completely transcended and spiritualized all that *worship* had hitherto meant. The fourth Gospel, in its narrative of the encounter of Jesus with the Samaritan woman, attributes to the Master the words 'The hour is coming when neither in this mountain nor in Jerusalem shall you worship the Father . . when the true worshippers shall worship him in spirit and in truth.'[2] This is not to say that worship ceased to be either local or visible: that would imply an opposition between the material and the spiritual which is foreign to the biblical outlook. On the contrary, it continued to be done visibly with such concrete objects as bread and wine. But it did cease to be locally *determined*; and its local aspect became the visible sign of something transcending place and vision. That is what is meant by calling it sacramental.

The contrast between the Jewish and Christian attitudes to worship may be summed up in this way: whereas for the Jew it is the local Temple that constitutes the worship, for the Christian it is the worship that constitutes the visible Church: wherever it may happen to be carried out.

The synagogue was a product of the gap between a central sanctuary and a dispersed people. It did not offer a substitute for the worship of the Temple, it was rather a means of spiritual communion with that worship. But if Judaism was a religion of one sanctuary it came to be equally a religion of one book, and this could be disseminated as its place of worship could not. Consequently the worship of the synagogue was dominated by the reading of law and prophets, together with their exposition, and prayer. As we can see from the Acts of the Apostles, Christianity, at any rate in its Gentile missions, used the synagogue as its spring-board. When, as always happened sooner or later, the local Christian community was obliged to separate

[2] John iv, 21.

Towards a Church Architecture

itself from the Jewish synagogue and use instead the private houses of its members, it took with it the synagogue pattern of the service of the word, but with the Old Testament interpreted in a Christian sense. In due course there came to be added to the Old Testament readings, first, passages relating to the life and teaching of Christ, which eventually became incorporated in the continuous narrative accounts known to us as the gospels; secondly, passages from former sermons of the apostles originally delivered *in absentia* as pastoral letters (or possibly, in some cases, actual sermons of persons unknown which were later dressed up as letters) which we call epistles. Thus the Christian service of the word is actually older than the New Testament as we have it, and in the formation of the New Testament liturgical usage played a significant part.

Religious rituals played a prominent part, as they still do, in the *domestic* life of devout Jewish households, the most characteristic of them being the *Berākāh*, or blessing of God for his mighty acts in creation and redemption, performed as a rule over material objects, and in particular as a grace over a loaf of bread at the opening of a meal, and over a cup of wine at the close of the more formal ones. The ritual of the passover supper is no more than an elaborated form of that belonging to Jewish meals in general, except for its direct association with the Temple worship through the eating of the paschal lamb previously sacrificed in the Temple precincts. Scholars remain divided on the question whether the Last Supper was actually a passover meal, but most would agree that it had at any rate paschal associations; certainly the rite which was instituted by it – by the command to perform the *Berākāh* ritual over bread and wine expressly in thanksgiving for Christ's own death – has retained for most Christians (though they are divided about the sense in which they would understand this) the aspect of a sacrificial rite as well as of a fellowship meal (of which only the *Berākāh* ritual now remains). The domestic table which has become the centre of the Church's worship is at the same time the place of sacrifice, the altar.

Christian worship thus inherited the centrality of the Temple in Israel, and transformed it by removing from it all considerations of place; it inherited the use of the word from synagogue worship, and transformed it first by Christian interpretation and ultimately by completing it with Christian scriptures; it inherited the domestic rituals already transformed by the new meaning imposed on them by

Jesus himself, and made them central where they had been auxiliary. To these must be added the requirement of initiation; as no uncircumcized person was permitted to enter the inner court of the Temple, so no person could join in the worship of the body of Christ until he had been admitted to that body; but the rite and mark of initiation was no longer circumcision but baptism in water, once an auxiliary ceremony of ritual purification, but now the outward sign of a new birth in Christ, which all, whether Jew or Gentile, had to undergo.

There is from the earliest times a polarity between Christian initiation and Christian worship which is fundamental both to the life of the Church and to the design of the church building. It is well illustrated by the earliest complete account of the worship of Christians that we have from a Christian source. The author, Justin Martyr, writing at Rome about the year 150, presents that worship in two phases He first describes how the new convert is admitted to membership of the Church, and then gives an account of the regular weekly worship of the Church to which his membership admits him.

Of baptism he says: 'All who accept and believe as true the things taught and said by us, and who undertake to have the power to live accordingly, are taught to pray and entreat God, fasting, for the forgiveness of their former sins, while we join in their prayer and fasting. Then we bring them to a place where there is water, where they are regenerated in the same way as we were; for they then make their ablution in the name of God the Father and of our Lord Jesus Christ and of the Holy Spirit.'[3] He goes on to describe the eucharistic offering in which the newly-baptized take part for the first time. We can here distinguish three elements: (i) the preaching of the word, which the convert has accepted; (ii) his response to it in prayer, culminating in (iii) his regeneration in baptism, which qualifies him for a share in the Church's corporate worship.

There is a close parallel between this and Justin's account of the corporate Sunday worship of the Church: 'And on the day which is called the Sun's Day, there is an assembly of all who live in the towns or the country, and the memoirs of the apostles or the writings of the prophets are read, as much as time permits. When the reader has finished, the president gives a discourse, admonishing us and exhort-

---

[3] Justin Martyr, *First Apology*, 61: as translated by H. Bettenson, *The Early Christian Fathers*, Oxford University Press 1957

ing us to imitate these excellent examples. Then we all rise together and offer prayers, and, as I said above, on the conclusion of our prayers bread is brought, and wine and water; and the president similarly offers up prayers and thanksgivings to the best of his powers, and the people assent with *Amen*. Then follows the distribution of the eucharistic gifts and the partaking of them by all, and they are sent to the absent by the hands of the deacons.'[4]

Here again we can distinguish (i) the reading and exposition of the word in scripture; (ii) the response to it in the common prayers of the Church, culminating in (iii) the eucharistic offering and thanksgiving. The parallel pattern will be evident, but it should be noted that whereas the eucharist is designed to be continually repeated, baptism is a single act, performed once for all; and, in so far as it admits to membership of the Church, it is strictly an act which takes place, as far as the candidate is concerned, outside the Church. Thus the proclamation of the word, which is presupposed both in baptism and eucharist, occurs as a liturgical factor only in the latter.

All other characteristic actions of the Church's corporate life can be related to one or other of these two. Confirmation is the bishop's blessing completing the baptismal initiation. Absolution of a penitent by a priest after confession of sin is a restoration of baptismal status. Other rites performed once for all, notably marriage and the bestowal of holy orders, bear a close analogy to the initiatory character of baptism, and like it have traditionally been followed by the eucharist as their climax. The communion of those absent through sickness or other urgent cause from the corporate worship of the Church (already referred to by Justin) is an extension of the eucharistic action. Preaching is strictly a liturgical activity, it is – or ought to be – an exposition of the meaning and relevance of the passages which have previously been solemnly read to the Church assembled for the eucharist, aimed at producing a response to these readings from the hearts of the congregation from which their eucharistic action will follow. The divine office, or daily meditative prayers of the Church – represented for Anglicans by the services of Morning and Evening Prayer – serves to extend in time the presentation of the word of God to the attention of the Church, which, as we have seen, is a constant feature of the eucharistic liturgy. The feasts and seasons of the Christian year have

---

[4] Ibid., 67.

the complementary function of concentrating the Church's attention on a single aspect of the Christian mystery at a particular time.

All these things collectively constitute, in its widest sense, the *liturgy*; but this word has become specially characteristic of the eucharist, to which – with its preceding service of the word, or *synaxis* – it is more usually restricted. The word liturgy denotes, first, an action, something done (not said, or thought, or felt), and, secondly, an action performed as a characteristic function or duty (thus the provision of a warship or a dramatic production at his own expense to which an ancient Athenian citizen was liable was described as his liturgy). This means, in a Christian context, that the action is one integral to the Church's understanding and realization of itself. The Christian usage implies, thirdly, that this characteristic action has a priestly quality, since it directly associates the Church with the priestly work of Christ its Head, and, fourthly, since the priestly character belongs to the whole body, not primarily to individuals within it, that the characteristic action is distributed throughout the body. All do it together, and all have an active part in it, but, since the body is hierarchical, all have not the same part. Thus, in primitive accounts of the eucharist (going back in one case into the first century) the bishop has one liturgy, that of reciting the eucharistic thanksgiving over the Church's oblations of bread and wine; the presbyters another, that of supporting the bishop in his liturgy (which grew into the practice of concelebration); the deacons another, that of receiving the people's offerings and carrying them to the altar, and of distributing the holy communion; the laity another, that of bringing their own individual offerings, and of communicating. And all the parts were integral to the corporate liturgy of the Church

The worship of the local parish church of our own day can only, at best, exhibit a more restricted hierarchical pattern. But the buildings designed to contain it should, at the least, promote, not hinder, the active participation of all present in the liturgy, according to their status and ability; as they should also make clear that the liturgy is literally the *raison d'être* of both community and building

Christian worship as we first encounter it in history is still domestic in character; partly because its most characteristic action grew out of a domestic religious institution, partly because there was nowhere to go but the houses of Christian people. The latter pragmatic consideration was long in becoming obsolete, and the earliest known church originally built for the purpose, at Dura-Europos on the Euphrates, is still essentially a house, with separate rooms for its different activities.[5] As the activities of the modern parish church extend far beyond its worship, the pattern is one from which we can again learn, though the subject hardly comes within the scope of a *liturgical* brief The considerations which dictated the construction of permanent church buildings from that time onwards, and especially after the influx of converts which followed the official recognition of Christianity in the fourth century, were the practical ones of the convenience of the householder and the numbers of the worshippers; it became an urgent matter for the Church's meeting for worship to find some alternative means of getting a roof over its head. And the basic reasons for having permanent churches remain practical. According to the conception of Christian worship outlined above, the Lord's service is equally effectual in the sight of God whether it is celebrated in a Nissen hut or in a great civic church, in Chartres cathedral or on the kitchen table of a priest-workman's lodgings. It does not matter whether Christian baptism takes place behind Ghiberti's doors in the great baptistery at Florence, or in a muddy tropical river, or with a tumbler of water beside a hospital bed; in each case it incorporates into Christ, neither more nor less. The word of God is not any more the word of God for being proclaimed from an ornate baroque pulpit, nor any less for being delivered from a soap-box. But, as every priest who has had to make do with a dual-purpose church building will know, the liturgy is not conveniently performed, especially by large numbers, in a building designed or habitually used for other purposes, nor do such occasions, with some moving exceptions, convey the full splendour of the mysteries by which the Church lives.

Full-time churches made their appearance hard on the heels of a full-time ministry, and for much the same reason: the pressures of an expanding church life. A type of secular building was ready to hand, and the basilica was readily adaptable to the exigencies of a liturgical worship which had already developed independently of buildings designed expressly to contain it. The basilica is not necessarily a

---

[5] On this see J. G. Davies, *The Origin and Development of Early Christian Architecture*, S.C M. Press 1952, pp. 20 ff.

A Liturgical Brief

model for those who build with the same intentions today, but the reasons why it was found suitable will bear investigation. It should be borne in mind that, if the ground plan of the basilica was a fairly narrow rectangle, the liturgical action carried out within it was thrown out much more into the body of the building than came to be the case in the mediaeval parish church, which was otherwise its descendant.

It was not unnatural that what had been established by pragmatic considerations should afterwards have reasons of symbolism attached to it; but we have suffered too long from the mediaeval welter of mystical significances that wholly divorced the inner meaning of a church's design from the function for which it was built. Actually, in so far as a church building has any justification over and above the pragmatic, it is as a visible embodiment of what the Church's worship really is. It is in this sense that a church should, as the *doyen* of Fécamp Abbey once told Sir Ninian Comper that his church did, 'pray of itself' – and, it might be added, preach of itself: for a church designed with a theological understanding of its *raison d'être* should have something to say not only to the worshipper but also to the unconverted person with eyes to see.

It would be incomplete, in view of what has already been said, to describe such a church, as many have, as simply 'a roof over an altar'; but its design will certainly focus attention at the points where the Church's liturgy focuses it: the font, the altar with the worshipping community gathered round it, and the place from which that community hears the word proclaimed.

In ancient times arrangements for baptism varied widely. The house-church at Dura-Europos had one room set aside as a baptistery, but in the west at the same period it was apparently normal to baptize in a river or wherever water, preferably running, was available. Hence the font, when it finally came to be provided for, was normally housed in a separate baptistery. (At Ostia, if Basil Minchin is right, the Church had its own bathing establishment adjoining the basilica, and baptisms were carried out there.)[6] If it was accommodated under the same roof as the main church building, it was always in a separate compartment of its own, as is still technically required by the rubrics governing the design of Roman Catholic churches.

[6] See *The Listener* for January 28th 1960, p. 181.

Towards a Church Architecture

There is therefore no traditional precedent for the practice, now on the increase in some new Anglican churches and many of the evangelical Protestant traditions on the Continent, of having the font close to the Lord's table and the pulpit. This is defended by two types of argument, one pragmatic and one theological. The pragmatic argument is that the majority of baptisms today are of infants, that it is desirable (as indeed it is) that they take place *coram populo*, and that the font should therefore be in full view of the people without any necessity for them to turn round. As an argument from convenience this has force, what it leaves unsettled is the prior question whether practical considerations of this kind shall be allowed to outweigh the theological objections, in particular to treating infant baptism not merely as common practice but as the norm by which the nature and significance of baptism is understood. The theological argument usually advanced is that the two sacraments of baptism and the eucharist are so closely associated that the places where they are administered ought, in order to symbolize this, to be as close to one another as possible. This, however, is to emphasize the closeness of their connection at the expense of obscuring what the nature of that connection is; for baptism *admits* to the community of which the eucharist is the characteristic corporate action and its source of renewed life. The arguments are therefore overwhelmingly in favour of placing the font not near the altar but close to the entrance, so that it not only is but is seen to be (by those who, in the majority of cases, cannot recollect their own baptism) the opening through which entry is obtained into the Church of Christ. I know of no more striking and significant example of the arrangement for which I am arguing than the great church built by the Oxford Mission to Calcutta at Barisal, in East Bengal, where an open-work screen divides the narthex from the body of the church, and sunk in the middle of the floor of the narthex is a large immersion font. The unbaptized must remain on the near side of the screen; none may pass beyond it until he has passed through the font. An arrangement produced in and for the mission-field may not be transferable as it stands, even to the increasingly missionary situation in this country; but the symbolism of the font's position and its polarity with the altar ought to be a a factor in the local Church's understanding of itself.

Next, the altar, its nature and position. The Christian altar is at once the table of the Lord, and, in some sense, the place of sacrifice:

the point at which the sacrifice of Christ and the self-oblation of Christians are mysteriously united. It should signify both these things by its design, position and construction. Too often these suggest a sideboard rather than a table, or an elaborate counter rather than an altar, and the fabrics which cover it seem intended to conceal rather than to adorn, since the piece of furniture underneath is neither a self-respecting table nor even remotely suggestive of sacrificial significance. The choice of material would seem to be ultimately a question only of emphasis, except for those whose rubrical directions provide otherwise, what is important is that the focus of the Church's worship should be as fixed and permanent as any item in the furnishings of the church The ornaments which stand upon the altar should not be disproportionate to it in scale, nor the altar itself out of scale with the man who is to stand and minister at it. If, because of the size of the building or for other good reasons, its dignity requires further emphasis, the ancient device of a canopy, whether standing on posts or suspended, has never been improved on.

The position of the altar must be related to that of the people in the church, for what happens at it is not the priest's action alone but theirs with him. It is not enough that they should be able to *see* the altar; the whole audience in a theatre can see the stage, but that does not make them actors, and in the Christian liturgy the whole people are actors: the presence of occasional spectators among them is not a factor for which the planning of a church should make special provision. Nor ought the position of the altar to suggest that what takes place there is something rarified, remote and unapproachable; for though the worship of the earthly altar is sometimes described in terms which imply participation in, or anticipation of, the worship of heaven, it is for all that a worship embodied in visible forms to which the faithful have entire freedom of access. Mystery there is; but it lies in the relation of the visible and earthly, bread and wine, and the words of a man, to the supernatural realities which they effectively signify: not in any artificially induced sense of the numinous. The altar should therefore be not only within sight and hearing but also within reach of the congregation as a whole; they should be so disposed round it that whichever side of it the celebrant stands (and the growing movement to have him facing the people should not be disregarded in the planning of churches for the future) his people are *en rapport* with him as the action proceeds. This implies

Towards a Church Architecture

almost any plan in preference to the conventional narrow rectangle with the altar at one end. For various reasons, some of them connected with other factors in the liturgical brief, the geometrical centre of the church has rarely been found an altogether satisfactory solution. But it is most desirable that the eucharistic room should be, in a general sense, centrally planned.

About the place of the proclamation of the word it is not so easy to lay down any hard and fast rule. One cannot with only a liturgical brief in one's hands decide between the claims of, say, twin ambos and those of three-decker pulpits. But it can usefully be pointed out that the exposition of the word of God (which alone has a proper claim to be called preaching) has not always taken such precedence, in the appointments of a church, over its reading or recitation as we have now come to assume. We think, today, almost unconsciously in terms of a lectern to read from and a pulpit to preach from; but in a primitive basilica the pulpit was the elevated place in the body of the church for the scriptures to be read (or rather chanted) from, while the bishop's sermon expounding them was usually delivered by him sitting on his throne in the apse. It would be merely antiquarian to advocate a return to this practice, but it does raise the question whether separate provision for reading and preaching (with the chief emphasis on the second) is really calculated to bring home to the lay mind that they are two aspects of the same thing. Apart from this it suffices that the people who are to hear the word (and this applies equally to the offices of Morning and Evening Prayer) shall be 'all gathered together in one place'; that those who read and preach to them – and it is desirable that the former function should be as widely distributed as possible – shall be easily visible and audible; and that the place from which they do it shall be closely related to the place from which the sacramental gifts are distributed.

Once the position of the altar in relation to the people has been settled, the disposition of the latter about the building settles itself. But a special problem arises in connection with the choir. The choir is not itself an order in the Church, but a section of the laity having its own specific liturgy, or part to play in the worship of the whole Church. Its position should signify this. It should by now be well known that the practice of robing the choir and placing it between the sanctuary and the nave in parish churches was a Victorian imitation of cathedral practice; and cathedral practice had extended to the singers the position in church originally occupied by the clergy only, in the period when the change from the primitive position of the altar had ousted them from the apse. This was reasonable enough when the literacy requisite for singers in choir (which included the ability to read Latin) was restricted to those with a clerical formation. But in Victorian England it meant that the choirs of parish churches, which vastly outnumbered the clergy present, were treated as an intermediate caste, neither clerical nor lay; and class distinctions of this sort are as inappropriate to the house of God as they are to the twentieth century. It is unfortunately easier to point out where the Victorians went wrong than to suggest a satisfactory alternative arrangement. To place the choir in a gallery may in some cases be musically very effective, but it isolates them unduly from the rest of the congregation. To place them behind the altar, as at Westminster Cathedral, for example, does mean that they no longer keep the main body of the people at a distance from the sanctuary, but it also retains and even accentuates the impression that they constitute an order on their own. To give them instead special places within the main body of the congregation (as is done, for instance, at the John Keble church at Mill Hill) emphasizes at once their distinction from and solidarity with the laity as a whole.

What has been presented so far is not so much an ideal as a theological and liturgical norm. But perhaps the greater part of the history of church design has consisted of deviations from this, and one can properly indicate what the norm is by some cautionary illustrations of what it is not. There have been three main types of distortion which the liturgy of the Church has undergone, and all of these have had their effect on church design.

1. There has been, first, the invasive influence of non-liturgical practices. Mission preaching, for instance, is not a liturgical activity though, in certain contexts, it is a necessary one, and it may even be desirable to build churches with this as their primary function; just as, in a rather different context, it is desirable to build churches for the reception of pilgrims, like Le Corbusier's chapel at Ronchamp or the vast subterranean basilica at Lourdes. It may be desirable, but experience would suggest that a tiered auditorium with a platform is a far more effective setting for ventures of this kind, and a stadium more effective still; and neither of these is strictly suited to

the fundamental functions of a parish church as I have outlined them. Mission preaching has invaded church planning in some unexpected quarters; we may be tolerably certain that the great pulpits halfway down the naves of Catholic churches of the baroque era, for which the congregation at mass must reverse their chairs, were originally intended for *ferverino* rather than for the liturgical sermon. And that indicates a certain reversal of priorities.

Another item in this category is the practice of public devotions to the reserved sacrament. This is not the place or the context in which to pass judgment on the practice. All that is relevant here is that it is by definition extra-liturgical, and any arrangement of a church or design of a principal altar in which it overshadows the eucharistic liturgy must be regarded as a deviation.

A third non-liturgical practice to which attention is often paid is the use of the church for private prayer. It is not generally realized that this practice took fully a thousand years to establish itself; and while it is altogether to be encouraged, and remains for many people their only opportunity of solitude for devotion, it is nevertheless properly regarded as an extension of the common prayer of the Church in which they take part on Sundays. It does not therefore require any special provision in the arrangement of a church over and above the place where that common prayer takes place; though the provision of a small chapel – which should be quite separate – for weekday liturgical use will meet the needs of private devotion as well: not only from such reasons of convenience as heating but also from considerations of scale. But a design deliberately aimed at bringing the casual visitor to his knees will probably, and deservedly, fail of its object.

2. Secondly, it is possible to perform liturgical actions in what can only be called an anti-liturgical manner, that is, in such a way as to imply that they are not central but peripheral. One sometimes comes across prayer-books printed in the eighteenth century with the second half of the communion service, the eucharist proper, printed in the small type reserved for the occasional offices; and an occasional office is what, as certain contemporary interiors remind us, it had become at that time. If this misconception is no longer current, it is by no means exceptional to find the central service of Christian worship treated as a kind of appendix to another service, and this has its effect upon the interior appointments of churches.

The logical expression of it would be the movable table which, in some churches of the Reformed tradition, is carried in and placed below the pulpit, and afterwards carried out again.

While recent Anglican practice has not gone so far as that, it is probable that the overshadowing of the communion service by sung Morning or Evening Prayer has contributed to the prevailing conservatism about the position of the altar; not because that position is regarded as positively good in itself, but because the practice of such churches, by keeping the function of the robed choir prominent, has inevitably relegated the altar, both figuratively and literally, to the background.

Again, the practice of treating baptism as a private occasion, attended by family and friends but not by the congregation of the local Church, is a deviation. But the distortion which has had most influence and done the greatest damage is unquestionably the mediaeval presentation of the eucharist as something done by the clergy and only seen (or sometimes heard) by the laity: the clericalization of the eucharist, as it has been called. This, as Father Jungmann has pointed out,[7] had the effect of reducing the main body of the faithful to the status of catechumens It has produced the long narrow church plan with altar and sanctuary, as often as not, screened off at one end; and, as we have seen, the further interposition of the liturgical choir between the eucharistic action and the laity. Whether the liturgy is performed with great splendour by a team of clergy and assistants, or said by one priest in solitary isolation, the effect has been, and is, in the clergy, clericalism; and in the laity, cut off from the action, discouraged sometimes even from communion, and in general left to their own private devotions, a ruinous individualism.[8] It has been largely responsible for the idea, so dear to English lay minds, that the fundamental activity of a Christian is *private* prayer; and that *common* prayer, being no more than a coagulation of individuals praying, is as such quite secondary. It was not without its effect on the way in which the importance of the word preached was re-established in the sixteenth century (for there is a clericalism of the pulpit not less damaging than that of the altar), and it was given an all too vigorous new lease of life by the romanticism of the Victorians.

[7] See *The Mass of the Roman Rite*, pp. 81 ff.
[8] A phrase used by Professor T. F. Torrance to indicate the inadequacies of the Reformation doctrine of 'the priesthood of all believers'.

3. Thirdly, it sometimes happens that in the heat of controversy one aspect of the liturgical whole is set up against another. This is specially characteristic of the legacy of the Reformation, and its effects in various forms are with us still. The Middle Ages had emphasized the mass to the exclusion of the sermon, so the reformers counter-emphasized the sermon, ultimately (though against their best intentions) to the virtual exclusion of the eucharist. Word and sacrament, which should be complementary parts of one whole, were set up against each other. Hence the characteristic Reformed church interior, in which, though provision is made for the communion, the whole is dominated by the pulpit. Another such dissociation concerns the place of the eucharistic celebration. The Middle Ages concentrated all attention on its sacrificial aspect and called it only an altar; the reformers said, not an altar but a table, and placed and arranged it accordingly. It is time now to realize that it is not one or the other but both: that the two concepts are not mutually exclusive, and that both should be expressed by the position, form and adornments of that which a church chiefly serves to contain.

It is against distortions of these three kinds, and on behalf of the principles which they distort, that the liturgical movement has entered its protest, in some countries for the past fifty years; and the effects of this upon church building on the Continent are already considerable. The Anglican reading public was introduced to the movement by Father Hebert's book *Liturgy and Society* as long ago as 1935, and one consequence of it, the institution of the parish communion, has long been gaining ground. But its implications for church planning and design have neither been rigorously thought out nor adequately publicized. A single essay such as this is quite inadequate to present them. It can only attempt to show in outline what, when a church architect proceeds to functional analysis, are the functions that he must take into account: basically, baptism, the eucharist, and the proclamation of the word.

6. Church Architecture and the Liturgy

CHARLES DAVIS

A church is a building with a definite purpose. That purpose is to house the Christian community when it gathers together to celebrate the liturgy.

For Christians, to meet together regularly is an essential part of religion. The meetings are not social or business gatherings, such as are held by all organized bodies, but religious assemblies with a sacred meaning. Christians come together to show their common life in Christ and to strengthen that life. When they are assembled as a community, they hear the word of God read and preached, they offer prayer in the name of Christ and they perform various symbolic rites, which bring those taking part into contact with the sacred realities represented. These activities of Christians gathered together as a worshipping community are called the liturgy. Its principal part is the eucharist, which is the centre of the Christian religion. The Sunday assembly to hear the word and to celebrate the eucharist is the chief expression of the life of each Christian community and the cause of its continued existence in Christ.

The Christian liturgy is not tied of its nature to any particular building or buildings; there are no material temples in the Christian religion. But from at least as early as the third century Christians have built special buildings to provide a shelter for the assembly and a suitable room for its liturgy. These buildings are the Christian churches.

A church, then, is a place where a community meets for its corporate worship. That is its meaning as a building. A church is not a monument; I mean, it is not an independent, self-authenticating expression of religious faith or emotion. It is tied to its purpose and must remain limited by it. Architects with aesthetic ambitions have no cause to complain of this limitation; for the purpose is a sublime one and brings us close to the heart of the Christian religion. To build a church designed for its purpose is a noble and challenging enough task for any architect. The obstacle to good church architecture is a wrong idea of a church, that divorces it from its proper purpose and substitutes a borrowed sublimity for its own sufficiently exalted meaning. We labour under the distorting influence of the cathedral image – the image of a church as, of itself and in abstraction from its practical purpose, a splendid testimony in stone to the majesty of God, the glory of Christ and the power and importance of his Church on earth. So a church might be on occasion, but that is not primarily what it is built for. To make one's first aim in building a church the expression, in stone, brick or concrete, of some religious theme, such as the kingship of Christ, is to make church architecture trivial because of social irrelevance. The architect is not there to indulge his poetic imagination, even if he finds his inspiration in the Christian faith. He is called upon to design a building to serve the particular needs of a particular social group. If his design is based on an adequate functional analysis and is directed by a genuine insight into what, after all, is a most sacred purpose, it will have of itself an appropriate religious significance and can do without the weakening effect of a superadded symbolism. And what will make great architecture, as distinct from merely good architecture, is not irrelevant imaginative flights but the depth of the relevant insight that lies behind the design.

To draw up a programme for a church is not easy, because the liturgy which the building serves is complex in structure and in meaning. Many problems have to be solved before a right ordering of the various elements is achieved. But the general principle that a church exists for the liturgy is beyond doubt, and it is lamentable that it should still receive so little attention, compared with the supposed claims of conventional religious feeling. When an architect builds a school, he is not asked to erect a symbol of the nobility of education or of the advancement of science or of the civilizing power of the humanities; he is instructed in detail to design a building with a practical social function as a place of education. If his building has architectural distinction, it will do more than provide a cover from the rain for the school children; it will give expression to its purpose as a school. But this expressiveness must emerge in the process of solving the practical problems presented by the programme, otherwise it is irrelevant or sham. A good school building will show us how society regards its children and what it wants for their education; it will reflect the contemporary understanding of education. But no school architect would set out with the intention of making his building a direct portrayal of some abstract theme or a means of arousing in us right feelings about education. It seems necessary to insist that the same principle ought to apply in building a church A church is not a complicated piece of sculpture or a shrine of religious art, giving form to a religious message and intended to have an impact on all, irrespective of whether they take part in Christian worship or not. A church has as definite a social purpose as a school. This purpose is on a higher level; it is heavier with meaning, with intellectual and emotional potential; further, it is proper to a particular community that stands apart from other men. But it is none the less a clearly defined purpose that demands analysis in a detailed programme and excludes any display of extraneous religious emotion. Since its purpose is sacred, a church must have a sacred character Church architecture can never be exactly equated with secular architecture, its purpose lies in a higher order, and so it makes peculiar demands on the insight and skill of architects. But a genuine quality of sacredness will not be given to a building by adventitious religious symbolism or by a trite repetition of what is popularly regarded as religious in tone, but it will come – when it does come – by a working out with sympathy and understanding of the problems involved in designing a building for the Christian liturgy. The first step towards a good church architecture is the recognition by client and architect that in building a church they must be concerned above all with the requirements of the liturgy.

That imitation of past styles, whether blatantly or by suggestion, which is still having such an inhibiting effect on church architecture in this country is due for the most part to a failure to get to grips with the fundamental purpose of building a church. The accepted ecclesiastical styles of the past are not imitated in the conviction that churches in such styles are better adapted to the carrying out of the liturgy. In most cases, this would be flagrantly untrue. The aim, even if unacknowledged, is to reproduce what has become a traditional religious symbol and to create again the emotional impact associated with ancient churches. The concern is with conventional religious effects, not with the real purpose and meaning of a church. The plain fact is that modern techniques and materials make it more possible than ever before to erect a building that will be truly suitable for the

Towards a Church Architecture

Christian liturgy The reason is the wide freedom now possessed by architects in enclosing and shaping space, which gives them much greater scope than their predecessors had in solving the problems involved. It is painfully true that most who ask that a new church should 'look like a church' have no real idea of what a church *is*. They have never reflected seriously on what a church is for They are simply looking for that immediate titillation of their religious emotions caused by certain buildings because of past associations The church architecture of every age must be traditional in the sense of embodying traditional insights about the meaning of a church, and, more basically, about the meaning of *the* Church and its liturgy; its special requirements will keep it somewhat apart from the modes of secular architecture· but none of this implies a restriction to past ecclesiastical styles. Indeed, to fulfil its purpose properly, a church must be built in a living language On the other hand, the use of modern materials to produce new dramatic effects of religious expression is as bad as the imitation of past styles Whether imitative or creative, the seeking after effect is a distraction from the real task of putting up a building suitable for the liturgical assembly.

What I have said so far about the right approach to the building of a church could have been said simply from the standpoint of good architecture. It says no more than a modern architect, unintimidated by the seemingly esoteric laws of church architecture, would have said without any special theological and liturgical knowledge. Find out what a church is for and build accordingly; do not strive after extraneous effects. that, I understand, is generally regarded as elementary good manners in architecture, however shy some have been of applying it to the building of a church. But that has not been my main reason for insisting upon it. My concern is with the liturgy.

There is taking place in the Church at the present time a liturgical revival: or better, a general revival in doctrine and life, but centred on the liturgy. Christians have rediscovered the central place of the liturgy in the Christian life and have reached a new understanding of its structure and meaning. Now, a new understanding of the liturgy leads inevitably to a fresh way of looking at the churches in which it is celebrated. That is what has happened; and the spectacle offered by our existing churches is depressing. A neglect of the liturgy and a defective understanding of it resulted in churches but imperfectly adapted to the needs of the liturgy and, indeed, has often put many obstacles in the way of its proper celebration. It would be unfair to blame the architects. The fact is that, until recently, no architect would have received a sound functional analysis of a church on which to base his work. The churches reflect only too well the inadequate grasp of the liturgy that prevailed for so long. So, efforts of the liturgical movement to restore a vigorous liturgical life had to include attempts to promote a new church architecture. These attempts have already had some success on the Continent. The many new churches built in Germany and France since the last war have attracted considerable attention by their modernity. They are not exercises in past ecclesiastical styles but buildings that are architecturally creative. This is indeed exciting, but it is less important than the fact that these churches – at least those that are truly significant, and not all are – embody a new apprehension of the liturgy and, consequently, of the purpose and meaning of a church. They translate into terms of church architecture what, owing to the liturgical revival, is now being said about the structure and activities of the liturgical assembly.

To appreciate the full weight of this fact, we must recognize that the liturgical movement is not a passing fashion but a movement of such force that it amounts to a modern reformation of the Church. It represents what is truly vital in Christianity today. No one whose commitment to the Christian cause is real can ignore it as something in which he is not interested; for, in the last analysis, it is simply the Church facing at last the demands of the modern world.

The movement, as has already been mentioned, began in Belgium in the first decade of this century under the leadership of the Benedictine monk, Lambert Beauduin, and almost at the same time in Germany at the Abbey of Maria Laach. It developed greatly in power and strength in Germany between the two wars, and after the Second World War the impact of the German movement on the rest of the Roman Catholic Church assumed significant proportions. The papal encyclical *Mediator Dei*, which is the authoritative charter of the movement, is closely related to the German movement and incorporates its chief principles. It was issued in 1947. The French were not really affected by the movement until the later years of the last war, but since then they have made spectacular progress, and their influence has done much to spread the ideas of the movement around the world. It has become a movement of universal significance. True, the practical results it has achieved are very patchy at the moment, they vary from country to country and from place to place within the same country. As quite a few of the so-called modern churches show, people often have a smattering of liturgical ideas but have not thought them through consistently. But this much is clear: sufficient momentum is being gathered to change the face of the Church and to bring about a modern reformation – this time, with a successful issue.

The movement had its origins in the Roman Catholic Church, and as a particular, clearly discernible movement it belongs to that Church. But other Christians have followed it with sympathy and interest and similar stirrings are taking place in the other Christian Churches. In fact, one of its results has been to bring Christians of different communions closer together, because the new understanding of the Christian liturgy is overcoming various distorting prejudices and defective ideas which all the communions of the west have inherited from the Middle Ages and which explain, in part, their divisions. In the Roman Church, the movement has been strongly pastoral in character, and it is the strongest force now working for the renewal of the Christian life among ordinary people, but it has stimulated an immense volume of historical research and theological thinking, which can be said to have permanently changed the Christian outlook on important doctrinal and liturgical questions.

Perhaps these brief remarks will have given some inkling of all that lies behind the new church architecture in Germany and France. Fresh doctrinal thinking, historical learning and deep pastoral concern have come together when thought has been given to the planning of new churches or the restoration of old. How much serious thought has in fact been given to the problems of church architecture can be seen from an examination of the directives for church building, published and recommended by the Liturgical Commission of the German bishops.[1] To appreciate them fully involves a mental transformation for many Christians; certainly, these directives bring us close to the doctrinal and pastoral preoccupations that are moulding the Church today. Many problems still remain, especially when we pass from general principles to their detailed application – the imperfections of many of the new churches show that – but, at least,

[1] See appendix, p. 248.

here is the fundamental approach to church building that we must follow if we are ever to build worthy churches.

People are often pessimistic about the prospects of church architecture in the modern world. The charges against the present age, which are considered to make the outlook for sacred art and architecture bleak, are familiar: subjectivism, a lack of a sense of the sacred, rootlessness and disregard for tradition, and so on. There is some truth in the accusations. But in other respects the present is a wonderfully favoured time for the building of churches This is because the advance in our understanding of the liturgy makes it possible to draw up a clearer and sounder programme for the building of a church than has been possible for centuries. The churches of the past have their glories as witnesses to the Christian faith, but many of them are very imperfect as places for that truly corporate celebration of the liturgy which Christians today are trying to restore. If we cannot recapture the glories of the past, at least we can avoid its defects and use our own advantages to the full

We must now examine more in detail the meaning and functions of a church as seen in the light of this new thinking. I can do this, of course, only as a Roman Catholic and with reference to the Roman rite. Clearly, differences of faith and rite must mean differences in the understanding and planning of a church. But much of what follows is, I think, relevant to Christians of other communions: at least it shows that we can plan a church properly only by considering its purpose.

Paradoxical though this may seem, I think it very important for a proper appreciation of the meaning of a church to realize that churches are not strictly necessary to Christianity. A basic trait of the Christian religion is that it is not tied to any sacred buildings. Churches do not and cannot have the place in Christianity that the temples had in paganism or the Temple of Jerusalem had for the Jews. Were all the churches of a country to be confiscated or destroyed, Christians would be hampered in their activites; they would have lost nothing essential. The mass loses nothing by its being celebrated in an ordinary house or hall.

The reality of the Christian religion lies in the Christian community, the Church – not in the church building. The Church as the body of Christ is the dwelling-place of God and the consecrated source of sanctity. Christians believe that the risen Christ lives on and that they are joined to him in a union of life, so that they form one body with him. It is Christ, the incarnate Son of God, made by his resurrection the permanent source of the sanctifying Spirit for all men, who is the new Temple of God. He fulfils all that the Temple of Jerusalem stood for. He is the dwelling-place of God and the meeting place between God and man. He is the priest and the victim of the sacrifice. He is even the altar: for the Jews and pagans the altar made the victim holy, but Christ has within himself the holiness that sanctifies him as victim. Christians are built into Christ as living stones of the new Temple. The Church, the body of Christ – Christ the Head and Christians the members – replaces all material temples and is where men must now meet God and receive power from on high; and this truth is part of the Christian message.

The union of Christians with Christ and with each other in the Church is permanent, but it is expressed and at the same time made more actual, given an intenser reality, when they meet together in an assembly. The liturgical assembly is the Church of a given place at its fullest reality. And Christ is there The word is proclaimed with the power of Christ, so that it is Christ who is speaking. The eucharist is celebrated as a memorial of Christ and of all that he did to save men: his passion, death and resurrection. This memorial brings present the sacred reality, or mystery as it is called, of what is represented in symbol. The Christian mystery is made present, so that all can enter into it, take part in it and make it their own. What was realized in Christ is now realized in his members. Thus the eucharistic assembly is at the centre of the Christian religion and is the source of the life and continued existence of the Church. The eucharist keeps the Church in being, and all the other activities of the Church depend upon the eucharistic assembly. What happens in that assembly affects decisively Christian life; its effects extend to the furthest reaches of Christian existence. The other sacraments, such as baptism, are more limited in scope. They are actions of the risen Christ on men and they bring the recipients into contact with the mystery of Christ, but they are each confined to a particular, limited purpose.

Such, then, is the reality of the Christian religion. But none of this is restricted to a particular building or buildings. No sacrament is tied to a sacred edifice. All the sacraments, especially the eucharist, are human symbolic actions carried out by a worshipping community. Human symbolic actions of a communal nature were chosen by

Christ as the means of perpetuating his mystery in the Church. The materials used in the symbolic actions – bread, wine, water, oil – are of the simplest and most universal, involving no restriction to a particular place or time. The reality of the Christian religion is a community of men living and acting in Christ.

Christians, then, do not build churches as dwelling-places of God nor altars as repositories of sanctifying power. The Christian religion is centred not on a temple or temples, but on the assembly of the community; not on a stone altar or altars, but on the risen Christ. Since, however, it is essential for Christians to meet together regularly in assembly, they normally need some special place in which to do so. This becomes a real practical necessity as soon as the Christian community in a place is of any size. So, although not strictly essential, the erection of special buildings to house the assembly was a reasonable development.

Any building erected for a special purpose will reflect and express that purpose. Hence a Christian church erected for the assembly and its liturgy should stand as a symbol of the assembly and reflect the sacred character of its liturgy. This is not an adventitious symbolism, but a significance that emerges from the proper adaptation of the building to its purpose. It is in accord with Christian tradition, which sees the material church as a symbol of the Church, the body of Christ. The church building, then, is an image of the mystical body, and our churches should be fashioned in the likeness of the assembly and express its mystery.

Notice that this is a very strong reason why they should be built in a way that is truly modern. A church has to be an authentic image of a living and active community that has a message for the present world. To imitate past styles is to convey the impression that the Christian Church is an anachronistic survival, irrelevant to the modern world and its problems. If the material church represents us, it must speak in our language. Unfortunately, it is probably true that our weak, nostalgic church architecture reflects well enough the ineffectual, fossilized state of our Christian faith.

While the basically inessential character of our church buildings had to be emphasized, it would be a mistake to reduce the need for a special building for the assembly to a mere matter of practical utility. A small community meeting in a private house has no difficulty in creating a suitable environment for itself, but a large community meeting in a public hall that is used for any and every event finds it very difficult to do this. Hence the provision of special buildings for the assembly arises from the need that is felt to withdraw some distance from an unconsecrated world and create a consecrated environment. In the conditions of this world, which have been worsened by modern secularism, churches are required to preserve the sacred character of the assembly and its liturgy. An architect must have a sensitive understanding of the situation of Christians, who are in this world but not of this world, if he is to strike a right balance between two requirements: a church must be built as a piece of genuinely living architecture, because it serves a living community with a relevant message for this world; but a church must also be different, because it is the symbol of a community that stands apart from this world and belongs to a new order yet to be made manifest. Church architecture, geared to a sacred purpose, can never be exactly equated with secular architecture.

We must grant, then, that special buildings for the assembly are a logical development within Christianity and a response to its needs, but it remains true that the sacred character of these buildings comes from the assembly. It is not walls that make the dwelling-place of God for Christians, but the assembly. A church is first and foremost a house for the assembly; it is not a shrine like a pagan temple – which usually left no room for an assembly of worshippers. A church is the house of God only because it is the house of the assembly which is the dwelling-place of God. The assembly not the church comes first, and the church is sacred in relation to the assembly. This primacy of the assembly, if really grasped, will be reflected in the building of a church. A church should be constructed so that its full beauty and meaning are given only in its relation to the assembly. It should not be a structure that can best be admired by individuals left in undisturbed privacy, or a structure so crushing perhaps in its power and splendour that it is a hindrance to a sense of community. Are the soaring vaults of Gothic churches really suitable for places where we go to God, not by lonely flights of mystical prayer, but with and through the assembly and its corporate worship?

Further, the primacy of the assembly means the adaptation of the church to a particular local community. The building is for an actual worshipping community, and it is the business of priest and architect to consider, indeed to analyse, the needs of this particular community.

It is obviously in this way that the size of a church must be determined and other practical matters decided; but other more intangible elements of form and style will be affected by the way the architect thinks of the church: in isolation from any particular community or in relation to a definite community. So often a church is conceived as a monument which provides space for worshippers but otherwise ignores them. A good architect will think first of the assembly and then the church.

It is the structure of the Christian assembly that determines the structure of the church building. Now, the Church is hierarchical in structure. Although all share in the priesthood of Christ and participate in the communal celebration of the liturgy, there is a ministerial priesthood which sets certain men apart to preside over the community with special powers. These men alone have the power to consecrate the bread and wine in the eucharist, and the great prayer of the eucharist, the canon of the mass, is reserved to them. Although all the faithful offer the mass, they do so through the priest, who alone performs the sacrificial action of consecration. He thus represents Christ as priest and mediator. He also has special functions and powers in relation to the other sacraments and in the proclamation of the word.

The celebration of the eucharist is not the exclusive purpose of a church, but it is in fact its chief purpose. Therefore the spatial arrangements of a church will be made principally to serve the requirements of the mass. We can say, then, that the structure of the Christian community assembled for the celebration of mass determines the spatial organization of the material church.

At mass all form one community and all take part in the celebration. There should be no spectators or onlookers; all should be drawn into a communal celebration. But the community falls into two distinct groups, each with a distinct function in the celebration. There is the priest, who is the president of the assembly and the officiant of the sacrifice, and with him we may group his attendant ministers; and there are the faithful who take part in the celebration through and with the priest. A church, then, must have two distinct parts: the sanctuary, which is the space for the priest and his ministers, and the nave, which is the space for the faithful. The distinction between the two must not be such as to destroy the unity of the assembly. The eucharistic room must have a structural unity that reflects the unity

Towards a Church Architecture

of the community. At the same time, the distinction must be sufficiently defined to keep clear the difference of office and function between priest and people.

Nowadays it is a commonplace to say that a church must be designed from the altar outwards and to insist that the altar is the correct focal point of the building, or, to put it in another way, that a church is a shelter for an altar. I should not deny the truth of this. The stone altar is the right focal point of the material building since it is, as the place of sacrifice, the focal point in the eucharistic celebration for which the church is principally designed. Moreover, tradition sees in the altar a symbol of Christ. If the church building is the image of the mystical body – the whole Christ, Head and members – then the altar has rightful prominence as the stone in it which symbolizes Christ himself.

But, while all this is true, it can be misleading, or it can be presented in a defective way. It is necessary to keep uppermost in the mind the truth that the Christian reality lies in the assembly as an assembly of persons, not in the building nor in the altar. The relationship between sanctuary and nave should be thought of as a relationship between two groups of persons. The relation between priest (with his ministers) and people, which is the primary feature in the structure of the assembly, is what the architect should first think about in designing a church. That comes before any consideration of the altar. We have here simply an application of the principle that an architect should first think of the assembly and its activities and then of the church building – and not vice versa – because the building is designed for the assembly. The basic architectural problem in designing a church is the translation into spatial terms of the relation between the two groups that constitute the assembly. That must not be lost sight of in the concern to give prominence to the altar.

If the problem is conceived in this way, the danger will be avoided of making an altar so large and dominant, with perhaps no adequate sanctuary, that it prevents the formation of the right relation between priest and people. And justice will be done to the other elements that go to make up a sanctuary, namely, the ambo and the presidential seat: granted, however, that the altar should keep its primacy among the constituents of the building. So, an altar should be conceived with the priest at it and the people grouped in relation to him at it; in other words, in the midst of an assembly – not impersonally, as an isolated sacred rock of sacrifice, dominating the assembly instead of subordinate to it as ministering to its mystery. Likewise, the principal division of levels in a church is between sanctuary and nave, and not between sanctuary and altar.

The altar, however, is the principal stone in the material building. As the place of the sacrifice and the symbol of Christ, it is the most sacred spot, the point of central significance in the church. One of the immediate and obvious effects that the new liturgical thinking has had on church building has been the new prominence given to the altar. It has been brought into full view without any obstacles to obscure it, it now stands free as its dignity as a sacrificial table demands; it has been brought closer to the people, so that their part in the communal celebration is rendered possible and manifest; unnecessary superstructures and trappings have been swept away, so that nothing might obscure its meaning. This is a wonderful advance. The altar had lost the place that belonged to it by right. Owing to the placing of relics of saints on or above the altar or the making of the altar structure a shrine for a statue or painting and owing also to the pushing into the background the sacrificial aspect of the eucharist by the stress on the adoration of the reserved sacrament, the altar had become little more than a shelf at the foot either of a shrine or of a permanent throne for the sacrament. These trends, added to the decay in the popular participation in the mass, often led to its being pushed to the far end of a chancel, so that there was little or no relation between it and the people in the nave. All this is now on the way out, even old churches are being modified to give the altar its due prominence, so important is this point. In any new church, the altar should be free-standing, in a position that brings the people into close relation with it, and not obscured as the sacrificial table and principal feature of the church by any reredos or superstructure. A ciborium or baldaquin is the traditional way of marking its dignity.

The desirable concentration of the interior of the church on the altar should not be disturbed by side altars. These lessen the meaning of the altar, and they prevent the church from reflecting and fostering the oneness of the community. Where they are necessary, they should be in side chapels that are marked off from and leave undisturbed the main eucharistic room, or they can be accommodated in a crypt.

Towards a Church Architecture

While I rejoice in this rediscovery of the altar, the present enthusiasm over it makes me a little nervous. I fear the danger of presenting an unbalanced understanding of the eucharist: the danger of too stark an expression of the mass as a sacrifice, with sacrifice understood in the narrow sense as the offering of a victim. The eucharist contains the *fullness* of the Christian mystery. If it is a re-presentation of Calvary, it is also a re-presentation of the resurrection and an anticipation of the *Parousia* The eucharist is our share in the painful sacrificial surrender of Christ on the Cross, but it is at the same time a joyful meeting with the risen Christ, a sharing in his glory and an anticipation of the wedding-feast of heaven. The harshness of some altars, or rather of their settings, is out of keeping with the Christian mystery. The church is a shelter for a people in exile, joined to Christ in suffering; but this people is already granted in the eucharist a foretaste of glory. The rock-of-sacrifice concept of the altar is dangerous; it can so easily be interpreted in a way that has more to do with paganism than with Christianity. The traditional approach is much more fruitful: it is to stress the symbolic function of the altar as representing Christ, who in the Christian sacrifice is in reality the priest, victim and altar: the altar as the meeting-place of God and man and the source of sanctifying power.

The question of the correct conception of the altar is an example of how nothing can replace a genuine insight into the Christian mystery in providing inspiration and guiding force for church architecture. There has been much progress in our understanding of the Christian liturgy, but we have not yet explored it adequately. Indeed, we are far from having done so. A critical examination of the new churches – I mean those that are genuinely new – shows how incomplete a grasp of the Christian thing still governs them. We can advance but slowly. However, a respect for the depths of meaning in the Christian mystery will safeguard us against the worst errors.

The second element in a sanctuary is the place for the proclamation of the word, namely, the ambo. The realization that the liturgy of the word is important came somewhat later than the rediscovery of the themes connected with the altar. Some churches have been built which give the altar its proper place but do not show any particular concern about the proclamation of the word. This is not surprising; for the first part of the mass, or the liturgy of the word, has been for so long a ritual formality. Our pulpits, distant from the sanctuary and having no relation to the altar, are visible expressions of a preaching unnourished by the liturgy and conceived in isolation from it. It is now seen that the liturgy of the word that precedes the eucharist proper is an integral part of the eucharistic celebration as a whole, and that the biblical readings that are its principal part have their own peculiar efficacy and value. New theological attention is being given to efficacy of the word when proclaimed and preached in the liturgical assembly. Christ acts upon us and is given to us both in word and in sacrament; in word as leading to sacrament and in sacrament as completing the word. The close link between word and sacrament in the liturgy calls for a place for the reading of the scriptures, conceived as an organic part of the sanctuary with a relation to the altar. This is what is meant by the ambo, which is the second basic feature of the sanctuary. The Roman liturgy envisages two distinct places for the epistle and gospel of the mass. This would seem to call for two ambos. However, in a church with a sanctuary of restricted size, it will often be inopportune to construct two ambos; one on the gospel side will be preferable. And I think that it is arguable that the provision of two always has a weakening effect.

As I have said, a reason for the frequent failure to provide a place for the word as an organic part of the sanctuary is the unsatisfactory state of the Roman liturgy at present. The priest stands at the altar and reads in Latin the scripture pericopes. If they are read in English, whether simultaneously or afterwards, it is a reading that is accessory to the liturgical proclamation proper. In all probability, this will be changed when the coming Council reforms the liturgy. The priest will not be at the altar for the liturgy of the word; he will proclaim the word to the people in their own language from an ambo.

The present unreformed state of the liturgy also explains the neglect of the third essential feature of any balanced sanctuary: the seat of the priest as the president of the assembly. According to the present rubrics, the one significant place for the priest is at the altar. True, he comes to the pulpit or ambo to read the epistle and gospel after he has read them in Latin at the altar, and he sits down during the longer periods of singing at a sung or high mass; but his one significant liturgical position is at the altar: apart from preaching, which was not until recently considered an integral part of the liturgy. This situation has been changed in the new Order for Holy Week; in this, the priest conducts the liturgy of the word from his bench.

Towards a Church Architecture

It is generally desired that this should become the universal rule, so that the celebrant should go to the altar only for the eucharist itself, presiding over the assembly during the other prayers and readings (unless he himself does the readings) from his seat in the sanctuary.

Certainly, an integral part of any sanctuary should be the presidential seat of the officiating priest. He presides over the assembly and he should be given a position that manifests this in visual and spatial terms. His seat should not be just an accessory piece of furniture. The justice of this requirement is evident as soon as sanctuary and nave are thought of with the assembly in mind. that is, in relation to persons and not simply in relation to the altar as a thing. In the early days, when it was usually a bishop who presided over the assembly, his chair was in the apse and was a focal point – indeed, the focal point – in the building. (Christians had not yet lost the sense of the assembly.) Some would like to see a similar position restored for the priest, who is now the normal president of the assembly. The reason is that the obvious position for the altar is between the celebrant's place and the people. Such a grouping on either side of the altar reflects best the structure and unity of the assembly. If this arrangement were adopted, it would be natural – though not necessary – for the priest, coming to the altar for the eucharist proper, to celebrate facing the people. The relation of priest and people in the offering of the sacrifice is expressed well enough whichever way he faces, but the wider need for a satisfactory grouping of the assembly favours the position facing the people. At present, the normal place for the celebrant's bench is on the south or epistle side of the altar. Even so, it ought to be designed as an organic part of the sanctuary. Sanctuaries which simply take into account the altar and ambo are incomplete. The priest in a reformed liturgy will lead the prayers from his place and listen there to the readings. He will even perhaps preach from there rather than from the ambo; the ambo, however, will remain the place for the scripture readings.

The sanctuary, then, or the space for the officiating priest and his attendant ministers, has three significant points· the altar, the ambo and the presidential seat. Both for practical purposes and in the achievement of a right relation between the sanctuary and nave, some kind of presanctuary may be helpful. Such a presanctuary would serve as a place for the commentator, who is now a feature of the Roman rite. He acts as an intermediary between sanctuary and nave, guiding the people's participation by short monitions. He has no function that puts him within the sanctuary nor does it accord with the dignity of the ambo that he should lead from there. A presanctuary is the obvious place for him. It is also at this point – the meeting of sanctuary and nave – that arrangements must be made for the communion of the faithful.

The second main part of a church is the nave. This is not just the rest of the church; it has its own significance as the place of the faithful. It should be such as to help the faithful to realize their union together as a community and to bring them into a close relation with the sanctuary and altar; and it should be designed in a way that makes active participation in the liturgy a practical possibility.

The chief problem is to relate the nave to the sanctuary and altar. The wish to bring the faithful close to the altar and the enthusiastic stress on the communal aspect of the liturgy led to some instances of centrally placed altars with the faithful grouped all around. This arrangement, however, is undesirable. It submerges the hierarchical structure of the community and makes difficult a proper relation of the people to the other features of the sanctuary, namely, the ambo and the presidential chair. It is a very good example of thinking simply in terms of the altar rather than of the sanctuary in terms of a thing rather than of two groups of people. On the other hand, the elongated rectangle with the altar at one end, expecially if there is a structural division between the nave and sanctuary and perhaps even a choir separating the people from the chancel, is equally if not more undesirable. The sanctuary and the nave must be distinct yet one. The faithful must be drawn within the action that is taking place through the priest at the altar. To achieve this means more than making the altar visible from every part of the nave. The altar may be visible and yet the design of the church be such as to treat the faithful as spectators: perhaps very well provided-for spectators, but spectators none the less and not participants. Many subtle factors in design are involved here, calling for great skill on the part of the architect, but let the aim at least be clear. the faithful must be brought within the eucharistic celebration as active sharers in it. Various plans and architectural forms have been used in the new churches abroad in the attempt to achieve this. They should be studied from this point of view, because the new solutions they offer are the most valuable contribution of our age to church architecture.

Towards a Church Architecture

As I have already said, modern methods of construction, with the ability they give of shaping space in almost any way, allow architects much greater scope in solving this problem than ever before.

Needless to say, in planning the nave, detailed consideration ought to be given to all the requirements of the liturgy. Thus, provision must be made for the solemn entrance procession of the priest and ministers through the nave to the sanctuary. Again, thought should be given to the communion procession a large congregation must be able to go to communion without an undignified disorder. I should not have to mention the imperative necessity of good acoustics, but this point is still often ignored – no doubt, owing to the concept of the church as a religious monument rather than a hall of assembly.

One of the difficulties in designing a church for communal worship is the varying size of the congregations that will assemble there: the throng on Sundays, the week-day few and the crowds for the bigger feasts. Churches in this country can meet the needs of a parish only by multiplying Sunday masses, so that quite frequently there are as many as six masses in a church. Here we confront a problem that is outside the purview of church architecture; it involves the organization of parishes, the supply of priests and so on. From the point of view of church building, it can simply be noted that there is a maximum size for a church that cannot be exceeded without detriment to its purpose. The principle given in the German directives is that the priest at the altar should be seen and heard from the farthest reaches of the congregation without mechanical aid and that the numbers should be such that the distribution of communion to all the faithful can be carried out without disrupting the mass. The size corresponding to this should not normally be exceeded except in special cases such as a cathedral or pilgrimage church

If a full-sized church is built and there are several Sunday masses in it, the problem of the bigger feast-days remains. This can be partially met if the design allows for a certain amount of spare space over and above the seating requirements, but distributed so as to avoid any loss of unity or sense of emptiness. This will provide extra places or standing-room when occasion demands. The problem of the week-day masses with the difficulty they create of achieving a sense of community among a few dispersed in a large church is best met by the provision of a week-day chapel. This can also be the place for the reservation of the blessed sacrament and for the individual private prayers of the faithful.

This brings us to a question that would demand a separate essay for its adequate treatment: the reservation of the blessed sacrament. In the German directives it is stated that a church must be designed chiefly for the eucharistic celebration, and not primarily for the adoration of the real presence. This simply corresponds to a correct understanding of the eucharist, and so this essay has rightly studied the church as the place of the eucharistic assembly. But it is also made clear in the same document that a church has several purposes, none of which must be excluded or forgotten. The purposes listed are: the mass, the sacraments, the word, the adoration of the real presence, non-liturgical devotions and private prayer. Among these purposes, the administration of baptism and the adoration of the real presence are the two that create special architectural problems. The question of providing for baptism must unfortunately be completely left aside here, for lack of space, but a few remarks must be squeezed in on the reservation of the blessed sacrament, because it has a definite bearing on what has already been said.

Though a secondary element in a sound eucharistic devotion, adoration of the real presence is a cherished part of Catholic piety. The Church has no intention of relinquishing what it rightly regards as a valuable development in the Christian life. At the same time, it occupied too large a place to the detriment of the more important purposes of the eucharist, namely, mass and communion. The bringing of these back into prominence has created the need to reorder our understanding of the eucharist and our eucharistic piety, so as to give due place to each element. This is not easy to achieve, and it has not yet been fully achieved in the Church. We must go cautiously, in order not to destroy anything of value. This situation is relevant in building a church, because the needs of a particular community must be kept in mind. There is not yet a definitive solution on the place to reserve the blessed sacrament.

The Holy See has decreed that the blessed sacrament must be reserved on an altar where mass is celebrated regularly. This insistence on reservation on an altar, and on an altar that is used, is in order to keep devotion to the real presence in a close relation to the mass and communion. It must not be divorced from these. Several writers have pointed out how devotion to the real presence, rightly understood, is a prolongation in our lives of mass and communion and, though much richer in meaning, is comparable in this respect to the devotion to the altar found in earlier centuries.

But does this mean that the blessed sacrament should be reserved on the high altar? There are reasons for doubting this. If the tabernacle is of worthy proportions, mass facing the people is hardly feasible on an altar of reservation and has for that reason been forbidden there by the Holy See. But there are solid reasons for wanting mass facing the people, at least in some circumstances. Again, the liturgy of the mass ignores the sacrament reserved in the tabernacle, mass being celebrated in the same way whether it is present or not. The fact is that, although the mass and devotion to the real presence are closely connected, they are two distinct forms of worship, differing in structure. The mass is *ad Patrem*. It is offered to the Father through Christ, so that its structure is *per Christum Dominum*. The adoration of the real presence has Christ as its term. If the worship of the mass is *per Ipsum et cum Ipso et in Ipso*, the worship of the real presence is *ad Ipsum*. Both forms of worship have their place in the Christian life and they are closely linked together, but nothing is to be gained and much is to be lost by confusing them. If the high altar were left free, it would allow an unambiguous expression of the meaning and structure of the sacrificial offering of the mass. The blessed sacrament would be reserved in a special chapel. The mass said there on week-days would ensure the link between the devotion to the real presence and the other, primary aspects of the eucharist. The danger of any obscuring of the basic structure of liturgical prayer would be removed by the clarity then given to the Sunday assembly. The blessed sacrament chapel would have to be richly decorated, both because of the honour due to the real presence and in order to counteract any impression that its removal from the high altar meant a diminution of respect. This solution to the problem of reservation is being advocated by responsible leaders in the liturgical movement.

Innumerable details have to be discussed in the actual planning of any church. Only the main principles have been dealt with in this essay. But perhaps the aim of driving home two truths has been achieved: a church is a place where a community meets for its corporate worship, and an understanding of the nature of that community and its worship is indispensable in the building of a church. To add a final word. We need to replace the cathedral image that lies behind so much of our thinking about churches with something humbler but more effective at the present day; namely with the image of the house or meeting-place of a community centred on the eucharist, a community that is closely knit by the mutual love of its members and their common life in Christ but at the same time open and radiant towards others with love and apostolic zeal.

7. The Theological Basis of Church Architecture

JAMES A. WHYTE

It is not the intention of this essay to argue that church architecture *has* a theological basis. It ought really to be obvious that just as educational theory and educational needs must inform and control the design of schools, so theological theory and the liturgical and other needs of the Church must inform and control the design of church buildings. If this thesis has not been obvious – and who can say, judging by the majority of our post-war churches, that it has? – the fault lies mainly with the churches, which have failed to relate their theology, their worship, and their church design; and, secondly, perhaps, with the architectural schools which have tended in the past (so one is told) to regard the church as a building which is uniquely without function or purpose, so that an exercise in church design is an exercise in 'pure form', unhampered by those mundane and practical considerations – finance excepted – which fetter the creative imagination in other projects. Of course, the attempt to state what the theological basis of church architecture is, and to illustrate it from past achievements and present trends, will constitute an oblique argument that such a basis is necessary.

I

It is a very striking fact that the great movements in the life and thought of the Church today are happening in their own way, with characteristic differences, yet almost in parallel lines, in all the churches. The liturgical movement, the layman's movement, the revival of biblical studies, and, of course, the ecumenical movement have touched all the major communions. This makes it possible for one who writes – as he must, and indeed, unashamedly – from within one theological tradition to hope that what he says will not be entirely foreign, far less offensive, to Christians of other theological traditions.

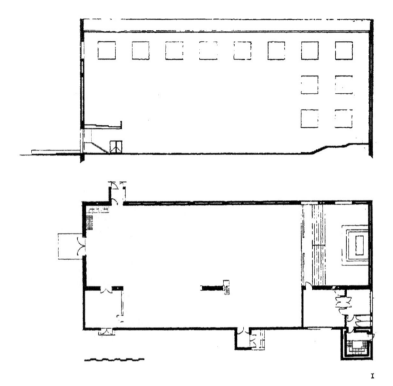

A house for a eucharistic community
Rudolf Schwarz's church of Corpus Christi (*Fronleichnamskirche*) at Aachen, 1928–1930, (nos 1–4), is a landmark in the history of church architecture a building in the mainstream of modern architectural development, which also exemplifies the renewed understanding of the *ecclesia*, its worship and its mission, stemming from the nascent liturgical movement. The eucharistic room, with its black marble altar, is a simple rectangular hall, nothing obscures its primary function as a place for the weekly assembly of the local Christian community. Secondary liturgical needs are provided for in a low *Nebenschiff* opening off the eucharistic room to the south and forming a distinct spatial entity Other ancillary buildings are grouped to the north of the church Cf the German Directives, conclusions, 1. 'the buildings which serve the various needs of a parish should .. form one coherent parish centre, so that the close links which inwardly unite church and priest, eucharist and *Caritas*, sacraments and education, are made manifest to the eye.
Corpus Christi, Aachen 1 Section and plan

2

3

2. Exterior from the south-west: the low structure on the south side of the church contains the porch, weekday chapel, confessionals, stations of the cross and sacristy.
3. Interior, showing pulpit and gallery for choir.

4. The eucharistic room. 'Table, space and walls make up the simplest church ... There have been greater forms of church building than this one, but this is not the right time for them. ... We must begin anew, and our new beginning must be genuine.'

5

5 Rudolf Schwarz Chapel of St Albert, Leversbach, 1932-1933 A liturgical shed of the utmost simplicity for a small rural community. 'It has been called a barn. Why not? Country folk have always celebrated their festivals in barns.'

6. Exterior from the south-west. The walls to the north and south of the sanctuary are glazed almost to floor level. A small sacristy, with a bell-cote, projects on the north side of the chapel

7. Entrance to the chapel The sandstone for the building was quarried by the villagers themselves and the chapel was built by voluntary labour under the supervision of one of the architect's pupils.

8

The revealed structure of Christ's body
A comparison between Schwarz's pioneer church at Aachen and a group of buildings designed by the same architect during the last few years of his life shows a significant growth in understanding. A deepened awareness of the priestly character of the whole *laos* is reflected in the trend towards a more or less centralized plan towards a more intimate relationship between the ministers in the sanctuary and the other members of the worshipping community, the relationship between sanctuary and nave begins to express both separation and identity. A new emphasis on the ministry of the word as an integral part of the Sunday liturgy brings the pulpit into closer relationship with the altar. In a few churches (see nos. 21 and 22) the sanctuary forms an organic whole, with altar, ambo and presidential chair brought into significant relationship. The choir is no longer set apart in a gallery, as it is at Aachen – an arrangement described in the Directives of 1947 as 'fundamentally wrong' The architectural setting of the baptismal liturgy begins to assume a new importance in the light of changes in theological understanding and pastoral practice. The reform of the archetypal liturgy of the Easter Vigil provides a new norm for church planning, though the full implications of this reform for the ordinary weekly assembly have still to be worked out

9

Rudolf Schwarz Church of the Holy Family, Oberhausen, 1958
8 Exterior from south-west The buildings which serve the various needs of this urban parish are grouped around two courtyards on a more or less square site. Some existing trees are preserved, and the whole complex is contained within a walled enclosure The eucharistic room, with square plan and central altar, is more than twice as high as the ancillary buildings It is approached through a forecourt, or *atrium* (see the German Directives, conclusions, 2), containing a place for the kindling of the Easter fire, a spacious porch, and a low room extending across the whole width of the building and housing the baptistery, confessionals and weekday chapel
9. The eucharistic room is a notable example of symbolic structure in which functional and symbolical are indissolubly united.

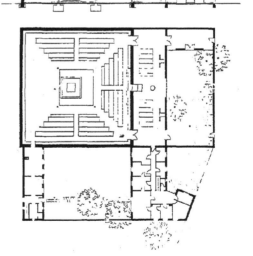

10 The seats for the congregation extend around the sanctuary on three sides The area to the east of the altar, which was still unfurnished when this photograph was taken, is intended for the ministers and the singers. The organ, in Schwarz's words, 'will not form part of the architecture, as a baroque organ did, but will be no more than a musical instrument, like a large harp.'

12 Rudolf Schwarz St Christopher, Cologne-Niehl, 1960 The sanctuary, with free-standing square altar, ambo and seats for ministers.

13

13, 14, 15. The church forms part of a coherently organized parochial centre for a new housing estate on the outskirts of Cologne. The large square porch shown on the plan has not yet been built, and the baptistery has been brought within the eucharistic room itself

14

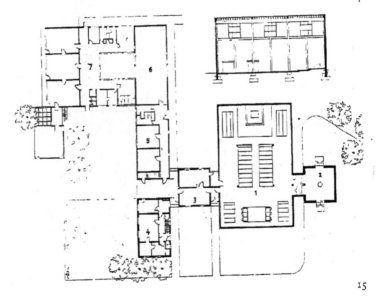

15

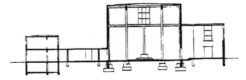

1 Church 2 Porch.
3. Sacristy. 4 Presbytery 5. Youth centre.
6 Parish hall.
7 School

16, 17 Rudolf Schwarz St Anthony, Essen, 1959 A new church incorporating the tower of a nineteenth-century building destroyed in the war Lofty T-shaped eucharistic room with seats on three sides of the square sanctuary Two ancillary rooms opening off the nave, to give a square plan to the building as a whole, contain the baptistery, weekday chapel, confessionals, etc. They also create a close relationship between the three groups into which the congregation is divided Here, as at Oberhausen (fig. 9), the exposed roof structure forms a vast canopy over the altar and fulfils a symbolic as well as a functional purpose (see *Kirchenbau, Welt vor der Schwelle*, p 272f)

18. Note the treatment of the ambo as an integral part of the sanctuary and compare with the position of the pulpit in the early church at Aachen

19 The baptistery, and 20, the weekday chapel, are located in one of the two spaces opening off the nave. Each is defined by a large square sky-light, and also by the treatment of the floor, which creates with great economy a strong feeling of 'place', persuading, segregating, emphasizing joining, dividing by surface pattern.

19

20

On the potentialities of the floor as a means of creating movement pattern see *Townscape* by Gordon Cullen, Architectural Press, 1961, p 128.

22 21

Rudolf Schwarz. St Andrew, Essen, 1957. An outstanding example of a sanctuary in which all the various elements are brought into meaningful relationship Cf. nos 23 and 24 for a similar but less satisfactory example of this eminently traditional layout.

23, 24 Rudolf Schwarz. St Michael, Frankfurt am Main, 1954: sanctuary and chair for the presiding minister.

25

Domus ecclesiae
Emil Steffann and Klaus Rosiny 'Maria in den Benden', Dusseldorf-Wersten 1959. This remarkable building is quite literally a house for the local church a house containing rooms of various shapes and sizes to accommodate all the activities in which the community engages. A complete parochial centre is grouped under a single low-pitched roof around a central courtyard The largest of the various rooms is that in which the community meets for the liturgy every Sunday, this occupies the whole space to the east of the patio One enters the church through a spacious baptistery (see no 29); the eucharistic room is twice as wide as it is long and the congregational seating surrounds the sanctuary on three sides To the east of the small cubic altar is an apse, the ceiling of which fulfils the function of a canopy or baldachino (this apse seems to have been designed to accommodate the seat of the president and those of his assistants, see no. 29) There is no permanent ambo, and the choir and organ are set apart in a gallery The church is lighted only from the west, and the glazed west wall (no. 28) separating it from the central patio can be opened when necessary to provide additional space for worshippers Around the remaining three sides of the courtyard are grouped the parish school, the presbytery, the weekday chapel and other ancillary accommodation.
25. Exterior from the south-east; note the prominent porch and the single bell hanging from the south wall of the church.

145

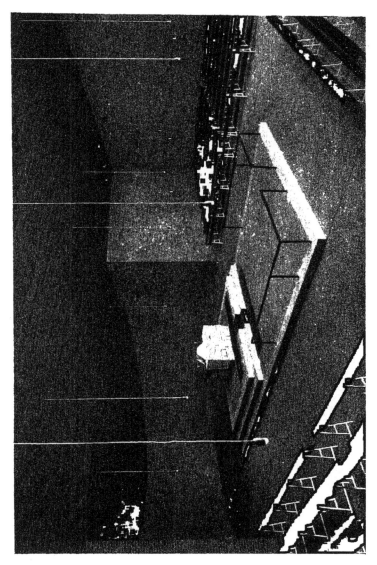

26

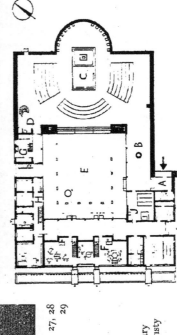

26. The eucharistic room.
27. Model.
28 Central courtyard.
29. Plan A. porch B. baptistery. C. sanctuary D. choir gallery E. patio F. school. G. sacristy H. presbytery J. chapel

30, 31. Emil Steffann. St Lawrence, Munich. The layout of this church is similar to that of the one at Dusseldorf-Wersten, but here the bench for the president and his assistants is an integral part of the sanctuary.

32

Two churches by André Le Donné
Each of these buildings by a former pupil of Auguste Perret is a parochial centre, designed to house the diverse activities of an urban community Each is a two-storey building standing on a rather cramped, sloping site, with most of the ancillary accommodation on the lower floor, beneath the room for the weekly liturgical assembly. At Mulhouse the church is set at right angles to an existing building, the upper part of which now serves as a weekday chapel where the sacrament is reserved.
32. Church of the Sacred Heart, Mulhouse, 1959. The massive square tower, beneath which the altar stands, is the only source of natural light, apart from the narrow strip of stained glass at eye level

33

34

35

33. Plan of church note the large narthex extending right across the west front and containing the baptistery The entrance to the chapel, on the north side of the sanctuary, is spanned by a choir gallery

34 The narthex as seen from the porch, and, 35, from inside the eucharistic room

36. Interior of eucharistic room, there are skeletal ambos on either side of the sanctuary, and the presidential seat is given a prominent position to

(Continued opposite)

37

36

the east of the altar (the seat was not *in situ* when these photographs were taken). The altar itself, 37, is a solid block of white marble The whole layout of the sanctuary assumes celebration of the eucharist *versus populum*, which has again become very common in France within the last decade.

38

39

St Clare, Porte de Pantin, Paris, 1959.
38 Interior of eucharistic room, which is square in plan (see no. 43). The apsidal sanctuary is flooded with light from a large semi-circular window, invisible from the nave.
39 Model, showing projected sanctuary layout with seats for the presiding minister and his assistants.
40 Principal altar. As at Mulhouse the sacrament is reserved in a separate chapel, thus facilitating celebration *versus populum*

40

41

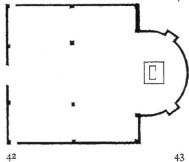

42   43

41. The apse is covered with *vercuivre* a thin sheet of copper on a glass and bitumen base.
42. Exterior from the west showing processional west door.
43. Sketch plan.

44

Two Anglican parish churches
44 Robert Maguire and Keith Murray St Paul, Bow Common, London, 1960
A church which exemplifies the radicalism, the 'readiness to go back again and again to the programme and to wrestle with its implications' which Sir John Summerson has noted as the hall-mark of serious modern architecture in Britain, a church which is modern, 'not in terms of current decorative clichés, structural acrobatics or fashionable formalisms, but modern in the sense of the hard core of moral conviction that holds together any number of formal and structural concepts on the basis of what Lethaby called nearness to need.'
The *Architectural Review*, December 1960 Since these photographs were taken a ciborium has been set up over the altar.

45

45 The free-standing sanctuary is defined by the large square lantern, a corona of rolled steel sections and a change in floor texture from precast flags to white flint bricks

46

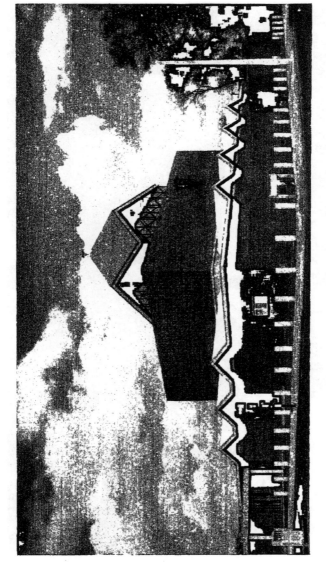

46 Interior from baptistery. 47. Exterior from south-west, the church will eventually be surrounded by eleven-storey apartment blocks.

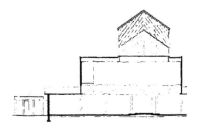

1 porch. 2 sanctuary
3 lady chapel 4 blessed sacrament chapel 5 baptistery 6 vestry 7 meeting-room. 8 kitchen
9 lavatories. 10 electrical sub-station

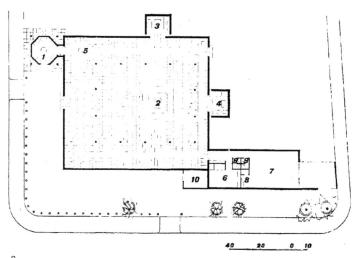

48

48. St Paul, Bow Common, cross section and plan. A parsonage house not shown on the plan, is to be built to the east of the church

49, 50. Robert Maguire and Keith Murray St Matthew, Perry Beeches, Birmingham; first project, 1959. A church for a housing estate on the outskirts of Birmingham at present served by a dual-purpose hall erected in the 'thirties, which is to be retained as a parish hall Note the relationship between the free-standing altar, the place for the ministry of the word and the baptistery the latter forming a distinct spatial entity but visible from the eucharistic room The font stands under the lowest semi-hexagonal roof From here the roofs ascend in a progression to the hexagon over the sanctuary

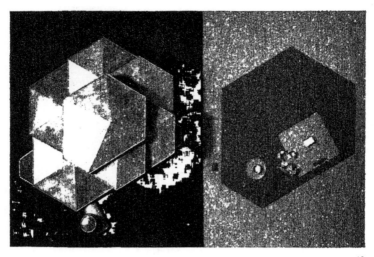

49
50

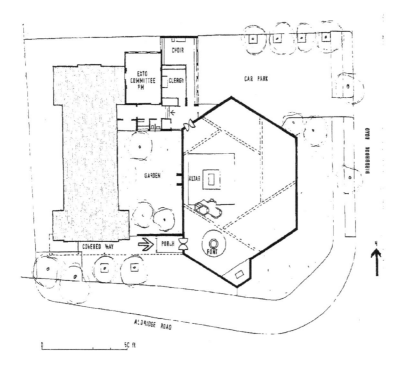

51 52

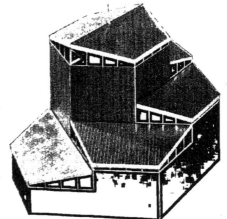

St Matthew, Perry Beeches, final project, 1961.
51. Plan, showing existing dual-purpose hall to the west of the church. The choir will sit on the north side of the sanctuary.
52. Model. As at Bow Common the bell will hang in a frame high on one of the walls.

53

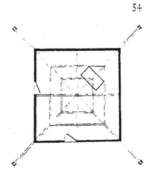

54

The spirit of poverty
53, 54 Rainer Senn. Chapel at Saint-André, near Nice, 1955 A chapel for the Companions of Emmaus, one of the Abbé Pierre's communities of rag-pickers It was built by the architect and two assistants in a fortnight and cost fifty pounds The chapel is 12 metres square and is constructed of four massive beams in the form of a pyramid 6 metres high, with the altar free-standing on a diagonal axis. The main source of light is at the apex of the pyramid, though there are also irregularly spaced apertures in the plank walls. The roof is covered with bitumenized paper.

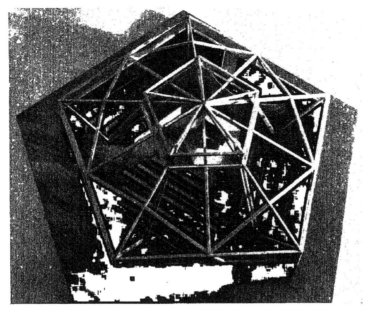

55

'The spirit of poverty is directly connected with material limitations These limitations can be the result either of outward necessity or of inner intention. When a building is the product of this inner intention it need not appear poor, in the sense of poverty-stricken, but, on the contrary, can radiate the spirit of freedom, a power that transcends the material. This is the key problem, as I have come across it in my various building tasks, and it has directly influenced my architectural solutions.' Rainer Senn

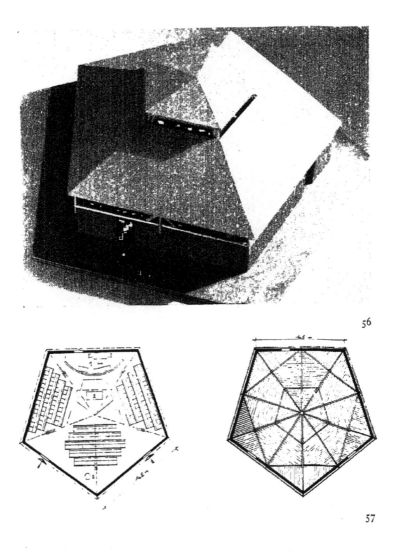

55, 56, 57. Rainer Senn Project for a small chapel, 1956. Timber construction. Pentagonal plan with sacristy behind altar

58

59

58–61. Rainer Senn. Our Lady of Lourdes, Pontarlier, 1959. The whole of the steel structure is visible within the church, the walls are of limewashed masonry, roof covering of copper.

60

61

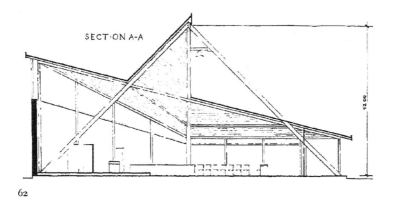

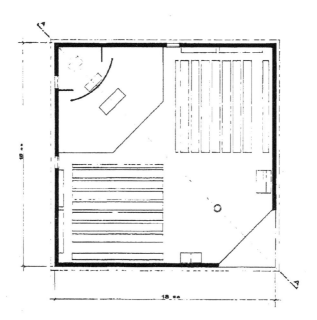

62, 63 Our Lady of Lourdes, Pontarlier Again the altar stands on a diagonal axis of the square plan and there is a small sacristy beyond the sanctuary Permanent furnishings have still to be installed

64

65

64, 65. Rainer Senn. Seminary chapel, Pelousey, near Besançon, 1961. Built on two levels on a steeply sloping site.

66

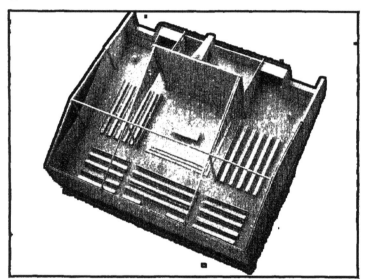

67 68

66–68 Chapel at Pelousey. 'The simplest materials are sufficient for building a church. The material gets its value from the function which it fulfils in the building, as the building gets its value by virtue of the men who live and move in it.' Rainer Senn

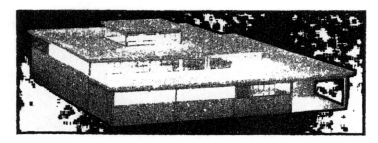

69

70

69-71 Rainer Senn Project for a prefabricated church, 1958 A project for a large, inexpensive, easily adaptable building which could be erected in a matter of weeks to serve as a house for the church in new housing estates Used simply as a church it could accommodate 800 people, but it could also be divided to create several rooms of different size, according to local needs A church for a *pays de mission* an admirable house for a parish which is aware of its function as a missionary community.

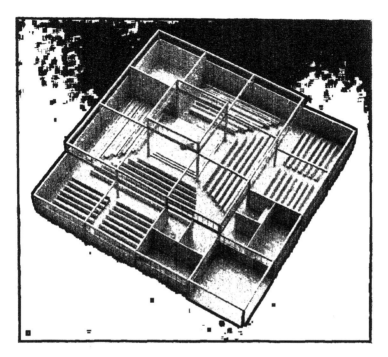

71

72, 73 Rainer Senn. Church at Villejuif, Paris, 1961. A large, inexpensive church constructed of steel Square plan with seats on three sides of the sanctuary Funds were so limited as to be just sufficient to provide four walls and a roof. You may think that this is a thankless task for an architect, on the contrary, it is a most rewarding task, for he gains the right of necessity to go down to the really fundamental requirements of the proposed building: he is obliged to examine what outward forms and traditions encumber men, which they can perhaps quite well do without. In this renunciation of outward forms it will become apparent that man comes into his own, that he acts directly on the enclosed space. The result is that an enclosed space, whether a house or a church, is only an envelope which should allow man as much freedom as possible to be himself'. Rainer Senn.

72

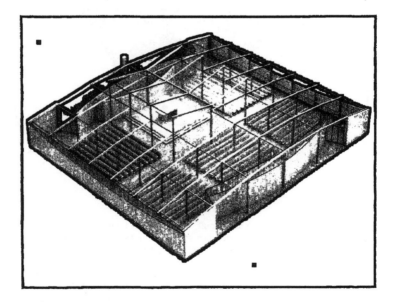

73

74

Architectural seriousness
Unlike the buildings already illustrated, neither of these modest chapels owes any obvious debt to the liturgical renewal within the Church. What they have in common with the churches of Rudolf Schwarz, for example, or those of Rainer Senn, is an architectural seriousness, an understanding of the means by which architecture can express meanings and values, without which church architecture can never fulfil its true function. There are no 'fatal overtones', both these chapels illustrate the three characteristic marks referred to in chapter 10 the sense of the provisional, the sense of economy and the sense of the continuing nature of space

74 Kaija and Heikki Siren. Chapel at Otaniemi, Finland, 1956 Exterior from the south-west (the chapel is not orientated).

75

75. Interior showing glazed north wall and skeletal holy table and ambo; an absolutely straightforward handling of timber and brick.

76, 77
76. Interior looking towards entrance
77. Exterior from south-east

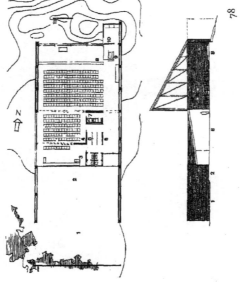

78. Plan and cross-section (scale 1 : 570) 1 Courtyard 2 Open-air altar 3 Clubroom 4 Parish room. 5. Coats 6. Entrance hall 7 Kitchen 8 Sanctuary 9 Organ 10 Sacristy 11. Cross 79 Model.

80, 81 Mies van der Rohe Chapel, Illinois Institute of Technology, Chicago, 1952 'A plain brick box with no tricks'.

The Theological Basis of Church Architecture

The ecumenical movement, the liturgical renewal, and the revival of biblical studies have combined to arouse in all the churches a new interest in the doctrine of the Church, and in the images of the Church in the New Testament:[1] the Church as the body of Christ, as the people of God (the *laos*), as the household of faith, as the temple, the dwelling-place of God through the spirit, as the royal priesthood offering spiritual sacrifices in worship and service. In some quarters there has been a tendency to take one image (e.g. the body of Christ) to the exclusion of others, and to make it the basis of logical, conceptual conclusions, in a way that is foreign to the thought of the New Testament. (For the New Testament, as Minear points out, the images are always images, never pushed to logical extremes, but always passing over into other images. there is no one like Paul for mixing his metaphors.) But what is being seen is that all these images refer to the whole Church, to the baptized, believing community.[2]

There are differences between the churches as to the relation between the institutional element in the Church – the outward form or organization without which no body can exist in this world – and the personal, spiritual element, the *koinonia*, the fellowship. It is clear that from the beginning some kind of organization was present, some kind of officers: apostles, apostolic men, bishops, elders, deacons and so on. The churches differ in their interpretation of this, and on the relation of the New Testament order to later developments in the Church, as well as on the relation of these possibly changing forms to the inner reality, the *koinonia*.

Again, the relation of Christ himself to his Church – the head to the members – is understood in different ways; whether he rules through

---

[1] See Paul S. Minear, *Images of the Church in the New Testament*, Lutterworth Press 1961.

[2] It may be noted that one result of the return to New Testament conceptions is a tendency, even in national churches, to begin to think of the Church as in some sense a gathered community. It is certainly questionable how far, in our secularized world, the Church can continue to be conceived as coterminous with society; but it is also questionable how far the situation of the early Church in the pagan society of the first century is similar to that of the Church in Britain today. If the similarity is pressed too far, the opportunities and responsibilities which remain to us from our Christian past can be thrown away. The large question of the relation of the Church to modern society can only be touched on, and very inadequately, later in this essay.

a Vicar, so that the church of which that Vicar is head in a sense is Christ, and is infallible in its teaching on faith and morals; whether he rules through his word, personally and spiritually; whether the body of Christ is to be regarded as 'an extension of the incarnation'.

While these differences remain, and will remain, there are emphases which, through the movements of our time, are finding their place in all communions today. There is renewed emphasis on the corporate unity of the Church, on the centrality of worship, and on the imperative of mission.

By corporate unity here, there is not meant the movement towards church union, but rather our departure from individualism, whether nineteenth-century or mediaeval, and our understanding of the Christian congregation in its worship and its life as a corporate unity. The coming together of the congregation for worship is its highest activity, in which all participate actively; the mission of the Church, to individuals and to society, is a responsibility which all bear together.

In the Church of Rome, through the influence of the liturgical revival, these emphases may be seen. The faithful are now enjoined not to pray at mass but to pray the mass: a direct contradiction of that late mediaeval view and practice against which the Reformers protested In recent directives for church building the view that the Church is hierarchical in character is, of course, maintained; but it is emphasized that this is not to be expressed in such a way that the unity of the Church is denied or obscured. In worship the whole Church acts together. The layman's movement expresses this same concern with regard to mission. The lay apostolate in the Church of Rome demands of the laity not simply passive obedience for the salvation of their souls, but active, responsible service in the world. Father Congar's book *Lay People in the Church*[3] is a notable attempt within the Roman tradition to express a view of the Church in which the word laity shall have a positive and not just a privative sense.

In the churches of the Reformation there is also today a rediscovery of the corporate unity of the Church. This had, of course, already happened at the Reformation. The Church as the people of God, the worship of the Church as corporate – common prayer or common order – involving active participation by the whole congre-

---

[3] Yves M J. Congar OP, *Lay People in the Church*, Geoffrey Chapman 1959.

gation in prayer and praise, in hearing the word, in table fellowship: these are clear enough emphases in the sixteenth century. The Reformers, it has been said, abolished the laity; and in Scotland, certainly, the word fell out of use; for the whole Church is a royal priesthood, and the whole Church is sent into the world. Within that Church, for the building up of the people in the maturity of faith and their ministry of love, is Christ's gift of the ministry of word and sacrament: 'to equip God's people for work in his service, to the building up of the body of Christ.'[4]

Later, however – and especially in the nineteenth century – the corporate nature of Christian life and worship was obscured by individualism, and at the same time (and this is surely no coincidence) there was a tendency to clericalism: not simply official clericalism, though like the poor, that is always with us, but the tendency, even in churches which theoretically held a 'low' view of the ministry, to lay the whole burden of the worship, the life, the 'success' of the congregation upon the gifted man, the eloquent preacher, the ministerial personality. All the significant things that are happening today in the Reformed churches illustrate a movement away from this unbiblical individualism, back to an emphasis on our corporate life in the body of Christ. If one may illustrate from Scotland alone, and leave it to others to see the parallels in their own situation, the liturgical revival which began one hundred years ago did a great deal of valuable work, but tended to remain an academic and mainly clerical interest. The great significance of the Iona Community as a liturgical movement, despite deficiencies in its historical scholarship, is that it alone has linked corporate worship with corporate congregational life and mission. Influenced without doubt by the Iona Community, there is an even more widespread movement or movements towards the active, responsible participation of the whole congregation in mission. 'The Church is the agent of mission' is a slogan which is accepted in theory, though not yet widely in practice. In the new housing areas especially, however, there is a great openness to new ideas, and an awareness of the needs and challenge of the parish; and there are signs that this attitude is spreading. There is a concern, variously expressed, for the witness and responsibility of Christian people at the functional levels of society: in industry, the professions,

[4] Ephesians iv, 12. *New English Bible* translation.

Towards a Church Architecture

local and national politics There is also, very widespread, and linked with all of this, a new need and a new experience of fellowship, *koinonia*, in smaller groups, for Bible study and service. (It is significant for our purpose that much of this is happening outside the church buildings: in houses and farm kitchens.) One's religion can no longer be regarded as one's private affair; it is fellowship.

II

It is not difficult to show the connection between these theological emphases and church architecture, because an illustration lies ready to hand. The influence of the liturgical movement on church building in the Roman Catholic church is becoming well known. The emphasis on the liturgy as the corporate act of the whole Church is being given expression in the arrangement of churches, so that the people are, to some extent, gathered round the altar: in some cases, round three sides. The altar comes appreciably forward (a central position for the altar has been rejected), and the celebrant begins to adopt the basilican posture: i.e. as in the early Church, and as in the Reformed churches, he stands behind the table The proliferation of subsidiary altars is discouraged, and the emphasis on the central significance of the corporate worship of the eucharist has led to a simplification – a shedding of much in the church and its furniture that was in danger of obscuring, or distracting attention from, its central purpose. There is, however, a new stress on the reading and proclamation of the word of God

For another illustration of the influence of theology on architecture and church design we may look at a much earlier liturgical movement which took place in Scotland: viz at the Scottish Reformation itself.

The Reformation, as has been said, saw the Church as the people of God, and ministry as a gift to the Church and a service within the Church – the ministry of word and sacraments for the building up of the body of Christ. The Reformation was inevitably a liturgical movement, because it was of necessity concerned not only with the reform of doctrine and of discipline but also with the reform of worship. Three points may be selected here as characteristic of the Reformed view of worship.

First, worship is corporate. It is the people's worship. It is their response of gratitude to the Gospel. Therefore the service is in the vernacular, service-books are in the hands of all the people, there is common prayer, and congregational praise. The Church is a royal priesthood, offering spiritual sacrifices to God through Jesus Christ.

Second, the Reformers stressed the centrality of the word of God. Worship is dialogue, it is address and response; but the primary word is God's word. When Luther spoke at the dedication of the Schlosskirche at Torgau in 1544 he asked that 'nothing else should take place therein than that our dear Lord himself should speak with us through his holy word, and we again speak with him through prayer and praise'.[5] The Church is created and is renewed by the word of the Gospel, the word of faith which we preach. Our relationship with our Lord is a personal one, and a present one; there is confrontation, address. The living God speaks his living word to the men of our time when there is a speaking and a hearing in faith in the midst of his people.

The intention here is not to argue this point, but merely to state it. Even in the Reformed churches today there is a tendency to separate preaching from worship; much more perhaps in churches where preaching is traditionally understood simply as human discourse, exhortation, instruction. Preaching so understood can only be seen as an interruption of worship, an addendum to worship, or an exhortation to worship, but not as itself worship But if you grant this other, dynamic view of the preaching of the word of God you can understand how preaching, so understood, became for the Reformers central to worship: because here 'our dear Lord himself speaks with us through his holy word'.

Third, they stressed the sacraments of the Gospel As W. D. Maxwell has pointed out, the aim of the Reformers was not only to give the Bible back to the people, but equally to give the sacraments back to the people. (In fact they held what might be called a 'high' view of the sacraments: 'And thus we utterlie damne the vanitie of thay that affirme Sacramentes to be nathing ellis bot naked and baire signes.')[6] The Lord's supper for them is a corporate act, and there is no eucharist without the communion of the people; and this com-

---

[5] Quoted by Karl Barth, *Church Dogmatics* I, i, Eng trans, G. T. Thomson, *The Doctrine of the Word of God*, T. & T. Clark 1936, p. 54.
[6] *The Scots Confession*, 1560, art. XXI.

munion is in both kinds, and is received seated at a table.[7] Baptism takes place at public worship, in the face of the congregation, the body of Christ, into which the infant or adult, engrafted into Christ, is received. The sacraments are sacraments of the Church and of the Gospel, and they are not celebrated without the people present and the word preached; but as they are the chief means of grace, great care is taken that they be not despised or taken unworthily, in ignorance or sin.

Let us consider how with this theory, the Reformers used the buildings which they had inherited from the past The important work on this subject is the book by George Hay, *The Architecture of Scottish Post-Reformation Churches.* Very many Scottish churches were in a grave state of disrepair before the Reformation, and the Reformed church was denied the funds either for speedy repair or for new building. The concern of *The First Book of Discipline* (1560) for churches to be repaired and ordered 'as apperteaneth alsweall to the majestie of the word of God as unto the ease and commoditie of the people'[8] – like much else in that book – was to be a continuing concern, frustrated by lack of funds. The churches in existence were of two main kinds: the simple, rectangular parish churches (the idea that every mediaeval church was cruciform is a myth), and the larger churches, such as the collegiate churches in the large towns, the cathedral and abbey churches. Some of these last-named were not needed for the people's worship, where an adequate parish kirk already existed, and some had already suffered destruction at the hands of English armies What was reparable and useful they did not hesitate to adapt for reformed worship. 'The adaptation of the smaller kirks' writes George Hay,[9] 'presented few difficulties. The pulpit, with a reader's desk or "lattron" before it, was set up against the south wall, its normal mediaeval site. For baptism, regarded as an essentially public service, the basin was bracketed to the side of the pulpit, and for the Lord's supper the table (or tables) was set up

---

[7] Practice varied in the churches of the continental Reformation, but, despite royal displeasure, the Scots clung tenaciously to the practice of receiving communion seated round a table.
[8] *The Buke of Discipline*, 1560, art. 'For Reparatioun of Churches'.
[9] Op. cit., Oxford University Press 1957, p. 22.

usually on the long axis of the building.'[10] Hay points out that when extra accommodation was required in the simple rectangular buildings, it was found by adding galleries at the east and west ends, and by pushing out an aisle on the north side, which was the origin of the T-plan, 'the classical design for new kirks up to the nineteenth century'.

The larger churches were never intended by their builders to be used as a single unit. The choir, or chancel, with the high altar, was a church for the clergy, the nave for the laity. Subsidiary altars abounded for chantry masses: there were twenty in Glasgow cathedral. How were these buildings to be adapted for the Reformers' purposes? The answer came from their theology of the Church and of its worship. The Church is no longer understood as divided into two parts, clerical and lay. The whole Church is the *laos*, the people of God, the *kleros*, the inheritance of God, justified by his grace, accepted in his beloved Son. In worship the people are participants, not spectators. The whole Church worships, hearing and responding to the life-giving word, gathering in fellowship round the table of the Lord. Not often in Scotland, and not for long, was the solution adopted of using the choir for communion, with the long tables set up its length, and using the nave for the service of the word. It may be that this represented a division between word and sacrament which was unwelcome. Usually the nave or the choir (according to the suitability of its size) was used, with the pulpit, as in the smaller churches, half-way down its length, and the tables for communion set in front of it on the long axis. (There was, of course, no fixed seating.) Sometimes the increased population of the burghs led them to use nave, choir and transepts (or croce-kirk) by dividing the building into two or even three separate places for Reformed worship. Hay argues, and very cogently, that this was not barbarism, as it has been called, but a practical and acoustical necessity, and that

[10] The use of the long table or tables, in the midst of the church, round which the people sat to receive communion, did not begin to be abandoned until the third decade of last century when it began gradually – though not to this day completely – to be displaced by the practice of receiving seated in the pew. According to one authority on Church law, the 'communion table' is the table at which *the people* sit to receive the sacrament. The custom of covering the pew-boards with a white linen cloth for communion suggests that they are regarded as 'the table of the Lord'.

'the contriving of the Reformers did in fact represent a much closer approximation to original usage than do the notions of vista loving Victorians and moderns'.

When new churches were able to be built in Scotland after the Reformation, one of them, Greyfriars, Edinburgh (built 1612–1620), was a simple Gothic nave, aisled and pillared, with the pulpit in the customary position half-way down its length. It appears that this was the only way in which so large a structure could be supported. But the earliest of them, Burntisland (1592), shows a completely new plan. With its central tower supported by four massive pillars, with its guild lofts all round, and its magistrates' pew directly opposite the pulpit, this church seems to have been designed to represent the life of the whole civil community gathered round the word and the sacraments. Architecturally, Burntisland, stands alone; it may have been copied in Holland, but not in Scotland. But in later Scottish building you find a great variety of architecture and design. The typical Scottish T-plan persists throughout the centuries, and from the eighteenth century on you have octagonal churches, oval churches, Greek-cross churches, and rectangular and square churches. Generally speaking, it may be said that these are all informed by a conception of corporate worship in which the preaching of the word has a central place, but in which the sacrament, though infrequently celebrated, was not robbed of its centrality, in the provision made for the long tables. (The character of many of these churches has been altered in the last hundred years, first by the introduction of the fixed communion table, following on the abandonment of the long tables, and above all by the introduction of organs in the worst possible place and the worst possible taste.) The nineteenth century saw not only the Gothic Revival, in which the aim became confused and romantic notions replaced the functionalism of the earlier buildings, but also the churches built for the star, and would-be star preachers. It is these churches, rather than any earlier buildings, which deserve the opprobrium of being called auditoria rather than places of worship, and when that happens preaching itself has become perverted into a personal performance which cannot be called worship.

III

Architecture has been defined as the fixing of relationships in space. Without arguing the adequacy of this definition, we can use it to

The Theological Basis of Church Architecture

ask what are the relationships which the theologian is asking the architect to express in spatial terms. It is convenient here to distinguish external and internal relationships.

By external relationships is meant the relation of the church buildings to their environment. This must rest upon the relation of the Christian community to the civil community in which it is set. Two examples from the past will illustrate this. Burntisland, four-square on its little hill in the midst of the town, seems both externally and internally to symbolize the whole community – i.e. the whole civil community – gathered round word and sacrament. This was not simply ideal, it was reality, here church and community are one. Think again of the great mediaeval cathedral, whose image still haunts us. What relationship between Church and community did the mediaeval cathedral symbolize? It is hard to escape the conclusion that, whatever the glories of its craftsmanship, it symbolized the domination of the world by the Church. You may put it in sweeter terms and say the domination of the temporal by the eternal order, but domination it remains. The question we have to ask is: ought the church to dominate? The statement issued by the 1959 ecumenical conference on architecture and the Church says, 'The serving and not the dominating role of the Church should be kept in mind.' This would seem to be a more Christian, and, in terms of economics, a more attainable value.

It is clear that neither the Burntisland nor the mediaeval solution of the external relationship is a live option in our modern, largely secularized world. Yet we have been planting congregations and building churches in our new housing areas without apparently asking the question: What is to be the shape of congregational life and its relation to the society in which it is set? Has the Church to be a centre of community life (the planners may not have provided any alternative), gathering its members, and others, into the church buildings for all their social life: badminton, amateur dramatics and the rest? (Some American churches include a cafeteria and a swimming-pool.) Or has the Church to serve and leaven the secular life of the community, sending its members out into secular organizations? The answer is by no means clear, especially since the nature of a geographical community, and its relation to more functional groupings of society, in days of rapid travel, is a live sociological question. Yet our needs in the matter of church buildings depend on some answer in each particular situation One thing is clear – the Church meets for other things besides the public worship of God. The exponents of liturgical renewal have reminded us that worship is the highest activity of the Church and the source of its life. This is true; but the relationship is also reciprocal; the quality of worship and of fellowship in worship will be determined by a common life outside of worship, a co-operation in various tasks of service, a personal knowledge of one another. Some of this common life will take place within the church buildings: in sectional organizations and church meetings; but increasingly it is taking place outside of the church buildings, in groups which meet in members' houses, at places of work and so on; and such groups will come together only occasionally for mutual conference and encouragement. One function of the church buildings that is often overlooked is Christian education. The Americans build a church school, with classrooms, as a first priority; we build a hall for badminton and fit in the Sunday school as and how we can.

The question of function will determine what is to be built in a given situation. How does such a group of buildings relate to the environment? Two things may be said. First, the church which is the church of Jesus Christ, of him who came not to be ministered unto but to minister, and to give his life a ransom for many, will express values that are at odds with many of the values round about it: in the new roadhouse, for instance Secondly, this foreignness must not be understood as if it were an anachronism, a stylistic hangover from earlier, nicer days. It is tragic if the suspicion, with which many people start, that the Church is simply an anachronistic survival, providing a comforting escape for those who find the modern world too frightening or insecure, is confirmed by the kind of building we erect. The Church as a human community can live only in the time and in the culture in which it is set. We cannot reject modern culture, yearning for a golden age in the past. That is impossible, for whether we like it or not we are modern men; and it is wrong, for our God is a living God, not a dead one. So it cannot be too strongly stressed that a modern church must be as much an example of modern architecture, must belong to the modern community, just as much as a block of flats or a shopping-centre. We must ask our architects to be bold, to be much less self-conscious than they have been, and to make full use of the possibilities opened to them by modern building techniques in expressing their idea. On the other hand we may

The Theological Basis of Church Architecture

not accept modern culture holus-bolus, for God is not only the Lord of all that is good in our mastery of nature and of techniques; he is the judge of all our false standards and values. It may be that the foreignness of a truly modern church would lie not in any striving after divinity, but in its deeper understanding of humanity. This is for human beings to use, it is the home of the new humanity. If we concentrated for a time less on the majesty of God and more on the humanity of Jesus Christ, we might build more truly to his glory, and more relevantly to the needs of society, to the humanizing of modern culture.

The building must also express in its internal relationships our idea of the Church and of its worship. There is no space here to consider the grouping of buildings according to their different functions; comment must be restricted to the internal relationships within the church building proper. The Reformers understood that they had to adapt existing buildings to express their new understanding of the relationships of minister and people to one another in worship. The Church is not divided into clergy and laity; the Church, the whole Church, is both *kleros* and *laos*, the inheritance of God, the people of God. Ministry – and no church more than the Reformed has valued the divinely given gift of ministry – is service within the body, not status over it. It is ministry of word and sacrament, whereby Christ himself rules and feeds his people. Both in worship towards God and in witness and service towards men, the Church, the whole Church, is called to active, responsible participation, in fellowship with one another and with Christ. This is also the conception of the Church, and of the congregation, which is being forced upon us today by all the movements, theological and practical, of our time, which many ministers and kirk sessions are seeking to embody in the life and worship of their congregations. Yet they are doing it often in buildings which negate this conception of the Church, buildings in which the congregation is set like the audience in the box-stage type of theatre, unified only by the fact that they are all looking in the same direction, with no relation to each other save that the building directs their eyes to the same point of visual focus. (The inevitable apsidal cross.) All the action takes place 'up there'. The conception of worship which such a building encourages is that which is all too common today: worship in which I remain an individual, I sit and wait for something to happen. What is being said and done up there may pull me in – just as a play may happen to grip and move me – but if not, I remain outside, a spectator, not a participant.

The internal relationships of the building, which are dynamic relationships between people, must surely express the reality of the fellowship, the fact that this is corporate worship, that we belong together and act together and help each other. The arrangement of the building will either help or hinder this. But a further relationship is involved: the congregation adores and worships its King and Head · he is active towards us. How is the relationship of the Head to the members to be expressed?

It is important to remember that the Church is the redeemed community; we do not worship a distant God at a distant altar. The Church is in Christ, and Christ is in the midst of his beloved people in word and sacrament. When the minister reads and proclaims the word of God, and when he takes his place at the head of the table, or at the font, he is representing Christ to his people. Yet he is still one with them. Preaching, for example, happens when both minister and people are hearing together what God the Lord has to say to them. The proclamation of the word in public worship[11] takes place in the midst of a believing people. They are not passive but active in the hearing of faith, and the minister stands with them under the word which speaks both to him and to them. How is this to be expressed? When a pulpit becomes too large and dominant it can easily cease to be a throne for the word and become a platform for the star personality. When it is too distant it can destroy the sense of personal communication, of unity under the word; when it is insignificant it can destroy the sense of the rule of the word in the midst of the people. 'The word is nigh thee' is indeed a good motto for the word of faith which we preach. Again, the sacrament is in the midst of the people. Christ has given us access into the holiest. Here again, the corporate unity of the Church must be stressed that his grace may be glorified. The whole people of God are gathered round the table of the Lord. For Presbyterians this is a table round which we sit, and those solid altars *manqués*, with ecclesiastical adornment, which we commonly set in

[11] It is important to distinguish between evangelism, public preaching and private witness to those outside the faith, and preaching in the context of public worship. The former may be the task of any church member, giving a reason for the faith that is in him. But the faith of the witnessing Christian is fed by the ministry of the word in public worship.

our churches, have no justification. A place must be provided for preaching, a place for the sacrament, and neither must be provided for in a way which denies or distorts the significnace of the other. This is not easy. But unless you have made significant provision for the preaching of the word you have not expressed the essence of Reformed worship.

The Scottish Reformers were bold in their treatment of the sacrament of baptism they annexed the basin to the pulpit, moving the font from the door, where it symbolized entry into the sacramental community, in order to proclaim the connection here between word and sacrament, and the public and corporate nature of the act – the congregation is also active in receiving the candidate. There is no space to consider the problems here, but it may be that one result of the theological work that has been done on baptism today should be a re-examination of the place and character of baptisteries, and their relationship with the other parts of the building.

These points are made in order to plead that the worship must determine the building, not the building the worship. Theological and spatial relationships are connected; indeed, it is difficult to describe theological relationships without using spatial terms (e.g. 'in the midst of the people', 'gathered round'). This is inevitable, but it must be watched, for we have suffered in the past from too rigid and stereotyped an idea of what a church is like, and it will not do to suggest by implication some other equally rigid and stereotyped plan, whether the T-plan or any other. The theologian must understand and describe the activity that goes on and the relationships which are involved; it is for the architect to express in his own terms the spatial solutions to the problems. One thing only is an absolute necessity. the acoustics must be good.

A final question must be faced. What about beauty and atmosphere? Is not the church the temple of God built to his glory? Ought we not to seek to create an atmosphere of awe in the presence of the *mysterium tremendum*? 'The Lord is in his holy temple, let all the earth keep silence before him' (as one city choir used to sing after their very pompous minister had ascended to the pulpit).

The answer must be brief. First, you fall into dangerous aestheticism whenever you think of beauty by itself. Beauty is an abstraction. The artist does not produce beauty, he produces a beautiful something; and the modern artist would be much more likely to use the word meaningful. Architects today tend to use ethical rather than aesthetic terms; to talk of integrity and honesty rather than of beauty, Doubtless artistic creation is controlled by a profound sense of the seemly – a crude functionalism cannot describe all that happens in architecture – but a self-conscious striving after the beautiful may produce only the pretty or the nice. To produce visual effect is not the main purpose of a building The living God is a God who speaks. We come not to contemplate him, but to hear his word. The Church cannot handle art today – and cannot understand modern art – because the Church lacks a truly Christian aesthetic whose standards will not simply be what is pleasant or what is nice.

Second, we must beware of giving the church building a significance it does not possess. The temple in which God dwells is the Christian congregation. 'Ye are the temple of God', says Paul, 'and the spirit of God dwelleth in you,'[12] 'God . . . dwelleth not in temples made with hands '[13] The church building is not made to house God, but to house the congregation. The *mysterium tremendum*, the numinous, is not an emotion produced by an aesthetic experience. It is the reality of God in the midst of his believing people. It is in the word of the Gospel and the silence of the sacrament.

Third, Reinhold Niebuhr has pointed out in one of his essays – with regard to the Episcopal cathedral in New York – the nemesis of human pretensions: that when a man sets out self-consciously to build a monument to the glory of God he ends by erecting what is also a symbol of human pride. 'Perhaps we ought not try to symbolize the truths of our religion in stone and steel. The result is usually some unhappy combination of the sense of divine majesty and human pride.'[14] For it is only humble, faithful work that truly redounds to the glory of God.

[12] I Cor., 3: 16.   [13] Acts xvii, 24.
[14] *Essays in Applied Christianity*, Meridian Books, p. 43.

8. Liturgy and Society

PATRICK MCLAUGHLIN

I

In English history books, and indeed in most books of European history, 'the Reformation' usually indicates the protest made in the sixteenth century against the abuses of mediaeval Catholicism, and more especially of the Papacy. Strict accuracy would require this term to cover also the corresponding movement of reform inside the Catholic remnant of Europe, but common usage ascribes to this the title 'Counter-Reformation', leaving the word 'Reformation' to denote only the Protestant half of it.

Both partisans and opponents of this reform are accustomed to treat the movement as an exclusively religious one; and to claim that it was probably the most violent upheaval and certainly the most radical change in the history of the Christian Church. That it was primarily a religious movement is true, this is manifest in the religious categories and language in which the disputes were carried on. But no movement in human history can be placed exclusively in one category. The Reformation, though immediately religious in purpose and character, was at the same time a movement of profound social, political and economic significance. Its causes were far more widespread than those of immediate religious scruple. Culturally, it may be seen as a reaction against the almost pagan humanism of the Renaissance. Socially, it represented and released the impetus of certain classes in the new mercantile society of the late Middle Ages towards a wider range of thought and freer scope of activity. Politically, it was clearly related with the emergence of the national state as an autonomous unit and its claim to sovereign independence. Economically, it adduced moral, if not theological sanctions for the emancipation of commerce from the constrictions of mediaeval customs and doctrine. That is to say, the Reformation cannot be properly studied, even as a religious movement, outside the social circumstance of the time.

Towards a Church Architecture

It is never easy to study phenomena in their full context. Indeed, without a measure of abstraction no scientific study would be possible. But, even when this is necessary, it must never be forgotten that abstraction is falsification. It is at best the deliberate positing of a premise upon which to make certain investigations or to base certain arguments; and *ex hypothesi* the validity of these observations or arguments is conditioned by the premise upon which they rest. This point may be illustrated by the Reformation itself in one aspect: viz., that the premises which had been posited for mediaeval trade and science had proved their insufficiency, and men were driven to repudiate these premises and to posit others which appeared more true to fact. In doing this they called in question the whole structure and ultimately brought about its collapse.

But however inadequate the premises of mediaeval society appeared to be in the sixteenth century, this inadequacy is as nothing compared with that of the premises laid down in that century, and accepted with very little modification through the succeeding centuries, in the light of experience today. As Henri de Lubac has written:

'For some time we have been assisting not merely at extraordinary events, which are changing the surface of the globe, but at an event at a deeper level which is changing something in man himself. In this universe of ours – a universe in course of psychic evolution – however fixed in essential framework since the appearance of the human race, consciousness expands at certain moments and perceives new values and new dimensions. It seems obvious that we ourselves are living through one of these moments of awakening and transformation.'[1]

He might have added also the word social; for there have been few periods in the recorded history of man which have witnessed such radical and rapid social change. Nor is this change to be seen only in the remote continents to which sociologists commonly direct our attention: Asia, Africa and America. It is no less rapid or radical in Europe. Forces unloosed in 1789 in the French Revolution gathered momentum throughout the nineteenth century, and have in the twentieth produced changes in the structure both of human society and of human sensibility which are virtually without precedent. Certainly they are far more radical than the changes made in the

[1] *The Drama of Atheistic Humanism*, Sheed & Ward 1949.

sixteenth century, far-reaching as those were. At that time the conscious appeal was behind the immediately preceding period of the Middle Ages to primitive Christianity.² Today the social critics or prophets speak rather of the end of our time, even of the death of God. One of them has suggested that to understand the depth and range of the changes in human experience today we must look for a parallel, not to the end of the Middle Ages, nor even to the death of the old pagan classical culture and its replacement by the Christian faith, but to the revolution in thought and feeling introduced by the first Ionic philosophers.³ For it was they who, in their desire to study scientifically (i.e. concisely and rationally) the universe in which they lived, first posited the premise that they were for this purpose abstracted from that universe, and put in the advantageous position of a detached observer scrutinizing through his telescope or microscope phenomena laid out, and even in movement, before him, whilst he himself remained unmoved.⁴ The importance of this premise or hypothesis cannot be exaggerated Upon it rests the whole corpus of scientific enquiry and discovery; without it men might well be still without even elementary knowledge of themselves or the world they live in. But it is to be noted that the extension of this method of knowing into the field of psychology has brought the instrument (i.e. human intelligence or man himself) under enquiry. This is what moved even so optimistic a social prophet as H. G. Wells to speak towards the end of his life of 'the death of instrument'. Other sages of the twentieth century have expressed this less dramatically but no less forcefully. L. L. White in *The Next Development of*

---

² Recent studies have shown how far removed was the sixteenth-century idea of primitive Christianity from the facts; and by inference how much less critical the reformers were of mediaeval doctrine and practice than they should or could have been. It is more difficult today therefore to make the same claims for radical change through the Reformation as were made by early historians, though there is no need to dispute the violence of the upheaval and the bad effects of the disruption of Europe.

³ H. A. Hodges, Professor of Philosophy in the University of Reading

⁴ There is a certain correspondence here between the role thus assumed by man as scientist and the *primum mobile ipsud immotum* of Aristotle; and an interesting echo of the serpent's temptation of Eve in the Garden of Eden that if the Adam ate of the Tree of Knowledge of good and evil they would be as gods.

Towards a Church Architecture

Man demonstrates the *cul de sac* into which human thinking of this kind has now come, and indicates the necessity of a new mode of knowledge which will go behind the abstraction of man from the historic process and place him once again within that process without suppressing the knowledge acquired meanwhile. The same thesis is propounded by R. G. Collingwood in his *Idea of History*.

Nor is this merely a game of ideas played by professional philosophers. All these writers were concerned to articulate what they saw to be actual processes of society, actual human experiences of today It is not difficult to see many instances of these in the people around us, or even in ourselves As a positive example, we may point to the emphasis on solidarity which may be discerned in the teams or gangs in which young people spend much of their time and find most of their satisfaction, or (on a large scale) in the labour movement; here men deliberately sacrifice their own independence of action, and even of judgment, to a larger group, in a fashion which would have astounded, and probably horrified, their ancestors, in the Renaissance and the Reformation. As a negative example, we may point to the tragically large numbers of people whose minds or nerves break down under the stress of the loneliness and isolation of the atomized society in which we still live, and supremely of the strains and stresses which this puts upon the individual unless he is immunized or insulated by membership of some group or gang. These are but some of the new social conditions and circumstances of our day and age. The catalogue could be extended almost indefinitely, the picture enlarged to the dimensions (and perhaps even to a replica) of Michelangelo's 'Last Judgment'. This chapter, however, is not an essay in social criticism but in the relation of religious thought and practice to the social climate and context.

For religion can no more be practised in abstraction from social circumstance than science. It is natural indeed that men should very often think of their religion as though it were abstracted or cut off from all other activities; natural because (as we have seen) this tendency to abstract is innate in man, and is indeed a necessary condition of certain activities at least; and because this tendency has most opportunity, if not most justification, in the field where man confronts ultimate truth. But whatever the justification, or whatever the temptation to abstract, religion remains in fact a human activity which like all others is conditioned in a large measure by the customs, ideas

Liturgy and Society

and movements of the age. It is not then surprising that the new experiences, feelings, thoughts and ideas of men in the twentieth century are reflected in new practices, doctrines, customs, and even structures of the Church. Not that they are there reflected immediately or just passively; for the Church is a factor in history as potent as any and more powerful than most. The Church therefore acts upon the movements of history and the structures of society as much as these act upon it. For the Church, like its Lord, has two natures: the one divine, supernatural, spirit-filled, the vehicle of Holy Spirit, an energizing force, the other human, finite, continually developing, and always conditioned by the circumstances of time and space in which it lives All the Church's acts therefore, and all its experiences are ambivalent; the effect of this is that since the Church exists and operates in time and space, it must and does continually develop and adapt its modes of operation, its structures and its self-understanding according to the varying circumstance of succeeding ages.

This is obvious today from any study of the Church's development in space. The history of that development during the last fifty years alone, in Asia and in Africa, is at once an exciting illustration of the Church's power of energizing society and of its power to adapt traditional structures, inherited customs, cherished formulations of belief, to new circumstances. But it is no less obvious from a study of the Church's development in time in its historic location in Europe. This century has seen striking developments in theology, and even in theological method, in every Christian tradition, whether Catholic, Orthodox, Protestant or Pentecostal. It has seen equally striking developments in the structure of the Church; even though in this country the diocesan and parochial structure retains an almost unchallenged monopoly, yet new forms are beginning to assert themselves, at least experimentally.[5] Abroad, where tradition is less respected and less strong, more radical changes have already taken place. The missionary demands of modern secularized society have issued in the creation of new structures of Christian operation (e g. the missionary priests in French industry, the *Mission de France*, the secular Institutes, etc.). Inevitably these developments import changes

---

[5] E.g. The Industrial Missions of Sheffield and Southwark; the 'house churches' at Halton, Leeds. Cf. J. A. T Robinson, *On Being the Church in the World*, s.c.m. Press 1960.

Towards a Church Architecture

both in rite and in ceremony. These changes are commonly grouped under the overall title of the liturgical movement; though it is important to remember that this movement is concerned with much more than the mere direction of liturgical action, and is in fact nothing less than a new reformation.

II

This new reformation, though still in its early stages, can already be seen to be both wider in range and of greater depth than that of the sixteenth century. First, the apparatus of historical research is far more developed than it was four hundred years ago; indeed, it is scarcely too much to say that history has developed its own methodology only within the last hundred years. It is this development which makes it possible for us today to discuss more accurately the customs of thought and practice, the social habits and patterns of the early Church, their development through the Dark Ages, the achievement of the mediaeval Church, and its degeneration and collapse. It enables us also to scrutinize the first reformation itself and to see how far the picture of the primitive Christianity to which it appealed, and which it thought it was recovering, is true, and how far it is false or at least romanticized; and it enables us to see both what was the real strength of the sixteenth century reform and what was its weakness. Its strength was not so much the removal of glaring abuses, but rather the deliberate attempt (which, though not wholly successful, yet was a marked improvement on what had gone before) to break down the barrier between the clergy and the people, and to give back to the laity, if not a fully active part in the Church's worship, at least the opportunity of intelligent participation by the use of the common tongue. Its weakness was that it carried over too many presuppositions of the mediaeval Church without adequate critical scrutiny; for example, the Anglican reformers at least, despite their laudable desire to encourage the laity to follow the service intelligently, none the less left the mediaeval distinction of clergy and laity unaltered; they continued to regard the sacraments (and so to teach and present them) in abstraction from any clear doctrine of the Church as itself the great sacrament, and so perpetuated controversies on the operation of sacraments which were largely meaningless and wholly sterile; by placing the Church under the jurisdiction of the King in place of the Pope, they changed King Log for King

Liturgy and Society

Stork and deprived the Church of England of any effective standard of social criticism or protest for the next four hundred years. The sixteenth-century reformation had other attributes which were both strength and weakness. For example, it encouraged in every individual a direct sense of responsibility towards God, a habit of Bible reading at home and personal prayer; but in doing this (as we can now see) it encouraged also the tendency to social atomization already strong in fifteenth-and sixteenth-century society, at the expense of men's roots in social groupings, customs and traditions, and, still more, encouraged the tendency to exalt the cerebral, rational faculties of man at the expense of his sensual, emotional and affective qualities.

Today the Church is beginning to experience a new reformation which it is tempting to regard as a mere reversal of the earlier. It is true that the tendencies today are away from the individualistic habits of the preceding age, and away from a purely cerebral or excessively rational understanding of religion. But this does not mean a total suppression of the ministry of the word in favour of the ministry of the sacraments, a surrender of all critical understanding to mere magical superstitions. Still less is this new reform a mere romantic movement away from an excessively intellectual or moralistic religion to a more sentimental or aesthetic atmosphere. The Church itself is not 'summoned by bells' whatever may be the experience of some of its members. No: this new reformation is rather a movement, partly conscious, but more largely unconscious, to recover that which has been, not lost, but lost sight of, during recent centuries – viz., the basic attributes of the Christian religion as communal, factual, dogmatic – without losing the fruits of their inherited experience. Hence, for example, the stress upon liturgy: for liturgy, rightly understood, is not merely a means of exciting pious sentiments, nor even an elaborate framework for the simple administration of sacraments. Liturgy is the Church's peculiar act (formal and public as the word denotes) whereby it proclaims its own nature, remakes itself week by week, and thereby remakes its several members into the mystical body of Christ. In doing this the Church addresses at once the mind and the heart or affections of men. In every liturgical rite there is a central act whereby something is *done* which *makes* things other than they were before; but at the same time both the sanction for and the meaning of this is clearly set forth by readings from the scriptures, and usually by prayers or homiletic expositions to draw the meaning out fully into the understanding of the participants. This function of liturgy was never better stated than in the words of Dr E. L. Mascall (speaking of the older controversies between scripture and tradition): 'The Church lives neither by tradition alone, nor by the scriptures directly The Church lives day by day by her liturgy, which is her living tradition but of which the scriptures are both constituent and normative.'

The liturgical movement therefore is more than a mere reform or corrective of the sixteenth-century reformation. It is a recovery of the communal, indeed corporate, character of the Church, seen no longer as a mere congeries of individuals, but as a living organism, whose head is Christ and in which every individual Christian finds not merely consolation or strength but a new nature, and with this a new understanding both of himself and of the universe. The liturgical movement is also a movement for the recovery of the factual aspect of Christianity. Christ came indeed to teach, but (more than this) to save: and salvation is an action Full salvation indeed must include the understanding and must therefore involve teaching But the understanding is only one part of man, and if man is to be saved in any significant sense, he must be saved in every part. Salvation then means a change in man's nature. This change is traditionally described as regeneration or rebirth. But just as natural generation or birth depends on more than mere feelings, or mere words, and involves a definite act, so regeneration, or rebirth, involves an explicit act. This act Christians believe to have been done in principle by the Lord and Saviour Jesus Christ, in his death and resurrection; but that act or event is made present in every place and every age through the Church, and actualized by the Church in its liturgy.

The Church therefore is primarily an agency for *doing* something, and only secondarily for explaining in words what is being done. And the liturgical movement is, among other things, a movement towards the re-establishment of language to its full function and power. For language has always a dual function. first, immediate: to convey a particular thought, wish, command, explanation, opinion, or whatever; secondly, ulterior: to speak through the ear to the whole man and to bring his mind into active harmony with his whole being. This second use has been dangerously ignored through recent centuries and sadly impoverished even in the realm of poetry, which alone was left to it Contemporary thinkers, however, have begun to draw our attention to the importance of this second function of language if it is properly to discharge its immediate function.[6] It is this use of language as both expository and evocative which is characteristic of liturgical language; and the Church in our day is coming once again to recognize the value and importance of this.

But these changes in practice or understanding are not isolated from the contemporary society in which Christians live. There is here, as always, an interaction whereby these new, or new-old, practices or insights may be seen as reflections of currents flowing in secular society, or equally as contributing force and direction to those currents. There is no question, however, of determining cause or priority The important thing is to recognize the impulse and direction of divine providence in both the Church and the world, and to see that, in the Church at least, its members shall be aware of what is happening, ready to change their attitudes, and even their habits, and prepared to accept changes in formal rites and ceremonies and in the actual planning of church buildings. We must not be surprised if there is some delay in this, and even at times considerable resistance. It can hardly be expected that all Christians shall move at exactly the same pace, or all adopt the same new attitudes at the same time. It is important in this as in all things to show patience and charity. But charity is not true charity if it involves sacrifice of truth. The apostle's injunction is 'to speak the truth in love'. This can never be easy. It is particularly difficult when the truth is hard to discern. We must be grateful if today it is relatively easy.

We have seen how social customs and attitudes change from time to time, and what are some of the distinctive features of the social changes of our own day. We have seen how the Church is already beginning to reproduce these changes in her own practice and structures. Our task is to apprehend these changes as fully as we can, to carry them out to the best of our ability, and to persuade our fellow-Christians of their validity and acceptability. Where, as very often today, we find an eager disposition to accept, we must thank God and press on; where, as sometimes, we encounter hostility and fear, our duty is to persuade our brethren that what is going on should

---

[6] E.g. T. S. Eliot, *The Use of Poetry and the Use of Criticism*, Faber 1933; Susanne Langer, *Philosophy in a New Key*, Oxford Univeristy Press 1942, A. M. Farrar, *The Glass of Vision*, Dacre Press 1948.

be regarded, not in fear but as a grace. We may also usefully indicate that this sort of change is not unprecedented. There have been other moments in the Church's history when changes almost as far-reaching have been made in her customs, structures, and therefore in her liturgical rites.[7] The first change came with the Peace of the Church, when the civil power ceased to drive the Church underground by persecution, and made available public buildings for public worship. Previously the local Church had been obliged always to meet in private houses. Sometimes there might be a room specially set aside for worship and never used for any other purpose; but it is probable that most often the local Christian community would gather for the liturgy in what would today be somebody's drawing-room or front parlour.[8] When Christians met for the liturgy in these relatively small and private circumstances they can hardly have failed to realize that the liturgy is the act of the whole family of God. The description of the eucharistic liturgy celebrated in or near Rome around AD 200 as given by Hippolytus shows clearly how everyone present had an active part to play; there was no question of a spectacle performed by professional actors whilst others looked on. There was scarcely indeed a recognizable difference in *kind* between all those present. The celebrant, or president, would of course play a larger part than others, and perhaps be treated with special honours even outside the ceremony; but he was not regarded as a being from a totally different social category or professional class, for the idea of a *clergy* was unknown at that early date.

After the Peace of the Church, when Christians were given the use of public buildings, the liturgy naturally became elaborated and more formalized Yet even in the time of St Augustine the diversity of functions was still maintained; every grade in the Church, indeed each several Christian, had his own special liturgy. Not until about the eighth century did the liturgical rites of the Church begin to take on that stylization which has characterized them ever since. Yet even then the diversity of functions was still maintained, and the pattern of the building much as it has always been. In the basilicas,

---

[7] These may be studied more fully in Theodor Klauser's *The Western Liturgy and its History*, trans. F. L. Cross, Mowbray 1952.
[8] A vividly imaginative picture of this is given by Dom Gregory Dix in *The Shape of the Liturgy*, Dacre Press 1945.

where the Great Liturgy was normally celebrated, the altar would still stand near the centre of the building or at least on the chord of the apse. The president, usually the bishop, would sit on his throne in the apse, with his presbyters or senators seated on either side in the semi-circle. Deacons would stand at the altar to spread the cloth, to receive the people's offerings and to prepare the eucharistic elements. The arch-deacon would have the task or privilege also of reading the gospel from an ambo in the nave. The sub-deacons would stand around holding lights and performing whatever other functions were required (much as servers and acolytes do today).

Not until the twelfth century (and then almost wholly in northern Europe alone) did this pattern of the church give place to the pattern familiar to us today, whereby the altar is placed against the east wall (where the bishop's throne used formerly to be); the presbyterium (or semi-circle of seats for the presbyters) turned into two ranks of stalls facing each other across a chancel; and a screen erected to divide the chancel from the nave.

It is not certain when altars were first moved from their free-standing position to the east wall; there is no doubt that this happened a great deal earlier than the twelfth century in remote chapels where Christian missions were established. It is possible that this pattern was adopted in the private chapels of bishops' houses, with the object of permitting the maximum number of people to be present in the room, and because in so small a room all those present could easily take an active part in the rite, even if they were no longer 'standing around' the altar, on three sides. It is possible in any case to distinguish between private and solemn celebrations of liturgical rites. We cannot here stop to question the legitimacy of private celebrations at all; he would be a very rigid purist, however, who would deny the legitimacy at any time of particular celebrations in particular places for particular groups or purposes. But a pattern which may be convenient for private celebration is unlikely to be suitable for public or solemn ones. The mediaeval innovations of east end altars, choir-stalls and chancel screens indicate a marked change in the whole understanding of what the liturgy is, and have been in turn the cause of much subsequent misunderstanding and malpractice.

We can now see that the impulse for these innovations came chiefly from two sources. First, the growth of monastic houses into large abbeys, requiring their own community churches yet carrying also a responsibility for the local Christians. What we now call the chancel would have been regarded then as the community church; and, since it was in effect a private chapel, the pattern of private chapels was not unnaturally reproduced. Where there was also a local parish church, this chapel remained a separate building; but where there was no separate parish church, the building would be enlarged to accommodate a local congregation in what we now call the nave. Since the occasions when these lay, or non-monastic, Christians were present, however, would be few and since the building would be used most often by the monastic community alone, it is not surprising if this community church or chapel (or chancel) was marked off from the nave, and sheltered from cold draughts by a screen. But, secondly, the breakdown of civil administration under the old empire, and the gradual imposition of these duties upon the Christian Church, led in the course of centuries to the elevation of the clergy into a separate and superior social class; and though for many centuries the great majority of clerks were not in priest's orders, yet in time it became a social and economic advantage both to multiply the number of priests and to exaggerate the superiority of the clergy over the laity. Again therefore it is not surprising if, by the high Middle Age, the monastic pattern of the church became normal even for non-monastic churches.

Even through the Middle Ages, however, the forms of liturgical rites were still flexible. Witness the diversity of rites still extant in the sixteenth century None the less the tendency to crystallize or mummify these forms continued; with the inevitable consequence that the Church's rites became more and more secret mysteries performed only by initiates, whilst the uninitiated were more and more excluded and had less and less understanding of what was going on.

It was one of the less happy features of the reformation that the gulf between clergy and laity, which had begun to yawn wide in the Middle Ages, was not bridged but yawned no less widely even after the sixteenth century. True, in Scotland the sons of Calvin and John Knox made great attempts to correct this error by ascribing to each Christian family the character of the local Church, and to the head of the household the attributes (if not the power) of a priest. Hence the custom of closing the local church building or temple during the week, in order to put the accent upon the house or family The intention was laudable; the effect less so. And in England there is little evidence that this habit ever caught on. Indeed it was in the state's

Liturgy and Society

interest that the local Church with its local parson should remain the focus of social interest and activity. Unfortunately, too, the growth of the national state, with its emphasis on the national monarch, introduced into Christian worship a further degree of elaboration [9] The ceremonies of the royal court were reproduced in the church. The altar, already placed against the east wall and there regarded more as a high place of sacrifice than as a table for the communion, now took on the added character of a throne Gradines were built up behind it and (in Catholic churches) the tabernacle enlarged so as to give the reserved sacrament the character of *le Roi Soleil*. Such changes could serve only to increase the sense of alienation between the personnel of the sanctuary and the people of the nave Hence the growth (from the thirteenth to the nineteenth centuries) of popular non-liturgical devotions such as the Christmas crib and the stations of the cross. Today, however, the new experience of community (as against individualism), of function or operation (as against talking or merely thinking), of the engagement of the whole person in both action and word, are making themselves felt not only in the rites and ceremonies of the Church, but in the actual planning of the church building. It is imperative that Christians should see the need for church buildings now to be planned on lines which express these insights and permit their realization in action

III

So far as the English-speaking world is concerned, there is as yet very little reference of church design to the social circumstance and climate of today. Of how many English architects who have designed churches in this century can it be said (as it was said of the German architect Rudolf Schwarz as long ago as 1939) that 'he made the church anew *a house for* divine worship, not an autonomous, architectural expression of religious feeling'?[10] The equation of religion with religious feeling is still so common in England as to be virtually a commonplace. The psychologizing of the Methodist movement, itself a notable reformation at a time when religion was, in effect, little more than an external observance of ethical rules or norms, has

---

[9] This is most evident in the Catholic half of Europe; but it may be discerned in milder form in England also.
[10] H. A. Reinhold in *Architectural Forum*, January 1939, p. 26.

developed to the point of virtually eclipsing any notion of external observance of any norms at all.

But no interior sentiment, no glow of religious fervour, can replace revealed truth. 'Enthusiasm' is no substitute for dogma. The Church's work is indeed incomplete until each of its members has assimilated the truth which the Church exists to actualize, to demonstrate and to proclaim, to the point of seeing all things in its light, and indeed living by it. But an end-product is always an end-product · it depends for its very possibility upon a long chain of production processes, and ultimately upon the raw material (*materia prima*) which inaugurates this chain. If the supply of this ceases, or if due care is not paid to its proper treatment, the end-products will themselves soon terminate.

If all men and women are to be saved by coming to the knowledge of the truth, then the first need is to demonstrate and declare that truth. The fundamental presupposition of the Christian Church is that this truth has to be declared and demonstrated if men are to see it, admire it, embrace it (or alternatively reject it); i.e. that it is *revealed* truth, inaccessible to the natural reason or sentiment of men. If it were not so, if in fact this truth were innate in all men and needed only to be elicited or articulated by simple teaching, surely a simple *stoa* or academy, or at most a small class-room, would suffice. If persuasive oratory is needed, then a meeting-room or a plain preaching-house would do. In neither case would a large building, with elongated chancel, elaborate screen, and remote altar or pulpit be needed. But if (as the contributors to this book believe, in common with the vast majority of Christians throughout this era, though the belief has been in eclipse in England for the past few centuries) the first business of the Church is not to evoke sentiment, but to declare truth: then provision must be made for that truth to be declared in its own proper mode. This truth was of course manifested originally and supremely in the incarnate word of God. By his ordinance and act it was extrapolated into the Church, known primarily as his mystical (sc. 'sacramental') body, *ipsa magnum sacramentum*, before it is heard as his voice. And the mode by which the Church manifests every day, every year, in every century and in every place, the truth which it embodies is in its sacraments, conveyed by its rites and ceremonies, of which, as we have seen, the reading and exegesis of scripture are constituent and normative.

Liturgy and Society

A church building therefore is primarily and essentially a building designed for the performance of specific rites and ceremonies, by a community or group of people who assemble or congregate for this particular purpose. (These rites are distinguished from psychic magic by the divine truth which controls and informs them, and by their address to the total being of the participant – his intelligence and reason, no less than his emotions or sentiments.) What matters most in its design, therefore, is 'the rediscovery of simplicity and basic needs, *not* the pursuit of whimsical fashions'.[11]

The primary task of the modern church architect should be to get back to essentials It is only too easy to design a building with strange new angles, exotic stained glass, and a hundred other exciting contemporary features, without producing a truly Christian church. It is equally possible to erect a building with a hundred helps to prayer, whose very lines induce a sense of being 'in tune with the Infinite', and yet fail to meet the real need. Only the marriage of a complete understanding of liturgy – its objectivity, its manifestation of divine truth through rite and action, its communality – with a scientific study of contemporary social fact can ensure that the Church may again be equipped with buildings adequate to its present needs and true to its eternal purposes.

---

[11] Patience Gray in *The Observer* for October 11th 1959.

9. The Church and the Community

PATRICK NUTTGENS

'In its religious organization, we may say that Christendom has remained fixed at the stage of development suitable to a single agricultural and piscatorial society, and that modern material organization – or, if "organization" sounds too complimentary, we will say "complication" – has produced a world for which Christian forms are imperfectly adapted.'

Since T. S. Eliot wrote that in *The Idea of a Christian Society*,[1] a world war and fifteen years of reconstruction and planning have wiped away some of the wrinkles in the face of modern society and carved others deeper. For all the re-thinking forced upon Christians by the second shattering of accepted values in half a century, and despite the marked revitalization of much church activity in the post-war years, few church people would, I imagine, consider that the fundamental situation has been much changed: that Christian forms of organization are, in Mr Eliot's phrase, imperfectly adapted to the contemporary world.

This essay is concerned with some of the basic questions raised by the physical fact of setting apart a special building for the service of God. In all the discussions on church architecture and its design such questions are quite the most elusive; they include the social and economic implications of this aspect of physical planning, or, to phrase it in another way, the relationship of the church and the community in terms of the physical environment. If this were an academic exercise it might be called 'The physical setting of a religious activity with an economic problem and social implications'. I am not here going to discuss the economic problem except indirectly; the more significant questions have to do with the sociological context of church planning. For if a church building itself has

[1] Faber and Faber 1939, p. 31.

a definite function and a programme, it is just as important to recognize its place in the social scene of town or country; to extend architectural matters into the wider field of planning. This is what the modern movement in architecture has consistently done in secular cases; it is probably a mark of the remoteness of church architecture from the modern movement generally, that a similar investigation has rarely been made in the case of religious buildings.

Because of this, it is easier to ask questions than to answer them, although, as in nearly all sociological queries, it is not at all easy to ask the right questions. This enquiry is really a series of questions from an outsider, arising from what seems to be a shortage of information of the sort relevant to anyone with Christian convictions.

I make this point because it seems to me important to recognize right away the essential difference in attitude of someone with a religious commitment and an apostolic vocation, from someone trying to make a so-called objective plan for a social situation. To some extent there is an inevitable antipathy between traditional Christianity and the ideology of planning, a suspicion among church people that the aims of planners are not entirely in their interest. This seems to me justified. Planning has been described as the translation of the work of the social planner into the finished product. This would not be an accurate description of planning in this country as we know it today, because social planning hardly impinges upon the minds of most physical planners, but it represents an underlying assumption. Contemporary planning, working from the survey, through its analysis, to the plan, may often consist merely in the preservation of the status quo (the survey renamed 'the plan') or it may be more creative in attempting to realize further some of the implications of the survey. In either case it may not be to the taste of the churchman.

'Men come together in cities in order to live', said Aristotle; 'they remain together in order to live the good life'. The churches ought to have a fairly firm view on what constitutes a good life, and there is not much evidence so far that that view has been shared with any real enthusiasm by the planning fraternity. Planning, in fact, has come to be mistrusted by many people. In its modern form it derives from nineteenth-century ideas of the benefits of a planned society, and has always had some difficulty in dissociating itself from certain forms of totalitarianism. More basically, it is associated with materialism, and with what William H. Whyte describes vividly in

The Organization Man under the heading of scientism. This is the 'promise that with the same techniques that have worked in the physical sciences we can eventually create an exact science of man'. More than ever, says this faith, 'the world's greatest need is a science of human relationships and an art of human engineering based upon the laws of such science'. It is a belief based on certain fallacies (two of those isolated by Hayek are objectivism and collectivism – the attempt to dispense with subjective knowledge, and to treat abstract wholes, such as society, as definite objectives, like biological organisms); and it founders on some awkward problems, such as the difference between good and evil, right and wrong.

In any case, these are attitudes which cannot belong to people concerned with the preaching of Christianity; nothing could be further removed from the ideal of planning than the Sermon on the Mount. Fortunately, planning in Western Europe has never been so logical or so extreme. But it still cannot be said to have resolved its relationship with the churches. In practice, nearly all town plans have had a section (often near the end) that recognizes the contribution of the churches to social life. But it is a recognition essentially different from the attitude of a convinced Christian, who is concerned primarily with something more than social life; it is equivalent to the attitude of people who read the Bible for the sake of its prose.

Nevertheless, there is an area in which the planning of churches and the problems of planning on a bigger scale come together, and in which each has much to give the other. If, as this essay suggested at the beginning, the religious organization has to some extent fallen over backwards in facing modern developments, a good deal of social organization has fallen over frontwards. It is now a truism that traditional forms of community have in many places broken down. Innumerable causes have been suggested: the failure of the family, the school, business, or the church to supply the individual with a sense of place and of belonging· the movement of people from one area to another in post-war reconstruction, the breaking up of old groups with slum clearance and city development Above all is the effect of urbanization, and its influence on the family, on education and on the complex of social relationships The traditional primary social unit of the family no longer encloses the functions and values it had in the simpler small communities of a century or more ago. Increasingly the local authority takes part in the parents' control of their children, in matters of health, education, and even indirectly in family planning. Work is no longer related to it, work and leisure are as separate as workplace from home. The family, it has been said, which was formerly production unit as well as consumer unit, is now only the latter. The fact of community, which grew over centuries on the terms set by the family and the village, has not survived untarnished the transference to vast urban agglomerations and the growth of the mass society. And neither has the parochial organization of the churches, nor the significance of their role in community life.

In the unoccupied areas between the individual and mass society we are increasingly aware of the need for something of understandable size to function as did (and sometimes does) the family, the parish and the village. 'We are learning', wrote Robert A. Nisbet 'that many of the motivations and incentives which an older generation of rationalists believed were inherent in the individual are actually supplied by social groups – social groups with both functional and moral relevance to the lives of individuals . . . there must be in any stable culture, in any civilization that prizes its integrity, functionally significant and psychologically meaningful groups and associations lying intermediate to the individual and the larger values and purposes of his society. For these are the small areas of association within which alone such values and purposes can take on clear meaning in personal life and become the vital roots of the large culture.'[2]

This is all of great relevance to the matter of the church and its community, or the church and the community at large; and right away there is the difficulty of knowing what a community really is. There is no shortage of definitions. George A. Hillery (quoted in Nels Anderson, *The Urban Community*, 1959) undertook a few years ago to collect them and found no fewer than ninety-four. Not surprisingly he found that those concerned with rural communities were more in agreement than those concerned with urban ones. I do not propose here to summarize these sociological definitions, which seem often to cast a good deal of obscurity on a subject that was dark enough already, but only to see how ideas of community have been used in the making of plans by planners.

To anyone unfamiliar with the education of planners, it may be a surprise to find that most of them accept the lack of a suitable de-

[2] *The Quest for Community*, New York, 1953, p. 70.

finition and do not even worry enough to question it. And yet community planning has been the slogan of virtually all the wartime and post-war plans, and of the early pioneers of the post-Geddes, garden city and suburb era. The fact is that what matters to a planner is a working assumption that may or may not be valid, a simple and fashionable war cry that enables him to get up energy and hack his way through to the nearest standard. In effect it is a useful notion for justifying the choice of some sort of geographical limit for working.

Thus three of the great plans: the County of London Plan of 1943 by Abercrombie and Forshaw, the Greater London Plan of 1945 by Abercrombie, and the Clyde Valley Regional Plan of 1949, by Abercrombie and Matthew, declare the principle of community planning but avoid defining community. On the other hand, they make great use of the concept of neighbourhood, a territorial group, working therefore essentially on the assumption that community and physical grouping are directly connected. 'The common environment provides an underlying unity', wrote Lewis Mumford in *The Culture of Cities*;[3] and this is a useful belief in providing a theoretical justification for the necessary planning proposals.

A much more serious study of the problem was, however, made in one of the outstanding advisory plans made in Great Britain· the *Middlesbrough Survey and Plan* by Max Lock, 1946.[4] In the section by Dr Ruth Glass (the social study) it does attempt to define the nature of community and its relationship with the neighbourhood in sociological terms. Thus a neighbourhood means either 'a distinct territorial group, distinct by virtue of the specific physical characteristics of the area and the specific social characteristics of its inhabitants', or 'a territorial group the members of which meet on a common ground within their own area for primary social activities and for spontaneous and organized social contacts'. The latter description seems to be much the same as that of a community, but for the territorial aspect; in use it covers a wider group than a neighbourhood. A community is essentially developed from common ideas; a neighbourhood is concerned with common social contacts in a geographical setting. So a definition of community is given: 'a territorial

[3] New York, 1938, p. 456.
[4] Middlesbrough 1946, p. 156.

group of people with a common mode of living, striving for common objectives' – and a neighbourhood may be a part of such a group.

It is interesting that this stresses the purposive nature of a community, a point made earlier by Lewis Mumford, and one which is of immediate concern to the churches. But first, without going into details, it is worth sketching in how this kind of general acceptance of the relation of the community and the neighbourhood has been worked out in some of the major planning proposals until very recently, under the heading of the *neighbourhood principle*.

In the two great London plans referred to earlier, Abercrombie sets this out, declaring that he has 'used the community as the basic planning unit', and that each community would contain one or more neighbourhood units. The basic elements in the urban structure are for him the living places and the work places, and the communication between them. Then come the social, administrative, educational and public buildings (including the churches). A residential neighbourhood may have 10,000 people, and a community plan would consist of a series of such neighbourhoods, each of between 5000 and 10,000 persons.

How are these dimensions established? The figures are based on school recommendations made by the Ministry of Education at the time. Thus 5000 people can provide material for one school for children aged 5 to 7 and another for those aged 8 to 11. Then a secondary (modern) school is necessary for each group of 10,000 people; since there is (or was) usually one for boys and one for girls. this gives two secondary schools for 20,000 people. This seems to suggest that a community of limited size could consist of two to four residential neighbourhoods.

The significance of this calculation is not only that it is empirical and practical. It reflects a more basic idea of the school as a central and integrative unit in community development. Lewis Mumford was emphatic about this: 'What are the new dominants in the opening biotechnic economy? They are not far to seek: the dwelling house and the school, with all their specialized communal aids, constitute the essential nucleus of the new community'. As for a neighbourhood, 'its size is determined by the convenient walking distance for children between the farthest house and the school and playground in which a major part of their activities are focussed.'[5]

[5] Lewis Mumford, op cit., p. 472.

Towards a Church Architecture

From this nucleus, or from the more administrative British type, the remainder of the necessary facilities can be developed for the service of the community or that part of it called the neighbourhood unit: the local shops and service trades, the community centres, youth centres and churches. Community and youth centres are usually mentioned first, the churches are sometimes referred to as important focal points. One wonders whether they will act as focal points in anything more than an architectural sense, as landscape features in space rather than fixed points in the essential social structure.

In such plans, what do the churches get? In general terms, about a tenth of the total acreage of a neighbourhood may be devoted to community buildings, including churches. The Greater London Plan estimated that church places should be planned for ten per cent of population. An average modern church has 500 seats; so there will be ten to fifteen churches for 60,000 people, (or perhaps two per neighbourhood), which is the likely size of a new town.

Here then is the new community as foreshadowed in the advisory plans. It is a serious and notable attempt to provide the geographical and architectural setting for social groups to form themselves and give a sense of unity. It is an idea drawn originally from the village, where, more easily than in the modern space- and people-greedy conurbation, the existence of community can be observed. Here too is the way in which the churches, hesitant in their functions, find their way, sometimes marginally or superficially, into the new plan: near the community centre indeed, but hardly integral to the structure. It is a just reflection of the decline of religion in the twentieth century.

So far I have been concerned with the background to the placing of churches as this has been affected by post-war planning in this country Considerably more thought has been given to the matter on the Continent by those actively involved in the work of the churches. There, the vitality of the liturgical movement and the serious discussion and co-operation between denominations hurried on by the upheaval of the Second World War have extended, rightly, to the necessity of the churches' part in the process of social reorganzation and development. It seems clear that one cannot argue long for the revival of liturgical practice inside the fabric of the church, for the participation of the faithful as a body, in common, in the mysteries which are as the still point in the turning circle of life, without studying the relation of that community to the community at large. The situation outlined in this paper is entirely understandable; but it is hardly satisfactory for the churches. At the same time, the attempt to foster community through the creation of neighbourhoods has been severely criticized on general social grounds. Looking at these may lead back to the churches' position It may be that where the neighbourhood principle is unsatisfactory for the churches is just where it breaks down generally; and it seems to break down on the facts of human behaviour.

Already it is being said that neighbourhoods do not exist in their planned topographical way. In the new towns, social groups cut across the artificial boundaries of areas, according to the interests and activities of their members. They even cut across very real boundaries, such as the wide main roads separating the neighbourhoods In some respects the school does not provide the necessary nucleus according to the physical plan; as soon as denominational schools are established they are no longer socially integrated with their neighbourhoods, but may serve a much wider and more diverse area. And there is little evidence that neighbourhoods make communities or that any numerical calculation of a suitable size is realistic. What makes a community depends on the distance of one's view; it can be anything from a group of families to a group of nations. Planners have differed radically in their evaluation of neighbourhoods. Some believe that breaking up a town into smaller units will encourage unity, others that it destroys the unity of the town. 'Fortunately,' remarked one American commentator, 'many planning decisions are unlikely to affect the happiness of new-town residents one way or the other.'[6]

So later trends have been towards the close-knit, higher density town, intended to counteract the spread of subtopia, to provide lots of townscape, and to make people happy and community-conscious because they are close together. The passing tribute to the mediaeval town, with plenty of cobbles and enclosure, the inevitable reference to the Piazza San Marco in Venice, the longing for the paved space where people will gather to engage in cultural pursuits and con-

[6] Quoted in William H. Whyte, *The Organisation Man*, Pelican edition 1960, p. 321.

Towards a Church Architecture

versation, are now familiar. It is all essentially visual and sentimental The mediaeval town was an expression of a functional organization that depended on the fact of the group rather than the individual as the unit of the social system – and we do not have that group now The visual attitude towards community is just as evident in the common argument from observation: in the old decayed place there was congestion and it was alive; in the new suburbs to which we have sent the people there is space and privacy, and it looks dead, let us have congestion. In fact what makes the difference is not the character and placing of the buildings, but the disruption of an existing community group.

This has a lot to do with the real nature of communities. In a remarkable series of lectures delivered in America a few years ago and printed under the title of the *The Decline of Wisdom*, Gabriel Marcel gave a powerful exposition of the inherited nature of the values which integrate social groups. The subject is too vast to discuss thoroughly here; I can best summarize what seem to me the most significant aspects of community existence as it affects the placing of churches.

The community is not exact and not quantitative, but depends upon a complex of inherited and often undefined values. It is concerned not essentially with a recorded assembly of facts and information but with an inherited way of seeing, thinking and behaving. In the literal meaning of the words it might be said that it expresses itself in the common sense of its members; common because it is those things which belong to the group rather than to the individual as such that give it its character: and sense, because such values are often known by sense rather than by rationalization and the collection of data. This seems to me clear from observation. In the gradual growth of a community one can look in vain for an exact definition of its nature that is applicable to more than a few of its aspects at a certain time. The apparent irrationality of groups, which is well known when an outsider is trying to do something good for them, like Lord Leverhulme in the Hebrides or some well-intentioned planner concerned with rehousing, is only a reflection of this. The nostalgia for the old court and tenement is not really different from the sudden opposition to proposals for new development and expansion, however much in the existing community's interests a reasonable outsider would consider them to be Faced with disruption or significant change, a community can reveal an unexpected unity and strength that is not much affected by dispassionate argument. It has a lot to do with inherited, accepted values and with the sense of belonging to a place As a more utilitarian environment is newly created and the family adjusts itself to this utilitarian pattern, something of the community sense is lost. The folklore dies, for the community is the residence of memories, both individual and folk ones, and it is not surprising that vernacular architecture disappears, for this is the expression of the community's inherited common sense in material terms 'Society', said Burke, 'is a partnership of the dead, the living and the unborn'; and this holds true for its smaller elements as well as the large one of society itself

To these characteristics of community I would add something to do with the existence of common aims and an element of common responsibility. There is a purposive character in a community, even though the exact nature of the purpose is not defined. It is doubtful if without some purpose a community can be said to exist. This is often the vacuum in new community centres and youth centres 'People do not live together merely to be together', in Ortega y Gasset's words, 'they live together to do something together '[7] It may be that exhortations to be public-spirited are not enough. The need for a degree of common responsibility is the complement of having some sort of influence on one's environment. In this connection local government and organization are important; it is interesting that Abercrombie remarks in the Greater London Plan that 'a strong point was made that a separate or defined community should be a unit in local government, at least for certain purposes'.

Now one of the traditional institutions with deep roots in society, concerned with values, and very definitely with common aims and responsibility, is the *parish*. It was also historically a unit in civil administration. As such its significance is no longer great, and the incumbent has been left with a collection of useful administrative activities of unknown importance, like the power to sign passport photographs. Nevertheless the parish is (or can be) one of the real integrating forces in certain parts of society. What is doubtful is whether it will remain so in the same simple way.

The problem is clearly put by T. S. Eliot in the book referred to at

[7] Quoted in Nisbet, op. cit., p. 61.

Towards a Church Architecture

the beginning. 'The traditional unit of the Christian community in England is the parish. . . . The parish is certainly in decay, from several causes of which the least cogent is the division into sects a much more important reason is urbanization – in which I am including also sub-urbanization, and all the causes and effects of urbanization. How far the parish must be superseded will depend largely upon our view of the necessity of accepting the causes which tend to destroy it In any case, the parish will serve my purpose as an example of a community unit For this unit must not be solely religious, and not solely social; nor should the individual be a member of two separate, or even overlapping units, one religious and the other social. The unitary community should be religious-social, and it must be one in which all classes, if you have classes, have their centre of interest.'[8]

In a world for which Christian forms are imperfectly adapted, he can offer two solutions to the problem at this stage. One is the return to a simpler mode of life. 'The other alternative is to accept the modern world as it is and simply try to adapt Christian social ideas to it. The latter resolves itself into a mere doctrine of expediency; and is a surrender of the faith that Christianity itself can play any part in shaping social forms.'[9]

Without going back to the simple life, we can surely take a less pessimistic view than this, and one that is less universal and more positive. Both for their own members and for others, the churches can make a positive contribution to the religious-social life of the place, and therefore to the creation of communities within the larger unit of society. What we perhaps need is a more flexible interpretation of the idea of the parish as the real unit in a Christian community. To start with, if the modern community or neighbourhood is not really topographically distinct, as was argued earlier, it may be that this applies also to parishes Already since the war, the moving of homes has increased the irregularity and artificiality of parish boundaries. Examination of the attendance at churches suggests that factors other than the proximity of a house are at work. One is probably the habit of attending a certain church after moving from the parish, but this may be short-lived. Others concern changes more radical in modern society.

[8] Op. cit., p. 29.   [9] Ibid., p. 32

It has been argued by some sociologists that there is need of a new conception of neighbourhood. Clearly the geographical framework is a necessary element; nevertheless relating neighbourhood with residential proximity does not fit the geographical realities of urban friendship and aquaintance.[10] Various investigations have shown the existence of contacts which are not limited by geographical distance. This is a familiar characteristic of middle-class society. But it is likely to be more general if present trends continue. The great social improvement of the last few decades, the supplying of education for all, the vast expansion of universities and now of technical colleges, are rapidly transforming a working-class into a middle-class society. In the traditional working-class area there was always a strong tie between community and place, as there was between workplace and home. There is an abundance of studies, both sociological and autobiographical, to show the significance of the street as the physical area of neighbourhood and the firm unifying bonds between several generations of the family in the same district. One's own experience of living in such streets confirms it over and over again. But this is not the characteristic of the middle-class society which is rapidly growing. The contraction of the family to two rather than three generations and a different range of social contacts, are reflected in the isolated house of suburbia; the half-way stage is reflected in the compromise residential areas of the new towns. The relationship between neighbourhood and place is no longer clear. Instead contacts are made across the lines of geography, through identity of interests and occupation, through professional activities, and so on.

Such a change is stimulated by the comparatively low densities of residential areas advocated on grounds of health and convenience; it is especially reinforced by developments in transport. It will not be long before there is a car for every family; as the car habit grows, the barriers of distance become strange. If there is a car outside your door, it is easier to drive half a mile than twenty yards. Increased mobility means that accessibility because of road patterns assumes greater importance. Nor are our contacts limited by accessibility. We find memories and values in common on a big scale through television and radio · on a smaller scale because of the telephone.

[10] Discussed in Nels Anderson, *The Urban Community*, 1959.

Towards a Church Architecture

So it may be that the community of the future should be viewed in a different light from the old ones which are easier to study, and it may be that the parish should move with the times. In the most recent of the new towns, Cumbernauld, the old neighbourhood principle has been abandoned; the town is tighter and more close-knit and is intended to be one community. In a pattern made by ring roads and radials, with a major town centre linked to the residential areas by a system of direct pedestrian ways, the churches are placed either in the centre or on these unifying pedestrian links. It is particularly interesting that the Catholic churches are related to the Catholic primary schools.

Here then is my first question concerning the point of contact between the church and the parish and the community. If the family and the school are, as Mumford suggested, the nuclei of the new community, and if the church is to have an integral part in that community, perhaps the planned relationship with the school is an important consideration. Here the family's aims and responsibilities converge; here too are made, through the less inhibited friendships of children, through parents' associations and other connected activities, a series of real social contacts.

Secondly, and to go further, should the new church complex be regarded as a basic community centre as well as a special Sunday-morning building? Is the accepted formula of church and church-hall big enough for the immediate parish, no longer a positive element in the plan? Obviously there are dangers to the Church as soon as it is seen as primarily a social organization, like some of the examples given in *The Organization Man*. Thus from one pastor, '... you get what we're after – a sense of community. We pick on the more useful parts of the doctrine to that end;' or, from a bulletin of the Protestant Council of New York City, 'In a very real sense we are "selling" religion ... can we not extend an invitation, in effect: "Come and enjoy our privileges, meet good friends, see what God can do for you."' This is certainly not what I mean from any point of view. What I am suggesting is that a community needs a purpose, and that the Church ought to be able to supply it; and that it is possible to have a community centre informed by the presence of the church itself as the chief element in the complex.

Ideas of this sort have been tried on the Continent by various denominations; they involve more than the church and its hall, and require a lot of thought in the preparation of the planning and architectural brief. A good example of this happening in an existing parish is the recent work of the Dominican fathers in Newcastle upon Tyne, where, with great ingenuity on a restricted piece of ground, a well-organized social centre and club, with very diverse facilities, has been built on the church site. There is now the whole complex of church, school and community centre, in a parish which has undergone considerable migration of its people; and its range of influence through social contact is by no means restricted to the old geographical parish.

Immediately this raises the further question of the size of such a centre and of the church itself. This would presumably vary for different denominations; in some cases it might be desirable to concentrate on one such complex rather than three or four little churches, and provide the facilities, for old and young, that could build it into society, and which smaller units could not economically support. Does this in its turn suggest the complementary need of smaller centres of worship: almost of the activities of the 'house church' to which some ministers in the Church of Scotland have been devoting considerable energy in recent years?

Such questions are surely important if the Church is to be seen as a real unit in society. They have yet to be answered, and they may not even be the right questions. One thing at least seems to me clear: that in the present building of churches, no quantity of crosses, fleches or campaniles, no collection of endeavours to make odd-looking buildings so bizarre that they must be churches, will make up for establishing a vital function in the total synopsis of a town or city. In the book quoted earlier, Robert A. Nisbet states this emphatically 'In the contemporary world the continuing reality of religion as an integrating force will depend on the successful fusion of religious impulse and religious organization with all forms of social life that implicate the lives of human beings. However fundamental and ultimately justifying are the private devotions within religion, the success of religion among large numbers of people, like the success of any structure of human faith, depends on the degree to which spiritual creed and values are integrated with *associative* purposes.'[11]

Will a modern church architecture ever be significant if it lacks an essential unity with its physical and social environment?

[11] Op. cit., p. 244.

10. Architectural Seriousness

LANCE WRIGHT

Churches in this post-war period present a peculiar problem to the architectural historian. As a group they are remarkably homogeneous. It is really not possible to detect any consistent difference between a Roman Catholic, an Anglican and a Free Church building. They seem inspired by the same motives: by a persistent yearning for modernity coupled with an equally persistent yearning for the past; and all are profoundly unsatisfactory.

This unsatisfactoriness is not to be explained simply in architectural terms. Clearly we are not up against some technical or design deficiency which is exclusively the fault of architects. We have to deal with some massive psychological defect which originates with those who use and commission churches, and which is so deep-seated and powerful that they communicate it to the architects whom they commission. If we can overcome this defect at the client end, then church architecture will develop naturally. If we cannot overcome it, then no *architectural* change can do any good, for no architect can make a living by giving his clients something which they are psychologically incapable of wanting.

It is unfashionable in architectural circles to speak either of architectural language or of architectural style. Of language, because to the good architect of today modern architecture, if such a thing exists, is no more than the unconscious result of applying a certain method to the problems of design; and the use of the word language suggests the existence of a set of ready-made 'words' which can be chosen deliberately to express this, that and the other. Of style, because style suggests to the architect the peculiar aberrations of the nineteenth century, when style meant a superficial architectural clothing which could be put at will over a relatively unchanging shell of building. Modern architecture, it is pointed out, is so different from any previous manner of building or designing that it is not to be included in this bracket at all.

Architectural Seriousness

Again, the good architect of the nineteen-sixties no longer insists on the revolutionary nature of modern architecture. This is partly because it is no longer necessary to do so. Over the greater part of the field of building the battle for the new method of designing has been won. But also because by insisting on the antithesis between modern and traditional methods of constructing and designing, an architect may find himself rejecting a traditional solution when it is in fact the right one.

For the architect all of these instinctive rejections are correct: of style, of language and of revolution; for all of these things are concerned with the effect his work has on other people, and for him to worry about them unduly would lead to self-consciousness. But it is sometimes important to remember that though these may be un-unprofitable realities for the architect to dwell upon, they are real nonetheless. The consistent application of scientific method to building does beget a consistent 'language' of forms; style need not be something superficial but is the inescapable result of any activity, the architectural revolution (and the technical revolution which accompanies it) is a formidable and continuing reality which is only beginning to have its effect on environment. Furthermore all of these things represent the way in which architecture strikes the intelligent, thinking beholder who does not happen to be familiar with the detailed manner in which architects view their task.

This essay therefore is written primarily for this intelligent, thinking beholder who has happened to live outside the specialized closed world of the architect, and for this reason it deals freely and unashamedly with these concepts of language, style and revolution. This approach seems the more necessary in this context of church building because the clergy as a group have hardly been reached by the ideas which have shaped modern architecture: a fact which is more the architect's fault than theirs.

From the point of view of architectural language, the Church today is the odd man out. There are, of course, a great many new churches which are considered by their designers and by their congregations to be very modern. But when you look at them carefully – or, indeed, when you look at them at all – you see that they are not of the same architectural family as other modern buildings. They have some affinities, of course; but it seems that architects designing a church, even good architects, feel obliged to infuse into their design certain overtones which are altogether contrary to the logic of modern architecture, and this produces a curious effect of silliness, of unseriousness. These fatal overtones arise because designers feel that they must bring in certain associations, usually historical associations, both in plan and in detailing. Questioned, they say 'but a church must *look* like a church mustn't it?' But however understandable and worthy the intention, the broad effect is that of a kind of architectural baby talk, analogous to the Gothic script in which *Ye Olde Tea-Shoppe* used to be written.

Needless to say, departures from seriousness are not all historical. There is another opposite and even more fatal departure, prompted by the desire to be modern in the fashionable sense. This, God knows, is a menace in its own right; but the other, the historical association, is the more widespread trouble; and if in this essay I concentrate upon it, this does not mean that I am unaware of the other opposing defect.

I know that many people feel that this is a small evil, at the worst a foible; but I would suggest that it is the outward reflection of a very great evil indeed. An evil not merely at the level of taste and culture, but at the level of morals and Christian understanding one which might be compared with the failure of Christians to respond adequately in the nineteenth century to the terrible social conditions engendered by the Industrial Revolution. It is the reflection of a moral failure, but it is at one and the same time the reflection of a theological failure, a failure to grasp the bearing of Christian belief on the problems of human culture.

Be this as it may, it is important to recognize from the start how weighty are the reasons which are often urged for preserving some measure of historical reminiscence in church building. My object in rehearsing these reasons is not to knock them down, still less to ridicule them, but to provide a realistic starting point to our enquiry. I will merely state them now and will return to them again later in my essay.

First then is the strong feeling for tradition among Christian people. Christianity is itself traditional, being handed down from one generation to another, even though its truths are verifiable by each. Ought not this fact to be instantly visible in church building? Allied to this sense of tradition is the sense of unity with past generations. All Christians are gathered together into a unity which is expressed for those in the Catholic communion by the doctrine of the mystical body of Christ. This unity is constantly being added to as each new generation is born, so that – to change the metaphor – the Christian community is like a net which is continually being woven at one end, and as it is woven is let down into the water: the water of death. We who belong to the little fringe which has not yet dipped below the surface are linked to the farthest members, to St Augustine, to the early martyrs and to the apostles themselves, by links which are even more strong and more certain than those which link us to our own parents. A Christian generation therefore is not alone but is one with all the others. In this perspective anything which looks like novelty seems out of place.

Again, there is a sort of functional traditionalism which points out that an evident continuity in the appearance of a church is as much a part of its material function as good planning and good hearing conditions, drawing people into a right frame of mind: 'a church must look like a church.'

Next comes that strong sense that a church is different from all other buildings, because what goes on inside it is different. It is, as it were, a sort of hiatus in environment. all else is secular, but within the four walls of the church only eternity matters. If this is so, then it is not surprising that the Church is odd man out in the architectural scene; it is wholly proper that it should be so.

Those who take this view go on to question the ability of the language of modern architecture to express the kind of thoughts that the Church must express. There are two lines here. There are those who say that our architecture is immature and incapable of expressing *any* thoughts properly: and there are those who say that it is designed only to express secular thoughts. Rejection of the monumental and severance from the visual tradition of the past together make it impossible to express that *time dimension* which is so essential a part of Christian perception. Comfort, convenience, even that kind of exaltation which comes from certain applications of modern architecture, all of these are very well in their place, but they are irrelevant in the business of church building. I will return to these points later. It is sufficient for the moment to say that all are of weight.

We are all conscious of living in a period of profound cultural change. This change has been maturing for a long time, if we read time in the human scale. People living one hundred or one hundred and fifty years ago were also conscious of this change, though as their relation to it was different from ours, it struck them rather differently.

We are always told to beware of generalizations, but they have their uses nonetheless, and as a generalization we may say that, whereas the last great age, that of the Renaissance, was characterized by the discovery of man, of man as a free, moral person living within a creation made for him; the succeeding age is characterized by the discovery of matter. I do not wish to defend this generalization now, but I think it is unexceptionable: in all that has to do with the Renaissance, man is so central a figure: the protection of his freedom of action, of his personality, of his liberty is the aim of all the period's arrangements and institutions. From that golden discovery we have passed to a second discovery which has proved even more momentous in its practical results, though less flattering: we have discovered the stuff of the created universe; and in discovering this we have discovered how intimate is the bond between man and the matter of which he is made, how close is the link between spirit and matter, even in so human a prerogative as the exercise of the will.

As you would expect, this discovery of matter has had a great effect on Christian thought and practice. Christian truth has often been likened to a statue part buried in the sand All is *there* from the beginning: but all is not equally evident: it needs the accidents of time – wind to blow the sand away and man's own exertions in excavation – to bring the statue fully to light. We have all experienced, I think, how some change in human circumstances has given added point to some passage in the scriptures which hitherto meant very little to us.

The effect of this discovery of the intimacy and continuity between mind and matter on Christian belief and practice has been to throw into relief an aspect of our religion which we have always known, but which we have perhaps slurred over, given insufficient attention to I mean the fact that God himself, in the person of his Son chose to enter his material creation. This gives to matter a dignity and importance which it would not otherwise possess and which religions which know no incarnation could not for a moment recognize. This means that the world of matter is not something completely external to man, an inanimate lump on which he exerts his will and which is of no intrinsic account, but it is continuous with him. his destiny and its are intimately joined

I think that this truth has always meant something to Christians, for in a sense the mere fact of western civilization is a testimony to it; but for the present generation it means something very much more precise than it did for earlier generations. For us, human institutions, human arrangements, the human arts and sciences, are seen to be far more relevant in the work of redemption than earlier generations had ever supposed.

It has led, to quote one example, to the great concern for sociology. Where Christians of an earlier generation were content that their social duties should stop short at doing good to their immediate neighbour, today's Christians see that it is really much more difficult than this, that they must find for social problems the technical solution which will reflect our Lord's teaching. For this it is not enough to have a good heart, you must have a good head also. If the intelligence is lacking, Christian activity is inclined to be rather disappointing, particularly when viewed from without. The comfortable Victorian gave sixpence to the ragged crossing sweeper. It did not occur to him that the only sufficient act of charity would have been to devise a society in which crossing sweepers, if there had to be such, were no longer ragged. Because he did not see this he has had a bad press ever since and his act of charity has been interpreted by the world as hypocrisy (which it almost certainly was not). This insufficient religious attitude of his has been stigmatized for our generation by the phrase (which I think is fairly general among all communions): a disincarnate Christianity.

A disincarnate Christianity, as I take it, is one in which, though the intentions are right, those intentions are not allied to a proper grasp of the actual human situation. Insufficiently alert to the present, people go on performing the practices and viewing life in the perspective of earlier times.

Let us be fair and admit that, to achieve a Christianity which is fully incarnate requires an immense effort of the intelligence. Christians brought up in the religious traditions of the Renaissance – whether Protestant or Catholic – have never been really accustomed to use their intellect on matters to do with religion. There is little doubt that the flight of the intelligentsia from the Church in the late nineteenth and the twentieth centuries has been due to their rejection of this disincarnate Christianity, which is in itself so immensely unattractive, alike in its fruits and in the futile claims which it makes on its practitioners.

We have then a concept of Christianity which is not confined to faith and morals but which is constantly pressing outwards, animating and forming the structures of the temporal order. The spirit of Christ, working through all believers, penetrates the world of matter, creating as it does so an environment which reflects the Redeemer. Needless to say, this concept has its dangers. If a disincarnate Christianity is a consequence of unawareness of it, clericalism is the consequence of being aware that Christianity must affect the temporal order but of not understanding the mode in which it must do so. We think of clericalism as a political evil because it has occurred most evidently in relation to political structures. But in truth it is an intellectual evil and can affect any sphere. Also, despite its name, it is not by any means confined to the clergy. It arises because of an inability to see, or an unwillingness to respect, the natural intrinsic values which reside in the material creation. In his desire to 'win all things for Christ' the clerical seeks to impose forms borrowed from the Christian past. Thus in the field of politics he will seek to impose political forms – eighteenth-century paternalism, for instance – which no longer apply. In fact the Christian can never foretell what will be the final visible result of Christ's action in any sphere. For him, for the Christian, it is an unconscious action; for he is the tool, though the intelligent tool, in the hand of another. He goes on in faith, doing his best according to his lights. He is all the time open, as we say: prepared to receive truth from the most unlikely sources. Newman wrote in that superb hymn of his Anglican days · 'I do not ask to see the distant scene, one step enough for me.'

If we are agreed on the importance of this action in temporal structures and if this is the mode of action, where then does architecture come in?

Few Christians today would deny the significance of sociology in the recreation of a Christian society. But equally few accept the importance of architecture in such a recreation. The reason for this of course is that architecture is still thought of in terms of style, as something stuck on to environment to please a few well-educated but not very nice people. It is not yet seen, though it is fast beginning to be seen, as a significant field of human betterment. It is not yet realized, though once more it is beginning to be realized, how much the quality of life stands to gain or lose by it. And of course such awareness as there is, is still only an awareness of the grosser defects of our everyday surroundings. Architecture has hit society mainly in the realization that there is not enough of it – there is not enough housing, for instance, or in the aspect of physical inconvenience, as in the disorder of our streets or the grotesque nuisance of the wireless next door. Until these nuisances have been overcome, the man in the street must be forgiven if he cannot look beyond the problems of material deficiency to the problems of visual quality, of architecture as satisfying, not the senses only, but also and particularly the mind.

But as this stage has not yet been reached, the architect urging the importance of architectural language is always at a disadvantage. Yet in the end the formation of a full and coherent architectural language is even more important to wellbeing than the sorting out of our physical problems of heat, light, sound and space planning. For only such a language can give us an environment which will reflect all that we Christians know about man and his destiny, and will use to the full all that we are discovering about matter.

It is my contention that the pursuit of architecture, like the pursuit of social justice, of which it is an aspect, is something which is enjoined upon us by our own religious attitude. This of itself deserves to give a new turn to church architecture. For to persevere with a separate language for church building as we now seem to be doing must abort totally the Christian effort in this field; it prevents Christ from entering into architecture and from exerting his influence upon it. Apart from this, it is a nice point whether the continuance of historical reminiscence in church-building is a hangover from the disincarnate Christianity of the nineteenth century, which we so strongly repudiate, or whether it arises from clericalism, from the desire to impose Christian memories on the face of secular architecture. In all probability it is an obscure and varying mixture of the two.

As our society grows older we develop a faculty of standing outside our civilization and of looking critically at it; and no aspect of our civilization is easier to look at in this way than that of architecture.

Towards a Church Architecture

Architecture is a revealing aspect of human activity because it offers visible and relatively lasting signs of a series of human decisions. For architecture and building is essentially a subject of deliberate choice, if only because the things made are among the most costly of all human artefacts.

Architecture is the subject of choice in respect of the shapes of the spaces which are to be enclosed, the materials which are to be used, and – in this last lies the distinction, if distinction there be, between architecture and building – the effect the finished work is to produce on those who see it. It is the choice made in respect of the third of these which is the most important and which determines what we call style. Style is in part personal to the designer and in part corporate, being a personal interpretation of ideas which are (usually) common to a whole society. Major changes in style – as from the Gothic to the Renaissance and from the Renaissance to the modern – are the outcome of a profound change in man's approach to the problems of life. These changes do not originate with architects (though architects may well share in their origins), they originate among scholars and thinkers. The first suggestion to remodel life on the classical heritage was put forward by Petrarch, Boccaccio and others in the second quarter of the fifteenth century. The change in architecture, when it came, was only a fulfilment, though a very important fulfilment, of a cultural change which had already been decided upon What we call modern architecture, too, is no more than the application to environment of the idea of remodelling life by the application of scientific method, which had been decided upon in principle at least since the beginning of the century.

Architecture is the dress of a society and the decision to make a really decisive change in it is made by society itself, as represented in its leaders, not by those whose business it is to tailor it.

The problem of church building turns on the attitude of the Church towards this dress of society's, on her relationship to society and on her attitude towards the ideas which have led society to dress as it has. This possibility, for the Church to take a different architectural dress from the society in which she is set, is something peculiarly Christian and derives from her theological position. If she were a theocracy, like Islam and indeed like most primitive religions in which religion, politics and culture were necessarily one, this distinction would be unthinkable. But the Church is in the world, but not of it. She is a free agent. She is under no compulsion to follow the world in this matter of architecural dress; if she does so, it is because she chooses to do so.

If there is no doubt about the Church's ability to stand apart from the world in the matter of architecture, it is also true that the nature of her mission is such that is it unusual for her to do so. Her mission is to inform human society, meaning by this at once to mould and to inspire. Other factors being equal, this is best done by her being within rather than without; and the practical effect of adopting a separate architectural dress is to place her without· to create a tension which makes her work more difficult. At the time of the Renaissance it might have been expected that the Church would have insisted on retaining her mediaeval architectural language. After all, this was a language which had been evolved chiefly through the impetus of church building. Classical humanism had much in its programme which was objectionable to Christians, and a proportion of its advocates looked on it as a liberation from Christian morality and sentiment. The Church could easily have decided that she wished to retain the mediaeval architectural language. Something of this sort did in fact happen in the Orthodox community, but in the west, both in the Church herself and among those who protested against her, the changeover was made as rapidly and as completely as technical skill would permit. There was no deliberate harking back. If conservative voices were raised in protest, there is almost no record of them.

Looking back, it is easy to see that this was a wise decision Had she decided to keep to mediaeval architecture the Church would have been visibly cut off from the intellectual life of the time in a very important particular. The church (regarded this time as a building) would have become the odd man out in the environment, and a tension would have been set up in the heart of western society which in the long run could have been more damaging than that generated by a divided Christendom.

What happened at the Renaissance established that in the western Church architectural form is not traditional. This is important in view of what happened at the next major architectural changeover, which took place at the relinquishment of classical humanism and the taking up of scientific method. This has been a slower change and much more complex. Its beginnings date from the Industrial

Towards a Church Architecture

Revolution and it is only visibly complete in our time, one hundred and fifty years later. The changeover has been marked, in architecture, by the rise and long continuance of romanticism. For the first one hundred and twenty years of the breakdown of the classical system no one thought of applying the new mode of thinking to the technique of designing buildings. In this one department of life – and in this one only – the quarrying from the past went on, but substituting for the single classical source the whole range of historical building. There was no sufficient excuse for this latter-day quarrying, for the people of the nineteenth century did not really believe that the people whose architectural dress they borrowed possessed a human wisdom which had since been lost. The underlying cause of this seems to have been a disinclination for the more difficult task of rethinking the problem of building and environment; for the motive, in client and architect, for choosing one historical style rather than another was usually no more cogent or profound than the motive for choosing a certain fancy dress in which to go to a ball.

It is in this social context that, in northern countries, mediaeval architecture was chosen as the most fitting dress for a church. In the one person most associated with this choice, A. W. N. Pugin, the choice itself was respectable, for he was wholly convinced that the entire mediaeval way of life was ripe for restoration; but this conviction of his was not shared by the hundreds and thousands of architects and clergy who used Gothic, or a reminiscence of it, for church building in the course of the next five generations.

Five generations is a long time: things done for so long obtain a false aura of tradition. This was doubtless the reason why, in about 1920, when ordinary scientific methods of thinking were first applied to architecture, church people were less willing than others to contemplate a change, and why today, forty years later, they still regard some reminiscence of the Gothic system as an essential mark of a building which is to be a church.

It is the belief of the writer that the choice of architecture for a church is a more serious matter at the pastoral level than it is commonly thought to be. We are now passing through an era of what might be called vestigial historicism in church building. Churches are now being built in great numbers which are believed by clergy and congregations to be modern, that is, framed in the universal language derived from the application of scientific method to design, but which are not so at all. What has happened in these churches is that modern building methods have been used to simulate effects characteristic of historical building. At first sight this seems an innocent, if not a praiseworthy quality, inspired as it doubtless is by the desire to be traditional, a response to a widespread (and in principle justified) feeling that 'a church should look like a church'.

It cannot be said too often that the choice of architectural dress is not a matter of 'taste' but is an indication of the attitude of mind of the building user. Today this turns chiefly on the acceptance or non-acceptance of scientific method. The continued use of an historical architecture, even of a faint reminiscence of it, is a sign of non-acceptance and of a reversion to that nineteenth-century romanticism which prefers to baulk the issue and to escape to fantasy. We have already seen that, in the nineteenth century, church people were not alone in choosing this escape; but it is important that they should not be too long in relinquishing it. For the kind of church to which they have grown accustomed during the last few generations is not traditional, nor is it traditional for Christians to be shy of cultural change. Today, acceptance of the importance of a close attention to fact is a mark of seriousness in every walk of life. Those who let themselves be guided simply by tradition, who claim to know the facts without having attended to them, or, worse still, who decline to notice them when they are brought to their attention, all of these are rightly thought to be unserious and therefore undeserving of influence or respect. The continued use of historical architecture, even in a vestigial form, is the outward sign of an attitude of mind which is lacking in seriousness in this sense. It is objectionable therefore, partly because it gives a false idea of Christian belief, but chiefly because the attitude thus represented makes impossible that profound reassessment of Christian life which our change of culture has made necessary.

Architects today like to insist that what they have to give is not a style, in the sense of the previous architectural styles; and they have some justification for this, for style has come to mean a change in outward appearances only. Though the difference between a Gothic building and a Renaissance building seems great, it is very much less than the difference between a Renaissance building and a modern

Towards a Church Architecture

building. No technical revolution accompanied the introduction of the Renaissance comparable to that which has accompanied the introduction of modern architecture. A building today is in a real sense a different sort of object, not merely from the buildings of thirty years ago but from all previous buildings. It is made differently, it produces a different environment, above all, it exists in a different social context. Traditionally it has been assumed that the client knows what he wants in the way of accommodation. So long as building was an unchanging product this was a reasonable assumption. But now that the techniques of construction and of the control of climate are so evidently on the move, the assumption is no longer reasonable. Several years ago Sir John Summerson pointed out that the essence of modern architecture lies in the importance which is given to the programme, that is, to what architects call the brief. If the process of design as a whole is the application of exact method to building, then this process must begin by reassessing what the client thinks he wants This reassessment of the brief is the most important single element in the design process, and the one which leads to the most surprising changes. It was this rethinking of the brief which changed our concept of a school from the overgrown Georgian mansion which it was in 1939 to the very different and far more apt school that we know today. This change, it will be noticed, has not merely meant a change in the environment of education, but a change in education itself. For this rethinking of what is to be done inside a building is of immense social importance. It is by far the greatest good which architecture has to give to society in this generation. A concept of modern architecture which only means the building of a fashionable shell round a pattern of behaviour which has not been re-thought from first principles, is something much less than the thing itself.

If the reassessment of the plan is at the heart of the modern architectural process, there still remains the question of expression. Architectural expression is commonly thought to be a matter of taste, but it is more accurately thought of as the reflection of certain perceptions of reality. It is perhaps still too early to say with certainty what are the characteristic perceptions which lie behind modern architectural expression, for some which we can now observe may prove to be ephemeral. But those which are founded upon the changed circumstances of building are likely to prove permanent, and, because they have a direct application to the problem of expression in church building, it is worth naming them here.

The three marks of modern architectural expression are then: *the sense of the provisional, the sense of economy* and the *sense of the continuing nature of space*.

The first of these, the sense of the provisional, seems to arise because the rapid rate of change in modern life has compelled the architect of today to take notice of the dimension of time in a way that has not been noticed before. Earlier generations of architects have always built 'as though for eternity' and this has led them to think of a building, not as something for passing use, but as a monument. This has been expressed in a great many ways: in the search for monumentality (i.e. grandeur) as we use the word today, but also in the use of moulding to give sculptural importance to architectural form. Today we have witnessed an unprecedented flight from monumentality. We have, after all, experienced the truth that man's building needs are not so unchanging as they were thought to be, and that to spend time and energy in providing this lasting-for-ever quality is to provide something which is not only unwanted but which may quickly prove an incubus. Above all, this search for the monumental no longer corresponds to reality as people see it today. To the Victorians a thousand years, the maximum life of a building, was a very long time indeed: to ourselves, brought up on a geological time scale, it is nothing at all and is not worth bothering about.

I have at home a copy of the Douai Old Testament of 1609: and this concludes, like so many bibles of the day, with a chronological table. This table states, with that confidence which only an exclusive preoccupation with theology can beget, that there were exactly 4034 years between the creation and the birth of our Lord. We are inclined to forget, I think, that it is in this cosy, human-scale time-perspective that our inborn desire for monumentality has been begotten and nurtured. For, if this is the order of the world's duration, then it is not altogether illusory to think of a building as lasting 'to the world's end'. It was an ideal well worth striving for. We know now, of course, that the world's time scale is not like that at all: and, if we are now millions of years from the beginning, why should we not be millions of years from the end? This violent change in the time perspective has begun to exert, and will continue to exert, a profound effect on our religious psychology. Some people find it infinitely distressing. But, if it leaves man poised between vast abysses at both ends, it also has the effect of making the birth of our Lord relatively so much closer. We have been taught to think of the incarnation as something which happened a very long time ago, and of ourselves as the latter day survivors of something very old. In fact, of course, the incarnation was only yesterday and we would be wise – and justified – in thinking of Christianity as something only in its beginnings. We must never forget that the sources of architectural form lie deep in human psychology and are not to be understood by reference only to design. For me, this hankering for monumentality is a wholly understandable atavism which must not be allowed to spoil our new church architecture. That our vernacular cannot produce this effect with conviction is really a sign of strength, not of weakness.

It is important to notice that, with all these marks of architectural style, we are dealing with the choice of a symbol, not with the choice of a real attribute. This sense of the provisional which is so persistent a quality in good modern buildings has no direct relationship to their actual life; some of them may last very much longer than buildings conceived as monuments. It is expressed in many ways, but particularly in the preference for the diagram, for informality and in the resolute exclusion of sculptural form from architectural surfaces.

The second mark of modern architecture is the sense of economy. This, like the first, contrasts sharply with the attitude to building which we have inherited from the Renaissance. Throughout the Renaissance and further back still, architecture and building have been associated with the idea of dominion. Though funds may often have been short, the objective, conscious or unconscious, has always been to make the building as magnificent as possible. The sudden retreat from this objective which we have experienced in this generation springs from a great social change, but also from a far more accurate perception by the architect of the nature of building and of the service he has to give. World population has increased, the needs of each person in terms of cubic foot of building *per capita* have also greatly increased, and though building methods have improved there hangs over the whole field of building design a sense that society will not get what it needs unless economy is the order of the day. Once again it is interesting to notice how a practical and general consideration like this has become a principle of design requiring symbolic expression even in jobs where expense is little object. Economy, it must be noticed, does not mean cheapness but value for money; and in terms of design it means simplicity and asceticism.

If the first mark of modern architecture derives from a sense of the historic reality and the second from the sense of the economic reality, the third derives from a sense of the spatial reality, from a sense of the continuous nature of space. This again contrasts strongly with a traditional architectural instinct, which is to enclose space, to cut off a room, an interior, from the surrounding spaces: to create a world apart. Up to now the heavy, opaque enclosure has been a technical necessity and it is perhaps true to say that the new ideal of openness and spatial freedom is little more than a celebration of the fact that this necessity is being fast removed. But it also corresponds to a change in outlook, an expression of the fact that as the world and human society unifies, the motive for privacy diminishes. Architecturally, this mark is expressed in a preference for planes and the reduction of framing and surrounds to a minimum.

The three marks which I have been describing do not represent the whims of a few individuals or of a professional caste, but the conviction, the way of seeing things, of a whole society. Because of this, it is to be expected that there should be some correlation between these visual convictions, as we might call them, and the way in which people see religious truth and interpret their religious duties. The content of the *depositum fidei* does not change, but understanding of it develops considerably with humanity's passage through time, and this development brings now one, now another doctrine into special prominence, throws up a special religious imagery appropriate to each generation or group of generations. There is no case for thinking that the imagery appropriate to one generation is more true, in an absolute sense, than the imagery of another; but equally it is unquestionable that the imagery proper to a generation is true *for* that generation and that the continuance of an earlier generation's imagery leads automatically to formalism. In the Church of the Counter-Reformation, Catholics tended to see their religious duties on the analogy with a subject's duties towards his sovereign. This arose in part as a natural outcome of the Renaissance orientation on the temporal prince, in part also because the upheaval caused by the Protestant Reformation made this kind of allegiance necessary. It goes without saying that this was, and is, an inherently possible imagery and one which the circumstances of the time made almost inescapable, but it is very different from the imagery commonly in use among Catholics today. Today Christ is seen not as dominating or seeking to dominate, but as informing The Christian people are not characteristically seen as an army, but as a leaven. For Catholics, since the main opposition, as it were, has shifted from non-Catholic Christians to those who have no Christian background at all, attention has turned away from apologetics and towards the need to re-create modern society on a Christian pattern. In other words, if architectural practice and modes of thought have changed, Christian practice and modes of thought have changed also; and though the circumstances prompting these changes are different, it is no coincidence that both are in the same direction.

The values which architecture represents are values in the natural order, but like all such, are capable of receiving a supernatural meaning. The idea of monumentality is of itself of no particular religious significance, but it is capable of receiving religious significance (e.g. as something enduring, like the word of God), and in fact much of our notion of what a church should be is based upon it. The question arises of whether this preference for monumentality is not related to the fact that earlier generations had a very different notion of time to our own. Christian symbolism of the church (regarded either as a building or as an institution) is exceedingly rich and it is surely inevitable and proper that Christians of each generation should pick on symbols which have a particular meaning for them because they correspond to some truth of the natural order of which they are particularly aware. Thus it is that the three marks of modern architecture mentioned above correspond with ideas which have a special religious meaning for Christians of this generation. The changeableness of things, of which people of today are so deeply aware, is paralleled for the Christian in the idea of the people of God as on pilgrimage, with no lasting dwelling place.

The second mark, the idea of economy, has an exact parallel in the spirit of poverty which, though a reality to all Christian generations, is a compelling reality in the present owing to the great concern for social justice.

The third mark, that of spatial continuity, is at first sight the most difficult to parallel, but it corresponds, surely, to the idea of the leaven. The parable of the leaven assumes that the leaven is one with and visibly undistinguished from the lump. For the first time since the days of the early Church the laity are called to put into effect an apostolate which has always been theirs, but which has been latent This means a considerable psychological change, both in the individual Christian and in the Christian community, requiring the adoption of a policy of openness, of emphasising the unity between Christians and other people rather than the difference. For a people pursuing such a policy it would be natural to adopt an ordinary secular architecture so as to make the Church one with the secular environment and to give the church building some measure of openness to the outside.

The case therefore for the adoption by the Church of an architecture formed by the use of the same method which is used for architecture in general is, first, that this method leads naturally to a re-assessment of needs, which is in itself so valuable a discipline; second, that the visual language which is the unconscious product of the use of this method is the only language capable of expressing the religious ideas characteristic of this generation of Christians.

We are now in a position to return to the arguments which I stated at the beginning of this essay in favour of continuity in church design, of the retention of historical associations and of the inability of secular architecture to fill the bill.

First there is the question of tradition. The first point that must be made on this head is that there is no formal architectural tradition in Christianity. This was proved, beyond all question, by what happened at the Renaissance. If ever it could be claimed that an architectural style was hallowed by Christian use, this could be claimed for Gothic. Yet when secular architecture changed, from the late fifteenth century, Gothic was shed without any difficulty at all. Though it would have been very easy to think up very worthy Christian objections to the revival of pagan architecture, it is striking that, so far as I know, there is no record of arguments of this kind having been put forward in ecclesiastical circles; and if they were put forward, they certainly were not listened to. It is also interesting to notice that in the use of classical architecture for church building there was no gothicizing distortion: if you used the corinthian order for the nave of the church it was the same corinthian order which you used for the market hall. Deliberate archaism, the desire to infuse an ecclesiastical flavour into church building is not therefore a part of the Christian tradition, but is something quite peculiar to ourselves This does not mean, I think, that there is no tradition in church building, but that it is a tradition of a kind which is not to be conveyed by the retention of externals. It is the kind of tradition which was so well expressed by Jean Jaurès when he said in the French Parliament 'It is in flowing down to the sea that the river is true to its source'. Each generation of Christians is imbued with the same thoughts, the same feelings, begotten by the same eternal truths. But human society changes, and it is the Christian instinct to encourage, not to resist this change and in any case to share in it, because it is only by so doing that Christians can influence society for good. For this reason the same instincts, the same truths, beget in the Christian totally different expressions at different times. So that when it comes to architectural form, the tradition is likely to be one of change, not of immobility. If therefore there is a tradition of Christian architecture it is a tradition of the acceptance of the current vernacular.

This does not quite answer the point of those who call for *visual continuity* in church architecture I think that for nine-tenths of history this condition will be fulfilled, but that when the reasons for it are grave enough, Christian communities will accept an abrupt change. The liturgical renewal, for instance, evidently presents a sufficiently grave reason for changing the plan shape, and it is my contention that the change in our ideas of the scope of Christianity which I have been outlining is a sufficiently grave reason for a change in architectural language. Some practical evidence for this is afforded by wartime experience when services had often to be held in extempore, secular surroundings. The effect of this was not to destroy but to heighten the impact and meaning of the liturgy. This must not, of course, be taken as an argument in favour of the particular architectural qualities of the Nissen hut and the NAAFI canteen. But it does show that for today's people the Christian rites become more impressive and full of meaning when they are shorn of a specifically ecclesiastical atmosphere.

A word must be said here of that very strong body of opinion which says that a church must be *different* from secular buildings because what goes on inside is different. This argument seems to go back to the old Renaissance and classical antithesis between sacred and profane. Because the ancient world did not know the incarnation it made so much more of this antithesis than the Christian view can really justify. But this antithesis was carried on into Renaissance religion, reaching a sort of paroxysm in nineteenth-century France, when the Church of France took such a remarkable and misconceived stand against secular society. For Christians of our own epoch the distinction, though real enough, is no longer of critical importance. For us it is not the distinction between sacred and profane which matters, but their continuity. For our generation has come to realize in a special way that the material universe and all that man does are capable of what Teilhard de Chardin calls divinization. Therefore the driving motive for this visible distinction between the Church and the rest of environment has disappeared.

We now come to the point of those who say that our architecture is insufficiently formed to be used by the Church, and of those who take the more radical view that it is inherently unsuitable. The second of these two objections is the more important. I am convinced that when this charge is made the real point at issue is that of monumentality. Up till now the church – in common with almost all secular building – has always been thought of as a monument, as something that is going to last for ever. Though modern buildings, if they are maintained, are probably no less durable than ancient buildings, this ideal of indefinite longevity is no longer held and this fact has had a profound influence on architectural form. A good modern building has an undeniable sense of impermanence and transience, and it is this, I think, that is felt to be at war with the fundamental aims of church building. You often meet with this, as it were, in reverse. Time and again I have found myself in a new church which the designer evidently meant to be a 'modern church'. And asking myself: why is this church outside the family of modern buildings? What is it that *grates*? I have reached the conclusion that the trouble all along has been that the architect, in response to the known requirements of his clients, has tried to build monumentality in: planes are less clear than they ought to be, mouldings abound where they ought not. Architectural style is a unity, however much it may vary in its personal expression. To break this unity by inserting overtones from an earlier age produces a result which is ugly in itself and – what matters most – fails absolutely to touch the heart.

Towards a Church Architecture

If the practical lesson of all that I have been saying is that we must use the pure vernacular in church building, that architects designing a church must not choose forms which they would not choose if they were not designing a church: my argument for this has not been based on what the French call fear of missing the bus-ism, but on the argument that there must be a concordance between our architectural approach and our religious psychology, and that since the latter has changed quite startlingly during the last half generation – and is certain to change still more startlingly during the next – we must expect our church architecture to change quite startlingly too.

For we are, of course, living in an *exceptionally privileged age*. New knowledge about matter has created a new religious situation, enabling us, as I believe, to roll up the ghastly religious controversies of the sixteenth century. I was greatly relieved to find, in writing this essay, that it was really no longer necessary to think in terms of religious differences – to keep interspersing my remarks with 'I as a Roman Catholic think this', 'you as Wesleyans or Anglicans will think that . . .' Though the theologians have still to take their time, at the level of culture and society Christian unity is already achieved. And that is something for a start.

Again, we Christians are so aware of the unity of Christian doctrine over the years that we forget sometimes how greatly our response to this doctrine changes. Take, for instance, our idea of the apostolate, of Christ's action in the world of men. When the great missionaries of the seventeenth century landed on the coasts of America, Asia or Africa, a man-of-war commonly stood out in the bay and they surged ashore to the crackle of small arms. It seemed natural and proper in those days that Christ should come accompanied by that sort of visible power, for was not the theocracy of the Middle Ages only just behind? Looking back from the vantage point of three centuries later, we see that, if their mission was only imperfectly successful, this may have been because their approach lacked something of the Gospel simplicity. It is easy for us to think this, rather priggishly, but we are right, for experience has taught us to see the action of Christ in the world as essentially *unseen* action: the leaven in the dough is the simile which exactly expresses this: the externals of things are not greatly changed by his coming, but their core and inner reality are transformed.

So it is with architecture. We often incline to think – certainly our clients think — that the building of a church is an end in itself. You take all that is best and make a masterpiece. Certainly a church is an important object in its own right. But there is another aspect to this. For the building of a church also offers a point of entry for Christian perceptiveness into architecture itself. We have all seen how modern architecture arose as a way of building utilitarian structures chiefly, and how greatly it was enriched and humanized by the mere fact of its being used after the war for schools. How greatly architecture would be enriched again if it were used on a large scale, straight-forwardly, for building churches. For we must never forget that the ultimate object of a Christian community in building a church is not merely to make a holy place for their own use, but to transform environment.

There is much lip-service paid by architects to the idea of applying scientific method to building, but as it is arduous, involving new techniques of design and in some cases a new relationship to the client, as clients are on the whole uncritical and do not know if it has been applied or not, and as the architect's own training does not fit him to do it, the thing itself is too often indefinitely postponed. A characteristic of this method is to reduce as many as possible of a building's requirements to quantitative terms. This resort to numerals is no more than a means of arriving quickly and surely at knowledge which would otherwise take a generation of trial and error to achieve, and it is made all the more necessary by the rapid rate of change in building technique At present the techniques for the ascertainment of architectural knowledge generally stop short at physiological data, at heat, light and sound, to which may be added some rather rudimentary data on space planning. These limitations are discouraging to some architects, who point out that when you have applied such techniques as we possess you are still not very far on towards the design of a building. Further, they point out, the usefulness of these techniques varies in inverse proportion to a building's symbolic content: in a utilitarian building, which is presumed to have a low symbolic content (though why this should be so is not clear), these techniques carry the architect a long way towards his solution; but in a building like a church they carry him, proportionately, only a short way. For a church (they point out) must appeal primarily to the mind, and a building which is perfect for heat, light and sound can fail deplorably as a church if it is an insufficient symbol.

Towards a Church Architecture

Ultimately this is an indefensible objection, for it implies a severance between functional performance and symbolic content which cannot be accepted. In reality, however, it reflects an understandable impatience with the shortcomings of such techniques as we now possess, which are still based on a comparatively rudimentary assessment of human needs. If we are discouraged it is sometimes as well to remind ourselves that only a very few years ago it was still thought that the only human requirement as regards heat related to air temperature, and that the only requirement as regards light related to quantity. But the really important shortcoming of the architect's existing methodology relates to user studies. Just as the rapid change in building technique has made it necessary to evolve quantitative techniques for keeping a check on physiological data, so has the no less rapid rate of social change made it necessary to evolve techniques for checking social requirements. User studies are concerned with finding out the social needs of a building type, principally but not exclusively in planning. They are pursued partly by an examination, in the light of first principles, of what is to be done inside the building, partly by a methodical recording of how certain planning arrangements in existing buildings work in practice. It is noticeable that where intensive user studies are carried out (e.g. in certain aspects of hospital design and in schools) a very different plan arrangement has emerged from that which was formerly assumed to be correct. It is noticeable also that the mere fact of user studies having been carried out has made the work of the architect better understood and appreciated and has had a tonic effect on all concerned.

It is a common opinion among church builders that the requirements of a church are well known and are unchanging. It is most unlikely that this is so. We are passing from an era of traditional Christianity to an era which, for lack of a better phrase, we may call one of Christianity by conviction. This means that Christian people, clergy and laity alike, but particularly the laity, have, in addition to their ordinary duty of living a Christian life, that of re-shaping human society. This is already reflected in a new interest on the part of the laity in the Church's liturgy and in their desire to take more than a spectator's part in it; and this in turn has led to a questioning of the validity of the long rectangular church plan. But the likelihood of change does not stop here. The fact that the Christian people are now embarked on a vast social and cultural effort brings with it the need for more accommodation. The greater part of the work of this lay apostolate is in the different secular milieux, but there is a residual demand, chiefly for office and committee room accommodation which ought to be related to the church, if not to form part of it. Modern architectural theory requires that church design should be considered not in the restricted sense of providing a place where the word of God is heard and the sacraments are received, but in the wider sense of providing for all specifically Christian activity. It is the architect's job to give form and coherence to needs which, without him, are met in a random and diffuse manner.

There are two practical difficulties which discourage user studies. The first is the difficulty of bringing those responsible for any given building type to realize that they have a common interest. The second is to persuade those who occupy existing buildings to take the time and the trouble to observe and record data. The owner of a new building feels very naturally that, so far as he is concerned, his building is a be-all and an end-all. He is not naturally inclined to the idea that it should be used as an experiment; nor, when it is built, is he inclined to spend much time recording how it works so that others may profit by his mistakes Apart from this it is beyond the means of any one client and of any one architect to bear the heavy expense of undertaking more than a very superficial investigation of what has been done before, and there is generally no machinery whereby future building owners may club together to undertake in concert investigations which will profit all of them. For this reason user studies have up to now generally been confined to large organizations with continuing building programmes. It is at best illogical for true architectural seriousness to be confined to government departments and the like, and some means must be found for furnishing lesser building users with an equivalent service. This ought not to be too difficult in respect of church building, as there is a common interest, even though church building itself may be a divided responsibility. If done on a national scale, a very small levy on each new contract would provide for the studies needed. Recording the distribution of cost, the validity of certain plan forms, the use of materials, of different systems of heating and lighting. all of these studies would provide a source of standing information on points which, though fundamental, are now left to each man's guess.

There is no doubt about the persistent whimsicality of church architecture as we know it. It is likely that the current church plan is also wrong. About the architectural language to be used there ought to be no doubt, for in the long run the vernacular of modern architecture is the only language in which today's Christian people can read their Christian thoughts. But the *content* of this church building, what is to be said in this language, is still hidden. It is hidden partly in the liturgy (in the current interpretation of which there seems much obscurity), and it is hidden partly in the Christian people themselves and in the response which they will make to the social and cultural problems of the late twentieth century. It is the Church and not the architect who must provide this content, nor can the architect discover it unaided. All he has to offer is a method It is the same method applied to architecture which everyone else is applying to life's other problems. There is nothing mysterious about it. In itself it is nothing if not prosaic, though, after a century and a half of romanticism, it may well produce unexpected results.

Appendix

ROMAN CATHOLIC DIRECTIVES FOR CHURCH BUILDING

Since the end of the Second World War two attempts have been made to formulate a statement of principle for the guidance of Roman Catholic church builders. The first, which owes a great deal to the pioneer work carried out in Germany during the 'twenties and 'thirties, led to the publication in 1947 of an official document entitled *Richtlinien für die Gestaltung des Gotteshauses aus dem Geiste der römischen Liturgie*, commonly referred to as the directives of the German Liturgical Commission. It was in fact drawn up by the distinguished liturgical scholar Dr Theodor Klauser in collaboration with the commission appointed in 1940 by the Catholic hierarchy in Germany,[1] and published by the Liturgical Institute at Trier. The document consists of a short statement of the theological and liturgical principles which should govern the design of *all* churches intended for the celebration of the liturgy according to the Roman rite, followed by twenty-one conclusions (*Folgerungen*) in which some of the architectural implications of these principles are drawn out. This is an important document which has exercised a most salutary influence on post-war church design in Germany An English translation was published in the American review *Worship* in December 1949, and this was subsequently reprinted as a pamphlet [2] The present translation is by Hildegart Nicholas, and is based on the revised text of 1955.

Ten years after the publication of the German directives the bishop of the Roman Catholic diocese of Superior, Wisconsin, set up a panel, consisting of architects, theologians, liturgists, a pastor, a canonist and an artist, for the purpose of drawing up 'a practical, concise statement of liturgical principle and architectural application intended to assist both pastor and architect in the important work of building a church'. The Superior directives were issued in 1957, and it was stressed that further study and experience would undoubtedly lead to revision and amplification.[3] The general outline of the document resembles that of the *Richtlinien*, but the architectural applications are rather more detailed.

[1] For the history of this commission, and of the Liturgical Institute, see Dr Johannes Wagner's article 'Le mouvement liturgique en Allemagne' in *La Maison-Dieu* no. 25, Les Editions du Cerf, Paris 1951, pp 75–82
[2] *Documents for Sacred Architecture*, The Liturgical Press, Collegeville, Minnesota, 1957.
[3] A revised text has recently been issued and a few of the more important changes have been incorporated in the version printed below, which is, however, substantially that of 1957.

Towards a Church Architecture

The significance of both these documents lies in the fact that they recognize the cardinal importance for church builders of theological and liturgical criteria; they start from the axiom that a church is a house for a worshipping community – not an autonomous architectural monument – and that the form of the building must be determined by the activities from which it derives its *raison d'être*. The *Richtlinien* begin by analysing the various purposes for which the people of God assemble, by distinguishing between what is central and what is peripheral. Without claiming that either of these documents provides an *adequate* statement of principle, they do at least provide church builders with a genuine liturgical brief and the approach which they embody is capable of serving as a pattern for further experiments on similar lines. Here the Church is beginning to fulfil its responsibility for providing the architect with a statement of the general requirements of the building type, such as is still unknown in most countries. This statement of general requirements is undoubtedly the most important single element in the various items which are required for the formulation of a specific programme for a particular church building.

The value of these directives for church builders is strikingly illustrated if they are compared with the wretchedly inadequate pamphlet issued as recently as 1959 by the English Church Commissioners.[4] This provides no guidance whatsoever where matters of theological or liturgical principle are concerned. In the section entitled 'Planning the Building', for example, there is no reference at all to the sacrament of baptism until one gets to paragraph twelve (out of a total of fourteen): the second of the two Gospel sacraments is mentioned only at the end of a catalogue of miscellaneous items including bells, vestries, cloakrooms, kitchens, cleaners' rooms, heating and lighting. It is hardly surprising if, in so many of our modern churches, the font appears to have been regarded as a mere piece of furniture which has been fitted into an existing building.[5]

Within the last few months it has been announced that a further statement of principle is to be prepared under the auspices of the *Centre de Pastorale Liturgique* in Paris. This, to judge by the published proceedings of the conference on church building organized by the C.P.L. in 1960,[6]

[4] *New Church Buildings: Notes on Procedure*, Church Commissioners, London 1959.

[5] The need for a statement of theological and liturgical principles was recognized by the National Assembly of the Church of England in 1960, and a panel of theologians and architects has now been appointed to draw up such a document, which will presumably supersede the *Notes* referred to above.

[6] See *La Maison-Dieu*, no. 63, 1960. The *conclusions* printed at the end of the proceedings provide the best summary of fundamental principles that has yet appeared.

Appendix

could mark a notable step forward from the two earlier documents. Since the appearance of the German directives there have been remarkable developments in liturgical scholarship, on the one hand, and liturgical practice, on the other; for example, in our understanding of the Christian assembly as an organic, hierarchical community (rather than as an amorphous body of lay Christians together with 'a celebrant'),[7] in our understanding of the ministry of the word, as an essential element in eucharistic worship, and in the fresh emphases which have resulted from the restoration of the Easter Vigil. I suspect that a French directive is likely to go a good deal further in recognizing the importance of these renewed insights than the document issued by the Superior Liturgical Commission which is somewhat conservative. Certainly the proceedings of the Versailles conference suggest that the next attempt to formulate a general programme for Roman Catholic church building may prove to be a document of major importance, the value of which will not be confined to one Christian community alone.

---

[7] Cf. *Richtlinien*, conclusion 6: e.g. 'emphatic opposition of priest and congregation'.

Towards a Church Architecture

GUIDING PRINCIPLES FOR THE DESIGN OF CHURCHES
ACCORDING TO THE SPIRIT OF THE ROMAN LITURGY

German Liturgical Commission, 1947

FUNDAMENTALS

1. The Christian church is a consecrated building which, even independently of the eucharist, is filled with God's presence, and in which God's people assemble. The purposes for which they assemble are, in the order of their importance, these:
   First and foremost, to celebrate the renewal of Christ's redeeming sacrifice;
   Secondly, to partake of the fruits of that sacrifice in the sacraments,
   Thirdly, to hear the word of God,
   Fourthly, to pay homage to Christ, present in the eucharistic bread;
   Fifthly, to participate in extra-liturgical devotions.

2. A church is not, however, simply a place of public worship, whether liturgical or extra-liturgical. It is also a place in which the individual may make his private devotions.

3. Such being its character and purposes, a Christian church must necessarily have a peculiar dignity:
   First, it is in a unique way 'the tabernacle of God among men' (Rev. xxi, 3), the place in which God allows his people to be certain of finding him; it is 'the Father's house' (cf. Luke xv, 17), it is God's royal palace (*basilica*).
   Secondly, it is the place in which the Church, the body of Christ, is formed, and in which it grows, and it is in consequence a symbol of that body.
   Thirdly, it is the place in which the ultimate union of God with his people is anticipated, and which has therefore been justifiably described as the heavenly Jerusalem descended to earth (cf. Rev. xxi, 2).

4. On the other hand, the multiplicity of the purposes which a church must serve creates special architectural problems. For each purpose makes different demands on the building. The celebration of the eucharist, the administration of the sacraments of penance and baptism, the preaching of the sermon, the devotion to the real presence, public prayers, private prayers: all have their special needs, and it is the function of the church architect to find a solution which satisfies each in the fullest possible way.

5. Of these acts which are performed in a church – the celebration of the eucharist, the administration of the sacraments, the preaching of the word, the devotion to the real presence: none is performed in exactly the same way everywhere in the world. In the course of centuries there has

Appendix

developed a number of different methods – the so-called liturgies or rites. By far the most important of these are the Roman and Byzantine, the former being proper to the western bishoprics and the latter to churches of the east. These two liturgies, although they agree in essentials, are entirely different in their outward forms, and a church which is appropriate to one cannot therefore be exactly the same as a church which is to serve the other.

6. A church is meant for a congregation of our own time. It must therefore be so constructed that men and women of today may feel at home in it. Their noblest aspirations must find fulfilment there: the urge towards community and fellowship, the search for the true and genuine, the desire to get away from what is peripheral to what is central and essential, the striving after clarity, the longing for peace, for warmth and shelter.

CONCLUSIONS

1. The buildings which serve the various needs of a parish – the church, the school, the hospital, the *Caritas* office [welfare organization], the almshouse, the parish library, the rector's house and the sexton's house – should not be separated without compelling reasons. Ideally they should all be placed together to form one coherent parish centre, so that the close links which inwardly unite church and priest, eucharist and *Caritas*, sacraments and education, are made manifest to the eye.

2. However necessary it may be to remind people, preoccupied as they often are with the externals of life, of the existence of God, it is best to avoid building a church so that it gives directly on a noisy shopping street. It is desirable that on one's way to church one should pass first through an enclosed square or a formal *atrium*, and should thus have a moment of silence in which to collect oneself in preparation for the stillness of God within the church.

3. The exterior of a church should not attempt to imitate contemporary secular buildings either in its proportions, its structure, or its decoration. Nor should it try to catch the attention of the passer-by with the architectural equivalent of the cries of the market-place. The aim should rather be to announce in a manner which is both dignified and eloquent the totally different nature of what lies within the church – totally different because belonging to another world – and yet at the same time to allow the building to take its place harmoniously in its surroundings.

4. In planning the entrances to the church it would be a mistake to consider only the problems of regulating movement in and out and excluding draughts. We must return to the idea that the treatment of the entrances, and especially the main entrance, should be so emphatic as to thrust upon the worshipper the parallel between the doors of the church and the gates of heaven.

5. In planning the interior it would be wrong to take as one's starting-

point, as some have, not the eucharistic sacrifice but the devotion to the real presence in the reserved sacrament, and thereby to give to the atmosphere of the church a one-sided emphasis on adoration and contemplation. It would be wrong because this devotion to the real presence in the reserved sacrament does not take first place among the purposes which a church must serve.

The conflict between the different purposes of a church can only be satisfactorily solved by making some separation, if this is possible, between the space allotted to the eucharistic sacrifice and that intended for devotion to the reserved sacrament. Likewise one should if possible make provision for separate rooms for the sacraments of baptism and penance. In this way each part of the building can receive the architectural treatment appropriate to its particular purpose.

6. There is a widely held opinion that one should endeavour to place the altar in the middle of the congregation, and therefore that the only satisfactory shape for a church is one that is centrally orientated. This is a mistaken opinion. A church is intended in the first place for the celebration of the eucharistic sacrifice. But, as it is understood in the liturgy of the Roman church, this celebration is an act. It is primarily the act of Christ and of his representative, the priest, but it is also the act of the congregation. The focal points of the congregation's part in the act are the responses before the preface and the 'Amen' at the end of the canon, as well as the movement forward to the altar-rails for the offertory and communion (though the former is rarely seen nowadays) The interplay of the different parts of the act demands a building which is in some way orientated to the altar, which clearly sets off the two actors – priest and congregation – and which opens up a way for processions in either direction. The ideal is therefore a church which fully satisfies all these requirements of the Roman liturgy – orientation towards the altar, emphatic opposition of priest and congregation, and provision for orderly processions in two directions – without placing too great a distance between the altar and the farthest limits of the space occupied by the congregation.

7. In its original significance the altar is the place at which earth reaches up towards heaven. In a Christian context it serves as the table for the sacrifice and supper of the faithful, and at the same time as the place at which God appears to us in the eucharist Moreover, because God made man becomes present on the altar through the consecration, the altar, even without a tabernacle, is the throne of Christ. And because a throne is the symbol of a ruler, the altar used in earlier times to be seen as the symbol of Christ.

From all this it is obvious how false it is to make of the altar a mere shelf against the wall, or to design it as if its sole or principal function were to provide a support for the tabernacle and the cross, for candlesticks and reliquaries, for pictures and statues.

Appendix

In the ideal church the altar is clearly marked out as the true sanctuary, as the heart of the plan. This is achieved in many ways. by giving it an isolated and raised position and by making it free-standing; by a balanced design and the use of choice materials; by according it a monumental character in relation to the rest of the building, and by skilfully leading the lines of perspective towards it, by placing it where the light is strongest, and perhaps by erecting a ciborium. In the ideal church the conception and design of both the interior and the exterior will start from the altar.

8. The traditional alignment from west to east should not be abandoned without good reason. We should rather try to revive in the minds of the faithful an understanding of the profound and beautiful symbolism of the act of facing east to pray, and thereby to bring back the significance of the orientation of our churches. There are some indications that in the church of the future the priest will once again stand behind the altar and celebrate facing the people (as indeed he still does in the old Roman basilicas), and this is the solution which seems to be called for by the desire, which is apparent everywhere, to emphasize the communal aspect of the mass around the Lord's table. To such a development the rule of eastward prayer would present no obstacle. For the focal point of the eastward attitude is God and his only-begotten Son, who are thought of as being, like the sun, enthroned in and coming from the east. This coming of God, this theophany, takes place, however, on the altar and it is to the altar that both priest and congregation must face

9. The altar should not necessarily occupy the same position in large churches as in small. In small churches it may be appropriate and necessary to place it at the extreme end of the building, as was sometimes done in the early Christian era, in churches of the basilica type (*Einraumkirche*) But in larger churches it would be more appropriate, and more in keeping with tradition, if the altar were placed in a clearly-defined sanctuary or choir. This should be rectangular, semi-circular or polygonal in shape, and visibly separated from the remainder of the church (*Zweiraumkirche*).

10. The back wall of the sanctuary should not be so filled with windows as to make it difficult to see the altar properly. Similarly, it should not be decorated with figurative pictures which have no direct bearing on the eucharistic sacrifice, or which are not appropriate to every phase of the liturgical year The architecture and decoration of the sanctuary should ideally be such that they do not draw the eye to themselves, but rather guide it to the altar and to the sacred act which is performed there. Where figurative representations are required, they should derive from the ideas of the central eucharistic prayer, i.e. the text from the 'sursum corda' to the final doxology. In any case, recourse should be had not to historical scenes but to timeless ideas.

11. Again, it would be wrong to arrange the interior in such a way as to deprive the congregation of the sense that in playing its part in the

Towards a Church Architecture

liturgy it is a single whole, a closed family circle. But it would be equally wrong to go to the other extreme and make it impossible for anyone to find a quiet corner for private prayer. The ideal solution is one which serves both purposes, which gives visual expression to the unity of the congregation – not only the large congregation on a Sunday or a feast-day but also the smaller congregation on a weekday – and yet which also provides those secluded corners in which individuals may prefer to make their private devotions.

12. It would be a pity to allow the congregation's attention, which should be concentrated on the altar, to be distracted by side altars and statues, by stations of the cross and confessionals, or by clumsily distributed lights and pews. Every accessory which is not strictly necessary should be dispensed with, and those which are unavoidable, such as side altars and confessionals, should, if at all possible, be placed in areas adjoining the main body of the church, or in a crypt. If this cannot be done, they should be so designed and arranged as not to interrupt the smooth flow of the lines of the building towards the altar.

13. The sacristy should be in the immediate neighbourhood of the altar, and not, as it was in early Christian times, for example, at the side of the façade of the church. But it would be an advantage if a connexion could be provided between the sacristy and the main entrance of the church, so that on Sundays and feast-days the clergy could solemnly process up the nave to the altar. The introit would then regain its full significance as an entrance-chant.

14. The size of cathedrals, pilgrimage churches, and churches in large cities has made it necessary for the sermon to be preached not from the sanctuary but from an elevated pulpit which is normally near the middle of the church, either standing at one side or projecting from the wall. This means that part of the congregation has its back to the preacher, an arrangement which, under the influence of these large churches, has unfortunately become universal. But the true liturgical sermon, that is to say the sermon which fits organically into the mass, is above all one which interprets and expands the epistle and the gospel of the day.
 since these are recited in the sanctuary, the sermon should be Preached from the same place, perhaps from an ambo standing by the altar-rails.

15. The choir has a clearly defined liturgical function to fulfil. it should lead the congregation in prayer, in responses and in hymns, it should share with the congregation in antiphonal singing and on occasion should entirely replace the congregation. From this it follows that it is fundamentally wrong to place the choir in a gallery at the back, invisible to the congregation. Ideally, in a church which was designed from a strictly liturgical point of view, the choir would be in the body of the church, next to the sanctuary. If it is really necessary to have a

Appendix

gallery at the back, then it should be occupied by the organ, since obviously the liturgical function of the organ is not to fill in 'gaps' in the action of the mass, like a soloist, but to give support to the singing of the congregation and the choir, and on occasion marginally to accentuate their spirit of rejoicing (The gallery would also be the obvious place for the polyphonic choir and for the orchestra, though the latter is of course alien to the strictly liturgical service.)

16. At baptism we are re-born as children of God and are thereby incorporated as members of the Church, the body of Christ. It is regrettable but true that this fundamental significance of the sacrament of baptism finds scarcely any expression in present-day parish life. The result is that the font is usually one of the most neglected features of our churches. In the ideal church this 'spring of baptism' (*fons*) would be given a monumental treatment and placed in a separate room near the entrance. According to a venerable tradition this room should be circular or polygonal, with the font in the centre, and the inward meaning of the ritual of baptism leads to the same architectural solution. For at the core of this ritual man appears not as an actor, but merely as the passive recipient of the mysterious action of God, and accordingly the appropriate architectural form is not a long room, which in symbolic language expresses action, but a room which is centrally planned, and which, since its axis is vertical, has a passive character.

17. The furnishing of a church should suggest neither the comfort of the houses of the well-to-do, nor the bareness of the houses of the poor. The interior of the ideal church should forcefully proclaim the greatness of God as something beyond all earthly standards. In this way it will lift the worshipper out of the atmosphere of his ordinary existence, while still allowing him to feel the warmth of the 'love of God our Saviour toward man' (Tit. iii, 4).

18. It is a mistake, though one which has very frequently been made in recent years, to leave the choice of the paintings or sculptures with which the church is decorated to the whim of the parish priest of the moment, or to that of the donor, or simply to chance. It is particularly important that this should not be done in the case of the decoration of the main entrance, the sanctuary, the altar, the font and the pulpit. For the making of the ideal church there should be not only a building plan, but also a plan for the artistic decoration, and this plan should be thoroughly thought out both from a theological point of view and from the point of view of the instruction of the congregation. It should ensure that the decoration of the finished church presents to the eye the world of faith, and presents it not in unrelated fragments but as a coherent whole, in a significant order and with the emphasis appropriately distributed

19 When planning new churches there is a common tendency to try

to make the buildings as large as the size of the site and funds available will permit. This is a mistake. A big church is not necessarily the best church. There is an ideal maximum for the size of any church: the priest at the altar must be clearly seen and heard in the farthest pew without the use of technical aids, and it must be possible to give communion to everyone present without disrupting the celebration of the mass. This maximum size should only be exceeded if there is a cogent reason for doing so (it is, for example, obvious that cathedrals and pilgrimage churches must necessarily be of larger dimensions).

20. The size of the sanctuary must be adjusted to that of the whole church. An average-sized parish church should not have a sanctuary so large that it could accommodate the numerous clergy of a cathedral, nor one so small that the altar-rails press up against the altar-steps. There must be sufficient space between the rails and the steps to permit of a seemly celebration of high mass.

21 The number and arrangement of pews must also be considered. One should, if at all possible, avoid having so many that they reach almost to the altar-rails in the front and to the walls at the sides. Ideally there should be passages in the middle, at the sides, in front of the altar-rails and at the main entrance, and these should be sufficiently wide to allow communicants to pass to and fro without any unseemly crowding, even when there are many hundreds of them, and also to allow free movement to the processions which the liturgy provides for on certain occasions (at the entry to high mass on Sundays and feast-days, at Candlemas, on Palm Sunday, etc).

Whoever is entrusted with the building of a church bears a grave responsibility. The success or failure of his work will determine whether generations of worshippers will love their parish church or not, whether they will go to the services which are held there eagerly or reluctantly. In such circumstances no planning can be too conscientious or too thorough.

Appendix

DIOCESAN CHURCH BUILDING DIRECTIVES

Superior, Wisconsin, 1957

I. THE CHURCH AND ITS ELEMENTS

Statement of Principle
A church is a sacred building dedicated to divine worship primarily that it should be at the disposal of all the faithful for the public exercise of divine worship. *Canon law*

O how awesome is this place; this is the house of God and the gateway to heaven; it shall be called the majestic court of God.

The mass of dedication

The Christian church, a house of God, is a sacred place filled with the divine presence, even apart from the holy eucharist, a place where the people of God assemble

First, to celebrate the re-presentation of the redeeming sacrifice of our Lord.

Secondly, to partake of the fruits of Christ's redeeming sacrifice in the holy sacraments.

Thirdly, to hear the preaching of the word of God.

Fourthly, to render homage and adoration to the presence of our Lord in the eucharistic bread.

Fifthly, to engage in various non-liturgical devotions

The German Liturgical Commission

The primary purpose of the church is to serve the sacred liturgy. The church is the home of the risen Christ, who under sacramental sign and sacred rite continues his redemptive work among us. In this sacred enclosure the glorified Christ offers expiation for sin, sanctifies, heals, announces the good news of salvation. The church is likewise the dwelling place of God's holy people· Christ's mystical body. In this sacred edifice the whole Christ, Head and members, offers perfect worship to the Father in heaven. Through sacred signs (the sacraments) Christ continues his divine operations in the living community. The baptized laity, the ordained ministers of the altar and the priest form this one body, of which the visible church is the unique symbol.

The church edifice must be inspired by these profound truths to be truly beautiful, meaningful, and functional on the supernatural level. Unless these truths are the guiding principle of sacred building, church architecture cannot escape becoming static and lifeless. The Christian church will convey a message to the men of our day only to the extent that the builders have understood the nature and spirit of Christian worship. No architect, therefore, ought to presume to build a church without first acquainting himself with the meaning and spirit of the

Towards a Church Architecture

sacred liturgy. Failure in this regard will lead inevitably to an architecture devoid of true Christian meaning.

Application of Principle

1. The architect of a church, the overseer of the entire plan, should be of outstanding competence in his field in creative skill. Conversant with the rich tradition of sacred building, he should be able to interpret that tradition in a living architectural form.

2. The architect, to execute a work of true aesthetic and religious value, must possess a true understanding of the meaning of sacred worship. He must be able to distinguish the essential from the peripheral and to subordinate lesser values to the higher.

3. The pastor or patron should make certain that the whole parochial complex is studied as a unit before embarking upon the planning of a new church. Rectory, school and church should be organized in a purposeful relationship.

4. The pastor or patron should work in close collaboration with the architect. He ought to make certain that the architect assimilates the theological and liturgical principles which he is to interpret in the church edifice.

5. The pastor and architect ought to work as a team in the planning and building of the church. Neither one ought to act independently of the other in matters which relate both to the science or art of architecture and the dictates of sound theology and liturgical practice. Each should respect the role of the other in his distinctive field.

6. Benefactors and donors of the church furnishings and sacred art should not be permitted to dictate their design and content, since the church's appointments must be related to the architecture and liturgical function of the church.

7. The church edifice is constructed to serve men of our age. Its architectural language should not be archaic or foreign but contemporary and genuine in expression. True Christian tradition accepts the true, good and beautiful in each age and culture.

8. When possible, materials indigenous to the locale or territory should be used in the construction of the church, if they are of good quality and serviceable. Both the architecture and materials should be related to the nature and character of the immediate surroundings. A pretence of magnificence or luxury by the importation of costly materials from foreign lands does not significantly enrich the sacred edifice. (This is above all applicable to the altar.)

9. The employment of a sacred artist or competent art consultant to aid the architect is highly commendable since sacred art plays such a significant role in Christian worship. This will ensure a unity of beauty and purpose which cannot be achieved by furnishing the church with

articles of an inferior prefabricated nature purchased from divergent sources.

10. Nothing false, profane or bizarre should degrade this holy temple in architecture or art. Shoddy craftsmanship and weak, stereotyped 'art-objects' of mass-production should be excluded as unworthy of the house of God.

11. The sacred art of the church must possess a certain symbolic character due to the invisible realities of faith of which it is the expository sign. Excessive naturalism absorbs the worshippers' activity in the object itself rather than the mystery it represents. The extreme abstractionist treatment of sacred mysteries renders their content unintelligible to the unschooled viewer.

12. The decoration of the church should be simple, organic and unpretentious. All deceit and false enrichment of the basic structure must be strictly avoided. The structural qualities of the architecture should carry the weight of beauty and purpose Art works and the furnishings of the church must find their proper place in the higher order of the architectural structure. The architect and artist should work in unity of purpose.

13 Since the Church is a hierarchical or graded society, not all of her members have the same function, but each participates in her worship of the Father according to his God-given capacity This hierarchical differentiation of function of priest, ordained ministers of the altar (e.g. deacons, altar assistants), and baptized laity ought to be expressed in elevation and articulation by the architecture.

The profound fact of the Church's unity, however, must not be forgotten in the attempt to achieve this visible gradation. Since the mystical body of Christ is a living, corporate society, the church architecture must possess an organic unity. Although many, we are one body. Functions differ, but the articulation of graded membership ought not to destroy the organic relationship of member to member.

Although distinct in treatment, the sanctuary which contains the altar and the nave which houses the community of the baptized ought to be visually and psychologically one. Visual or architectural separation should be avoided. The arrangement of space relations should lend itself to the active participation of the laity in the sacred action of the liturgy. Clear vision of the sanctuary and easy dialogue between priest and people should be readily possible Long, narrow churches which remove the laity from close contact with the altar are undesirable.

The *schola cantorum*, or choir, should be no exception to this oneness of the community in worship. The choir ought not to be placed in a loft apart from the assembly but should form an integral part with it. The choir's proper place is in an intermediary position between the priest and people. A space at the left of the sanctuary ought to be provided for the *schola cantorum* so that the director of liturgical song is visibly accessible to both the choir and the entire assembly.

14. As Christ is head of the Church, the altar is the heart of the sacred building Nothing should hinder the architectural initiation of the entire building toward the altar. Stations of the cross, lighting fixtures, ornaments and statuary, rather than break the continuity of the converging line ought to maintain it.

15. Shrines and areas of particular non-liturgical devotions ought not to conflict with the church's higher purpose of serving the official worship of the church. More private areas ought to be provided for the individual devotional needs of the community. These can be located at any part of the nave providing they do not disturb visible or physical access to the altar.

16. Architects should strive to attain good acoustical qualities and proper lighting to avoid the audio-visual strain of the members of the community. Stained glass and diminutive windows which make electrical substitutes necessary even during the day hours are to be avoided.

17. Since full participation in the liturgy implies procession of the faithful on various occasions, (e.g. procession to receive the eucharist) the facility of easy mobility by the entire assembly is to be preserved. The kneeling benches and aisles must not be an impediment to processional movement.

18. Since the word of God is proclaimed to the faithful in the liturgical assembly, the ambo or pulpit, rather than being a portable stand for notes, should possess dignity without being unduly massive. A step of elevation properly depicts the apostolic office of announcing the good news of redemption. The pulpit should be located in the sanctuary on the gospel side near the communion rail.

19. Second in importance to the altar is the baptistery of the church. Each church is to have a baptistery of reasonable size to accommodate the minister and participants with ample space.

20. The baptistery is to be located near the entrance of the church. The holy font should make a strong statement to the community entering for divine worship since it is a continual sign of the Christian's rebirth in Christ and his membership in the mystical body. An open grill with locked gate is required by rubric, unless the font itself is locked. The baptistery should not be used for any purpose (e.g. crying room) other than the administration of this holy sacrament of Christian initiation.

21. The sacred font should be strong and dignified with a certain suggestion of massiveness to indicate its importance. A bath of regeneration and font of life-giving water, it should be stationary and permanent rather than provisional or portable.

22. A step of descent toward the font is commendable to portray the rich Pauline doctrine of baptism. By this means the inner meaning

Appendix

of baptism as a mystical descent into the death of Christ and the corresponding ascent with him into the Easter life of resurrection is visually symbolized.

23. The entrance to the church ought to be prominent and significant of the redemptive mysteries which are re-enacted within. A space of transition (fore-court, vestibule or atrium), of peace and quiet between the outside world and the inner sacred space, has been traditionally observed. The vestibule is a physical aid to those who enter to dispose their souls for the sacred mysteries of the liturgy. It should be spacious and share the atmosphere of reverence of the church proper.

24. The sacristy should provide ample space for the many works of a practical nature in preparation for the sacred liturgy. A more solemn entrance to the altar should be provided for Sundays and feast-days so as to lend greater significance to the entrance procession (introit).

II. THE ALTAR AND ITS SETTING

Statement of Principle

The altar of holy Church is Christ himself.	*The rite of ordination*
Christ Jesus is the Priest, the Victim, and the Altar.	
	The Roman Breviary
The altar stands for Christ.	*St Thomas Aquinas*
The tremendous table.	*St John Chrysostom*

As Christ is the Head of the Church, the altar which represents his presence in the Christian assembly is the heart and centre of the Christian church. This sacred stone of sacrifice and holy table of the eucharistic meal must possess absolute prominence over all else contained by the church. Above all the furnishings of the church, the altar stands as the symbol of Christ *par excellence*. It is the most expressive sign-image of Christ's mediatorship between God and man. Standing between heaven and earth, the altar sanctifies man's gift to God and brings God's gift to man. Thus the altar is the most sacred symbol of the priesthood of our Lord Jesus Christ and a permanent sign of his presence among the holy people of God.

The altar, rather than a supplement or ornament of the church, is the reason of its being. The church is constructed to house the holy table; the altar is not furnished to complete the church. The church edifice is the extension and complement of the altar of sacrifice.

Application of Principle
1. The design of the church begins with the altar; the altar must be the unchallenged focal point of the sacred building. The church must

not only 'contain' the altar but also complement the altar in its architectural organization.

2. The altar, the holy symbol of Christ's priesthood, ought not to be needlessly multiplied. Where auxiliary altars are necessary for the private celebration of the eucharistic sacrifice, they should be placed out of view of the congregation. A portable altar of reposition can be furnished when liturgically required.

3. The altar's autonomy is to be secured by preserving its centrality and independence. It should not be placed against the sanctuary wall as a mere object of furniture but ought to be free-standing as required by rubric. A minimum of three feet from the wall is to be observed. A greater distance is recommended

4. The altar should be accessible from at least three sides. The predella should be constructed to allow free circuit around the altar on a single plane.

5. Retables, reredos, gradines, and other superstructures should be excluded from the altar since they tend to obscure the altar proper. The sanctity of the altar precludes the use of the holy table as a pedestal or stand for multiple accessories.

6. The structure of the altar should be notable for simplicity, integrity, and beauty as befits this holy symbol of Christ and his redemptive work. The *mensa* (table) and the *stipes* (supports for the table), the essential parts of the altar, should be expressed boldly and directly in the visible structure.

7 The material of the altar (the stone or the wood extension) should not be denatured by over-refinement or high-gloss polish treatment. The preservation of the natural surface texture of stone or wood, rather than weakening the solidity of the altar-image, strengthens it. Materials and finishes of 'dainty' colour ought to be rejected as incongruous with the altar's dignity and function.

8. An unnecessary overstatement of the altar's size ought to be avoided. The significance of the altar as the stone of sacrifice is achieved not so much by size as by the strength of the altar's architectural statement. Small churches ought not to emulate the size of altars in large churches. The relations and proportion of altar, sanctuary and church having been duly considered, altars varying from six to eight feet in length will be adequate.

9. Since the altar itself is the symbol of Christ and his sacrifice, symbolic ornamentation of the altar is unnecessary If symbolism is applied, it should be visually uncomplicated and legible to the worshipping laity. Simplicity and directness is the norm for the form and content of the symbol. The symbol should be immediately related to the meaning of the altar or the sacrament-sacrifice.

10. The use of natural light should play an important part in main-

taining the altar's focal position in the church. The altar should be the centre of light concentration. Since artificial light does not supplant the need or beauty of natural light, architects should strive to achieve light emphasis without the use of electrical substitutes. Recessed or shielded source-lighting, a precaution against sanctuary glare, is commendable. Windows should never be located on the terminal wall of the sanctuary.

11. The altar's appointments (tabernacle, altar cross, candleholders, and canopy) should not detract from the altar's primacy of position. *The altar dictates the scale of proportion.*

12. Unduly large crucifixes or wall crucifixion groups ought to be avoided since they tend to usurp the altar's primacy of position. (The altar's primacy as an object of veneration is derived from the inherent sacredness bestowed by the constitutive blessing or consecration.) The altar cross, formerly a portable processional banner, is an extension of the altar.

13. The altar crucifix secured for the setting of the eucharistic celebration should not express a naturalistic interpretation of the sacrifice of Christ. Rather than emphasize the dramatic and emotional aspects of the crucifixion, the ideal crucifix depicts the dogmatic realities of this act of redemption. The Saviour's interior sacrificial will and external physical oblation, which suggest triumph through death, are important notes of true representation.

14. The canopy or baldaquin should form one visual unit with the altar. The baldaquin's purpose is to enhance and enrich the altar in dignity as 'God's dwelling place among men'. The canopy should not draw attention to itself, reserve and simplicity of execution is required.

15. Care must be exercised that the sanctuary be not reduced to an abbreviated appendage to the church as often occurs when the roof or wall line is broken at the sanctuary, e.g. for the intrusion of the sacristies. The spatial unity of the sanctuary and nave must be preserved.

16. The sanctuary which serves the ministers of the altar ought to be spacious, lightsome, uncluttered, and furnished in good taste. A solemn serenity, sobriety and purity achieved by the direct use of natural materials should characterize this sacrificial space as well as be the distinguishing mark of the church as a whole.

17. The communion rail (not required by rubric) should not serve as a visual barrier between altar and people. Rather than separation it should suggest the distinction of function between the ordained ministers of the altar and the baptized laity.

18. The sanctuary should not house shrines of particular devotion. The sacred art contained by this reserved space, more than simple portraiture, should recall the great mysteries re-enacted in the sacred liturgy of the Church. Rather than relating to the cult of the saints or a particular feast of the liturgical year, art themes of the sanctuary

should be universal in character developing the rich signification of the eucharistic sign. Eschatological themes of which the eucharist is the prefiguration are especially appropriate. The art of the sanctuary, however, must remain subordinate to the church's most important possession, the altar.

Lightning Source UK Ltd.
Milton Keynes UK
UKHW020824300922
409697UK00005B/464